Women, War and Peace in South Asia

Beyond Victimhood to Agency

Editor
RITA MANCHANDA

Sage Publications
NEW DELHI ■ THOUSAND OAKS ■ LONDON

First published in 2001 by

Sage Publications India Pvt Ltd
M-32 Market, Greater Kailash, Part 1
New Delhi 110 048

Sage Publications Inc.
2455 Teller Road
Thousand Oaks, California 91320

Sage Publications Ltd
6 Bonhill Street
London EC2A 4PU

Published by Tejeshwar Singh for Sage Publications India Pvt Ltd, typeset in 10/12 Garamond by Deo Gratis Systems, Chennai and printed at Chaman Enterprises, Delhi.

Second Printing 2002
Library of Congress Cataloging-in-Publication Data

   Women, war, and peace in South Asia: beyond victimhood to agency/ editor, Rita Manchanda.

     p. cm.

   Includes bibliographical references and index.

     1. Women and peace—South Asia. 2. Women and war—South Asia. 3. Women in politics—South Asia. 4. Women—South Asia—Social conditions. I. Manchanda, Rita.

JZ5584. S65 W66   305.4'0954—dc21   2001   00–065809

ISBN: 0-7619-9539-0 (US-HB)   81-7829-018-9 (India-HB)
      0-7619-9540-4 (US-PB)   81-7829-019-7 (India-PB)

Sage Production Team: Jaya Chowdhury, O.P. Bhasin and Santosh Rawat

Women, War and
Peace in South Asia

Contents

Acknowledgements

This study was made possible by the South Asia Forum for Human Rights (SAFHR) and in particular, its secretary ge₁eral, Tapan Bose who had the vision to take seriously women's experiences of conflict situations and the faith that women's perspectives can open up alternative ways of negotiating conflict and building a just peace. My sincere appreciation goes to the Swedish International Development Agency (SIDA) for supporting the project.

The idea of the project grew out of my many conversations in Kathmandu with Paula Banerjee to whom I owe an enormous debt of gratitude for helping to conceptually define and refine the adaptation of a gendered analysis of conflict to the South Asian reality. The project, being an experimental one, was in many ways also a collaborative initiative, with the contributors to the volume actively engaged in shaping it. I must also acknowledge the encouragement of Urvashi Butalia who in the initial stages gave me excellent advice on how to listen to the silences in women's voices and not discard what on first hearing appears banal. Sumanta Banerjee was, as he has always been, encouraging and insightful in his comments.

I should also like to express my appreciation to the many women who shared with me their experience and conceptual ideas at the London conference on 'Women and Violent Conflict: Global Perspectives' and Harvard University's 'Women Waging Peace' network. Their vision and indomitable courage was inspirational, and their solidarity supported my flagging spirits on days when the dominant security paradigms threatened to overwhelm my search for alternatives.

My heartfelt thanks go to my family, friends and colleagues who patiently bore with my obsession during the last couple of years when this book was taking shape. And to my husband, Tapan Bose whose impatience at what he feared might become a lifelong project prodded me on to finish. It was an impatience which in no way lessened his encouragement and belief that the study needed to be done. Finally, this book would not have been possible without the hundreds of women who trusted us with their stories. It is to them that this book is dedicated.

Where Are the Women in South Asian Conflicts?

1

Rita Manchanda

In the meta-narrative of histories, the dominant motif of women in violent conflict is the Grieving Mother. Women of Sorrow make up the chorus in war, outsiders to the battle front. Traditionally, history provides no chronicle of women's experiences of organised political violence, ignoring as inconsequential the differentiated way violence impacted on their lives, forging survival strategies, resistance and peace building; and how it effected a social transformation in gender roles. However, as master narratives give way to the recovery of nomadic narratives of people's lived experience—as remembered and interpreted by them—the focus shifts to make visible the multiplicity and complexity of women's narratives of the war story.

At the international level, feminist scholarship[1] has combined with peace studies research to challenge the exclusion and marginalisation of women's experiences and perspectives of conflict and women's agency in conflict transformation. Challenging the centrality of men's experiences and theories and paying attention to the women's experience, it is argued, sheds light not only on the gendered[2] aspects of social and political life but provides acute insights into other forms of structural inequalities at the heart of conflict. The postulate being that the women's experience represents an alternative reading of history, the possibility of non-violent ways of negotiating conflict and agency for reconciliation and peace. In the background, the theoretical debates around women and peace lurch from the biological to the cultural, to reasons of 'justice', and finally to the flat assumption that women are for peace because they are the worst sufferers in conflict.

It is argued that women, because of their socialisation and historical experience of unequal relations, bring different insights into the structure of power relations and different values to the process of peace building. Women's peace activism and feminist critical consciousness has questioned the centrality of the dominant meaning of peace as defined in the strategic discourse as an absence of war, and of security as national security. Instead, women's perspectives tend to privilege the notion of a 'just' peace, as defined from the perspective of the discriminated and disempowered. The elite form the national security constituency the world over[3] while it is the less privileged, the poor and the marginalised, the majority of whom are women, who are most concerned about a just peace and human security.

International peace and gender research initiatives have focused largely on Africa, former Yugoslavia, Northern Ireland, Middle East and South-Central America. In South Asia we are yet to pose the question: Where are the women in South Asian violent conflicts?[4] This volume grew out of our need as academics and peace activists in South Asia to understand the role of women beyond victimhood, women's variegated negotiations with conflict and their capacity to emerge as agents of social transformation, in other words, women's agency in war and peace. In the bubbling cauldron of ethnic and regional conflicts in South Asia, the old conflict resolution paradigms have failed and there is dire need for new perspectives and untapped experiences in promoting non-violent ways of dealing with difference. Clearly, our peace politics has been invested in this research.

Making visible women's experiences in situations of violent conflict, their agency in managing survival and reconstruction and women's notions of security and peace, is necessary to get due recognition for women's experiences as a resource and a space in formal politics for mainstreaming gender in the peace building process in South Asia.[5] Beyond the icon of Mother Sorrow, there are many faces of women in conflict in South Asia. Women have negotiated conflict situations by becoming citizens, combatants, heads of households, war munitions workers, prostitutes, producers of soldiers and war resisters and political leaders at the local and national level. In South Asia, at one end is the Woman of Violence represented by the Armed Virgin of the Liberation Tigers of Tamil Eelam (LTTE), at the other end is the Woman of Peace, symbolised by the Naga Mothers Association (NMA) in the nationalist struggle for an independent Nagaland.

In India's Northeast, the Naga Mothers have taken the lead in the process of building peace and have called for a halt to all killings. In 1994–95 when killings by the security forces and internecine violence between rival factions reached a peak, the Naga Mothers launched a campaign—'shed no more blood'. In a symbolic gesture of the rejection of violence, irrespective of who the perpetrator, the Naga Mothers persist in covering with dignity the body of every victim with a shroud. It is in keeping with the old Naga tradition of women peace makers (*phukhrelia*) during conflict. Peace teams of Naga women have walked remote tracts to appeal to rival factions to stop the violence. Once the 1997 ceasefire was declared between the Indian government and the dominant militant faction, the National Socialist Council of Nagalim (NSCN) Isak-Muivah, the Naga Mothers have worked with the Naga Council of elders, the church and a myriad women's organisations in the region to mobilise support for the ceasefire and the peace process. In September 2000 when the ceasefire was in danger of being broken, the Naga Mothers along with the Naga Women's Union of Manipur appealed to Indian Prime Minister Vajpayee and the chairman of the NSCN Isak-Muivah to heed the people's cry for peace and sustain the peace process.

The Naga Mothers Association's peace initiative turns to the moral authority of the mother and socially sanctioned space available within the Naga tradition of women's activism for peace in the informal space of politics. It is precisely as mothers that women have this space to appeal to the powerful and move them to compassion and shame. The NMA's initiative represents the use of motherhood for women's political mobilisation and also its limitations. Naga women still do not sit in the village council of elders where the decisions of formal politics are made. Their activism in the informal sphere of politics needs to be legitimised by men before space for women can be made in the formal sector. However, Naga women, through their peace activism in the informal space of politics, have acquired publicly recognised space for themselves in mobilisations for peace in the civil society, making their presence in the dynamics of the formal peace process significantly necessary. In July–August 2000, when the peace process was threatened by the arrest in Bangkok of top Naga militant leader Thuingaleng Muivah, en route to the peace talks in Geneva, the NMA president was camping out in Bangkok. Her presence was recognised as a necessary and legitimate part of the democratic mobilisation for peace.

Does the Naga Mothers story direct us to an alternative reading of the master narrative of the 45-year-old Naga armed struggle around a separatist national identity? Do women's experiences, as we shall explore in this volume, open up the possibility of an alternative way of negotiating the construction of conflictual identities and nationalities? Does the Naga Mothers narrative hold out the possibility of women constituting a group which could organise movements around issues of peace, reaching across the conflict divide? Historically, women have been excluded from power and decision-making processes, fostering an ambivalence towards issues of citizenship and national identity. Women's problematic relationship with the politics of exclusion of national identity struggles is epigrammatically expressed in Virginia Woolf's assertion 'I have no nation'. At a more pragmatic level, it is argued that women, because they are excluded from 'politics', have less stake in the ideological or political positions on which conflict thrives. It may be less important for women to display appropriate political attitudes. In Kashmir, women across the Muslim–Pandit divide rush unthinkingly to save a boy being hauled away by the militants or the police. The men stay inside. Dan Smith argues, 'if there is a female propensity for peace it may be because of a male propensity to exclude women from politics'.[6]

There is need, however, to guard against sentimentalising the phenomenon of women bonding across the ethnic or communal divide.

True, 'some mother's son', is a metaphor and a reality as we see in the chronicles in this volume. But equally, they demonstrate how in conflict situations, women who are traditionally cast as embodying community honour, are pushed to embrace markers of an exclusivist community identity, as for example, in the veiling of Intifada women or Kashmiri women. But women are not just passive sites for reproducing community identity. In the struggle for an independent Naga nationality based on the cultural and political survival of an exclusivist identity, women are careful not to challenge but do innovate within their traditional identities. Among the Naga Mothers, agency is manifest through 'stretched roles' of women within the Naga social tradition.

A critical analysis of the way the gender issue is configured in community/nationalist struggles in Kashmir and the Northeast in India, the Chittagong Hill Tracts (CHT) in Bangladesh, the Sri Lanka Tamil conflict and the Muttahida Quami Movement (MQM) violence in Pakistan, reveals a central paradox. It is precisely at the time of dramatic shifts in gender roles, brought about by the societal upheaval attendant on conflict, that the impulse to promote women's social transformation and autonomy is circumscribed by the nationalist or communitarian project itself. For these projects need to configure women as the guardians of the community's accepted and acceptable distinct cultural identity and tradition, thus circumscribing the processes of desirable change and even pushing back women.[7] This may also explain why peace is invariably conceptualised as a return to the gender status quo irrespective of the non-traditional roles taken on by women in conflict.

Conflict in South Asia

South Asia is one of the most conflict prone regions of the world. It has witnessed three inter-state wars, two partitions, intermittent low intensity conflicts and a powder keg of intra-state class, caste, communal, ethnic and nationality conflicts. In the post-colonial nation states of South Asia, the majoritarian nation-state building project of these multi-ethnic and multi-cultural political entities has produced violent struggles and military repression. The ferocity with which smaller groups are asserting their right to cultural survival and political power has seriously challenged the state as the sole source of legitimate political power and the concept of the state as a neutral umpire. Resurgence of ethnicity and nationality has pockmarked South Asia's history with civil wars. Politicised religion has fostered cultural violence undermining the impulse to promote social reform in the position of women. Globalisation driven economic policies have deepened the poverty divide (and feminised poverty). The failure of the democratic agenda to make a difference to the grinding poverty and underdevelopment of the majority of the people, has radicalised politics.

Revolutionary class struggles have plunged Nepal, and Bihar and Andhra Pradesh in India into peoples' wars. Separatist and autonomy struggles have, in the north-east of India, produced five decades of violent conflict. In Sri Lanka, the ethnic conflict is in its 18th year; in Bangladesh, after 16 years of armed struggle for autonomy in the Chittagong Hill Tracts a fragile peace accord has been negotiated; in Pakistan, chronic cycles of violence continue to wreak havoc in the urban areas of Sindh pitting Urdu-speaking immigrant peoples against the state, the Sindhi community and others. Communal and sectarian violence is endemic in India and Pakistan. Twelve years of conflict in Kashmir have turned it into a flashpoint for violent conflict between India and Pakistan which could plunge South Asia into a nuclear war.

Technology and the strategy of total war have resulted in civilians becoming the overwhelming casualties of war. Warfare is no longer something which happens far away on the front, an empty space functionally differentiated for conflict. In South Asia's internal conflicts, as elsewhere, modern organised political violence rests on creating institutional terror which penetrates the entire fabric of grassroots social relations as a means of control. The sites for confrontation with the enemy are the market-place, the community water tap and bathing space, sites largely visited by women. The counter-war objective is to undermine the social fabric of society, psychologically demoralise the community and alienate their support for the 'enemy' as a viable alternative. Women who are the social bulwarks of the family and the community, invariably become targets of heinous violence in counter-insurgency operations and wars of attrition.

Beyond Victimhood

Traditionally, women have formed the humanitarian front of the war story. They are the mothers grieving for sons dead and missing. They are the widows or half-widows struggling to survive in female-headed households bringing up orphaned children. They are refugees displaced from homes. They are the raped and murdered in war. Essentially, women are visible as the overwhelming victims of war. But beyond the passivity and powerlessness of victimhood, conflict has seen South Asian women come out and mobilise resistance, confront the security forces, the administration and the courts. Women have formed Mothers Fronts and coalitions for peace, women have become guerrillas and soldiers and women have emerged as agents of social transformation and conflict resolution.

Violent conflict opens up for women the public sphere predominantly controlled by men. As the security forces and armed groups spread institutional terror, civil society is suppressed and the public sphere of men collapses. Men literally and metaphorically retreat into the private sphere, traditionally the domain of women. In these conditions when the organisation of survival becomes critical, men often have to abdicate their roles and female management of survival assumes crucial importance. As we see in the lived narratives of women in the Kashmir conflict or in the Chittagong Hill Tracts of Bangladesh, protracted curfews and high risk security regimes obliged women to innovate survival strategies for the family and community. It was the mothers, wives and sisters who made the rounds of detention centres and torture cells looking for the disappeared and entered into negotiations of power with the institutional power structures, the army, administration and the courts. Women used their traditional invisibility in the public sphere to create space for their activism. As they are seen as less threatening, they are less watched. Violent conflict blurs the divide between the private sphere of the family and the public sphere of men and politics and in so doing calls into question the validity of the divide. Indeed, the chronicles in this volume look at the gender politics inherent in the assertion: 'Oh, women, they don't want to be political.'

Theorising about Women and Peace

In the iconography of war, the woman of peace is the Mother. The electronic media has powerfully reinforced that image. In the first phase of the Chechnya conflict in the 1990s, the media reported how Russian mothers went to the front to take back home their soldier sons, away from the fighting. The *motherist* narrative highlights the conservative logic of the biological connection in the binary stereotype of women and peace, and men and war. Feminist peace analysis is uncomfortable with the *motherist* logic which ends up implicitly affirming the structural inequality between men and women at the heart of patriarchy. As Brock-Unte defines it, patriarchy is 'a form of social organisation based on the force based ranking of the male half of humanity over the female half, patriarchy has to do with power over people, mostly power to control women and nature'.[8]

Also, the *motherist* or testosterone logic flies in the face of empirical evidence which demonstrates that there is nothing essentialist or inherently peaceful about women. Women make up a third of the combatants in the Maoist insurgency in Nepal and the Somalia conflict. Women in Rwanda and the LTTE in Sri Lanka have been perpetrators in the ethnic/communal attacks and massacres of women and children. However, it is a fact that men predominate across the spectrum of violence.[9] Perhaps it is more useful to think not of women's 'natural' commitment to peace but of the profound depths of violence in masculine culture and institutions.

The cultural argument rests on the psycho-social construction of feminities and masculinities in patriarchal societies which connects women to peace. The cultural logic spotlights women's socialisation as primary child rearers and nurturers which privileges values such as the ethics of care and rewards cooperation and not competition and conflict, privileged in the socialisation of men in patriarchy. It is argued that militarisation relies on patriarchal patterns and patriarchy in a sense relies on militarisation.[10] Structurally, women are excluded from decision making on security issues and indeed from politics. Culturally, militaries need men and women to behave like binaries, i.e., women need men to protect them and men go to war to protect women. The false consciousness or ambiguous logic of 'protecting women', was exposed during an Africa regional meet on child soldiers in Mozambique. Defending the conscription of children, government officials—all men—asked, 'What will happen when all of us are dead? Somebody has to protect the women.' Representatives of non-governmental organisations (NGOs)—all women—replied: 'Women will protect themselves.' At stake was not only how to tackle conflict but how to avoid it. 'If a child at 14 is fighting, who's to say at 24 he won't want to go back to fighting and look for excuses to do so.'[11]

Amidst the ambiguities of peace as a women's issue because of biology or culture, is the argument that peace is a women's issue because of reasons of justice. Cynthia Cockburn, a feminist researcher and peace activist maintains that 'if women have a distinctive angle in peace, it is not due to women being nurturing. It seems more to do with knowing oppression when we see it.'[12] Knowing what it is to be excluded and inferiorised as women, gives them special insights into the structure of unequal relations at the root of conflict. Women, therefore, are more likely to see a continuum of violence, because they experience the connected forms of domestic and political violence that stretches from the home, to the street to the battlefield. A 'feminist' culture of peace fundamentally critiques unequal structures of domination and is built on learning to live with difference without aggression. In short, peace politics are crucial for everyone in unequal relations. The question of women and peace and the meaning of peace for women cannot be separated from the broader question of unequal relationships between women and men in all spheres of life and the family.[13] It is a radicalisation of the women and peace connection. A feminist peace politics thus connects with the struggle against racial, ethnic and class oppression.

Clearly, peace here is much more than an absence of conflict or an absence of fear of direct physical violence which Brock-Unte calls a 'negative peace'. A 'positive peace', she argues, includes absence of structural inequalities in micro structures leading to unequal life chances and an absence of economic structures built up within a country or between countries so that the life chances of some are reduced and the environment irretrievably degraded. As we explore below, women's notion of peace is mediated by the vision of a 'just peace' and a 'positive peace'. Women's peace movements have been a major influence on current trends towards the redefinition of security. They have argued that real human security lies in protection against harm of all kinds, in a healthy environment capable of sustaining all life and respect for human dignity of all. Women's experiences of providing for day-to-day human security and their more comprehensive perspectives on what constitutes security are essential to the redefinition of security.

In the ultimate analysis, understanding the women and peace connection is to understand the gendered impact of militarisation and the violence of armed conflict on women. It is a truism that in the modern forms of organised political violence, women are the worst sufferers. Women are victims of the physical and psychological violence of dislocation, fragmentation of families, loss of children and men, and the predatory masculinity and misogyny of war, rape and murder. Women experience the economic violence of conflict even before its physical outbreak. Militarisation entails a diversion of scarce resources from the social sectors of greatest concern to women. The disruption of armed conflict makes the socially assigned responsibility of women to feed and care for the children and the aged, all the more difficult. While the men go underground and join the militias, it is the women who remain in the home, unless forced to flee. Indeed, for women the negotiation with conflict begins 'after the bombs stop falling'.[14] Conflict produces women-headed households in a patriarchal society where women are structurally and socially disadvantaged.

Cultural violence against women gets magnified as conflict promotes macho values which legitimise misogyny. Rape is not an accident of war. In the case of the Palestinian conflict, 'The violence used against Palestinian men has made them violent at home, in the work place and in their free time', observed Palestinian Member of Parliament (MP) Dalal Salmeh. In Karachi an MQM woman observed that after the conflict began her normally timid husband would threaten her with his gun. Men compensate for their loss of power by hitting out at women. Moreover, with women seen as symbolic and physical markers of community identity, there is the pressure (on both men and women) to embrace identity constructs which undermine women's autonomy of being, as in the veiling of Palestinian women after the Intifada uprising or in India's Kashmir after the outbreak of insurgency. This practice recedes as the intensity of conflict eases.

There is need, however, to guard against sentimentalising the issue of women and peace politics. Women have been known to actively support violent and sectarian organisations and have been guilty of perpetuating the 'them' and 'us' divide at the heart of conflict. Mothers have risen to oppose a conflict that kills their sons, but equally they have raised sons to be soldiers to be sacrificed in the name of nationalism. And yet in the end, as Thandi Modise, an MP from South Africa observed,

> For women, it doesn't matter which side you are on, on both sides children get maimed and killed and women get raped. It makes it difficult for women to choose sides and enables them to reach out across the ethnic divide. This is particularly so when the violence is perceived as illegitimate, that is violence for violence's sake. But the neutral space is a contested one with competing ideologies at play of nationalism, community, class, race and gender.

Arguably, the fact that the women's historical experience is one of living disarmed (in a monstrously armed world), as the feminist historian Bernice Carrol describes it, 'gives women special skills to assess the role of weapons and war and to offer alternative models of behaviour in dealing with conflict and social change'.[15]

Problematising Gender, War and Peace in South Asia

This volume has a consciously exploratory character. The overarching theories of gender and conflict have been hewn in the critical analysis of women in conflict situations in Africa, former Yugoslavia, Northern Ireland, South America and the Middle East. Given the historical, regional and cultural diversity of the South Asian experience, there is need for specific empirical studies to constantly test assumptions in what is an experimental field of study and a germinal state in the theory and praxis of women's culture of peace politics. Locating South Asian women's experiences of conflict and addressing the dualism of women's agency turning to violence or to peace, requires us to innovate tools of analysis. In giving primacy to women's voices, we have to learn to listen to women's language of resistance encoded in their cultural space of being.

The six chapters in this volume make visible how women's lived experience and responses have been shaped by violence, how in turn women have reconstructed new meanings in the interiority of their lives and stretched them to the public realm. We question how women's engagement with everyday violence has led them to think of issues of security, peace, conflict management and transformation. The assumption is that the impact of violence on women is gendered, their response is gendered, and their notion and praxis of peace building too is gendered. A gender sensitive analysis of conflict and peace inevitably runs the risk of over-determining the category of gender. Also, a gender analysis tends to reinforce as essentialist the categories of feminine and masculine underlying patriarchy, rather than moving towards a solution within these socialised dichotomies. In its defence, it should be said that the 'over-determination' is necessary to make women's historical invisibility, visible.

Underpinning these six chronicles is our understanding that women's negotiations with violent conflict create historically and situationally specific economic, social, cultural, ethnic and national realities that form a new knowledge base and resource. We claim space for a women's narrative of the war story. In Kashmir, is there a women's war narrative which challenges the dominant narrative structure of binaries—nationalist and pro-separatist, soldier and militant, grieving mother and martyr's mother? How do women, historically excluded from formal political space, negotiate the ambiguities of ethnic and national identities? Controlling women's sexuality is central to demarcating ethnic and national boundaries and women have both accepted and contested embracing visible markers of communal identity, e.g., the veiling of Kashmiri women. But women's multiple narratives also reveal a capacity for alternative ways of negotiating the construction of conflictual identities.

What conditions foster women's agency in creating neutral spaces and reaching across a hostile ethnic divide as in the case of Bodo women talking to Santhal women in Assam in India or the weakness of the Sinhala Mothers Front in Sri Lanka to forge solidarity with the Tamil Mothers Front in the north? Does the absence of autonomous and secular women's groups in Kashmir limit the possibility of women's independent activism and the possibility of transcending the communalisation of the struggle? In Sri Lanka, however, secular women's groups have been unable to survive the hostile ethno-nationalist climate and ended up getting co-opted by political parties. But in Karachi, Pakistan, an initiative by a mainstream secular women's group, the Women's Action Forum (WAF), has demonstrated the possibility of forging solidarities with 'other' women trapped in MQM violence and the possibility of bringing the women of divided communities together.

Violent conflict renders women without men, vulnerable to the predatory masculinities a war culture fosters. But what about the opportunities for intended and unintended desirable changes wrought by protracted conflict in opening up empowering spaces for women? What social transformations have been effected as a result of the structural implications of nearly a quarter of the households in Sri Lanka being women headed or in Nepal's villages without men and in Karachi, where men have retreated from a violence bombed public sphere? A spontaneous civil society mobilisation against violence sees the emergence of groups like the Hill Women's Federation (HWF) in the CHT conflict, but why do they get politically marginalised? Is it because like the Muslim Khawateen Markaz or Dukhtarane Millat in Kashmir, HWF lacked autonomy and when

political alliances were brokered by dominant masculine organisations, they too became allied and marginalised?

Does the induction of women in the fighting ranks of rebel forces
with an ultra-nationalist ideology like the LTTE or United Liberation Front of Assam (ULFA) have liberatory implications for reworking gender relations or are they just cogs in the wheel? In
revolutionary class struggles such as the Maoist Peoples War in
Nepal, has the large presence of women at all levels resulted in women
reshaping the programmatic agenda to take on the women's question and not postpone it till after the revolution? As Darini
Rajasingham-Senanayake reminds us, feminist scholarship has shied
away from engaging with women's agency turning violent except
to locate it as a male patriarchal project. Women make up a sixth of
the LTTE fighting force and a third of the guerrillas in the Maoist
strongholds in Nepal. Gautam, Banskota and Manchanda examine
the dynamics of how the revolutionary ideology of the Peoples War
has created a space for women to claim rights, but the women joining the movement have given a substantive material reality to that
ideology at the grassroots level.

Mobilisation of women in conflict and even induction of women
in the guerrilla ranks is recognised (by men) as necessary in democratic struggles. New role models are configured by the propaganda
machinery of war as for example, in the projection of the martyrdom of Malathi by the LTTE in Sri Lanka. Annually on her death
anniversary there is a public commemoration of her sacrifice, the
first woman Tiger to be killed upholding Tamil rights. During the
latest celebration on 10 October 1999 women dressed in the colour
of blood carried placards proclaiming 'Women! Break barriers ex-
pedite liberation'. Two teachers carried a huge cut-out of the LTTE
supremo Velupillai Prabhakaran.[16] Ultra-nationalist and fascist movements like the LTTE and the MQM often involve women pledging
personal loyalty to the supremo, in the case of the latter—Altaf
Hussain.

A recurring theme in the six chapters in this volume is the instrumental relationship forged by struggle movements with women,
dramatically illuminated in the title '"They Use Us and Others Abuse
Us": Women in the MQM conflict'. Women raped by the security

forces are exploited in the propaganda war to expose the human rights violations of the state. But as in Kashmir, the pro-separatist political ideologues fail to take on the challenge of locating rape in gender politics, reinforcing the notion of feminisation of honour, thus condemning the raped women to social ostracism in a patriarchal society. In Assam in India, studies have shown that victims of army rape were later liable to be sexually violated by their own patriarchy. In the MQM conflict in Pakistan, in the case of rape the notion of family/community honour remained the dominant discourse, not the violation of a woman's body and her social being. Anis Haroon questions patronising quick fixes like the leadership calling for boys to come forward and cover 'her shame' with marriage.

The politics of rape in conflict is imbricated in women's bodies being both a metaphor and the material reality of markers of the identity of the community/nationality. Meghna Guhathakurta explores, through the poetry of the Chakma women in Bangladesh, how in their consciousness the politics of the struggle for CHT self-determination is internalised in their physical being, and their personal humiliation and harassment by the state security forces is experienced as the humiliation of the community/nation. This explains the refusal to acknowledge sexual violation by one's own armed groups and the hostility to mixed marriages.

These empirically based chronicles seek to understand the nature of the women's experience of political violence as direct and indirect victims of physical violence, economic violence and cultural violence. The emphasis, however, is on how it shaped women's responses. We focus on why women, whose mobilisation was so visible in the spontaneous part of the struggle, get marginalised and post-conflict women get pushed back to their sewing machines with the gendered statement: 'they don't want to be political.' Women are projected as the victims in the humanitarian front of the war story but their activism in conflict situations is undervalued.

Part of the difficulty is that women themselves see their activity as non-political and an extension of their domestic concerns, i.e., stretched traditional roles of the nurturing and protective mother. Women's activism in conflict flows from their everyday concerns of keeping the family together. But in conflict, women's everyday activity as reproducers and nurturers gets highly politicised because it ensures community survival. Its corollary is the specific targeting of women and family as a task of war to destroy the community, as we explore in the Kashmir conflict.

Domestic activism[17] challenges the conventional notion of the public and private sphere. Paula Banerjee in her analysis of the conflict politics of the Northeast in India, shows that women denied space in formal politics creatively expand informal political spaces to negotiate and transform conflict. There is an implicit questioning of the dominant (western) assumption that women's power in their non-public roles is usually depoliticised because this power, in the private sphere, does not give women authority to legitimate their action in society. Arguably, the common experience of women across the region is that their activism, grounded in the informal space of politics, does get undervalued and marginalised as the struggle gets more militarised. However, the Naga women's initiatives show the scope and limits of transcending the public–private divide and using the authority consolidated in the informal space of politics to legitimise a measure of authority in the public space of formal politics.

Women's activism is further obscured by the fact that women's language of support and resistance flows from their cultural experience, especially of being disempowered. Women are not strong in the classic rally and speech variety politics. Women's strategies of protest often use the symbol of mourning and motherhood both for moral authority and political mobilisation. In Sri Lanka, in the aftermath of the suppression of the Marxist-nationalist Janatha Vimukthi Peramuna (JVP) in 1989–90, the Mothers Front drew upon a culturally recognised strategy of ritualistic cursing in public—the traditional weapon of the disempowered—to challenge the government over the fate of the disappearances of 40,000 people.[18]

In the Maoist insurgency in Nepal, the refusal to mourn is forged into an empowering symbol of protest by a widow whose 'innocent' husband was killed by the police in an anti-Maoist action. She wears the social markers of a *suhagan* (a married woman) as a symbol of quiet resistance. In revolutionary or nationalist struggles in

Nepal, Sri Lanka or India, the faithful are exhorted not to mourn for martyrs. The LTTE has specifically proscribed mourning for LTTE cadres killed in action. A mother forbidden to grieve secretly gives a photograph of her son to a priest and asks him to pray for his soul. It is a reminder that for the disempowered, agency can be passive. Private sorrow becomes politicised when it is taken into public space as in the strategy of the Mothers Front or the Women in Black. The creative anarchy, the sporadic nature, the non-hierarchical and non-conventional forms which mark women's initiatives, challenge traditional notions of what political action should and can be about.

In public space made barren by institutional terror such non-formal initiatives open up the space for political mobilisation. But a clear political vision is necessary for human rights initiatives like Parents of the Disappeared in Kashmir to become the frontline of a peace mobilisation lest they get co-opted as happened with the Sri Lanka Mothers Front. The politics of motherhood are ambivalent, they are available for mobilisation for human rights and peace and for raising soldiers. As Cynthia Enloe frames it, there is need to understand 'when a community's politicised sense of its own identity becomes threaded through with pressures for its men to take up arms and for its women to loyally support brothers, husbands, sons and lovers to become soldiers'.[19] Culturally, militaries depend on the acceptance of the logic of men protecting women by arms and women needing protection. The ambiguities inherent in action framed within this binary logic is ironically exposed in Anis Haroon's comments on the huge gates put up by the MQM in affected settlements, in the name of protecting women and children when they were actually installed to defend the militants whose action is endangering women.

It needs to be emphasised that women's critical consciousness about political violence is linked to their construction of the legitimacy and illegitimacy of violence. Women's experience of conflict is not a homogenous experience, it is contextual and shifting. Women's response strategies are also shifting. In Kashmir we see women actively support armed conflict and then turn their backs on the armed struggle. In the CHT conflict, human rights violations mobilised civil society activism, e.g., the Hill Women's Federation, and opened up the possibility of democratising the struggle and empowering non-armed actors in the conflict transformation process. In the Peoples War in Nepal there is a sharp contrast in the differentiated attitude towards political violence between the Maoist widows and the widows of the victims of Maoist violence.

In a comparative study of conflicts in the Northeast in India, Paula contrasts women's support for the 'just' struggle of the Naga peoples and their alienation from the corrupted violence engulfing Assam. In both situations though women have been in the forefront of a kind of politics which has helped to limit the impact of armed conflict on the fabric of society. What then is a woman's peace politics? As a peace activist from Northern Ireland Carmel Roulston observes, women's peace building efforts have laid the foundation for a future where the two warring groups 'can learn to accommodate each other and to express their differences without aggression'.[20]

Women forge survival strategies, build dialogue, co-existence and reconciliation at the grassroots level, but get marginalised when formal politics takes over at the negotiating table. In the negotiations for the Bangladesh–CHT peace accord of December 1997, no weightage was given to the Hill Women's Federation. At the negotiating table were only representatives of the armed group. Meghna Guhathakurta suggests that the accord is flawed because it sidesteps issues necessary for the reconciliation process to take place, that is, issues of human rights violation and justice. Increasingly, women activists across these conflicts are questioning their exclusion from the negotiating table. Women are active in healing and reconciling at the local village level through informal sporadic initiatives but are powerless to shape the big questions which again plunge their communities into destructive conflict. The lessons of the recent history of war and more war in Bosnia, Northern Ireland, Rwanda, Burundi or closer home in Sri Lanka, Pakistan and India emphasise the importance of women moving beyond the humanitarian front of the story to take a seat at the negotiating table. Women need to be present to discuss issues of genocide, impunity and security if a 'just' and enduring peace is to be built. The luxury of Virginia

Woolf's 'outsider' position in *The Three Guineas* is just not tenable if a peace politics is to be built.[21]

Patriarchal structures which exclude women from formal politics predicate that their experience of negotiating conflict and maintaining survival is not recognised as a significant resource either nationally or internationally. The challenge is to tap and consolidate the myriad spontaneous and sporadic women's initiatives in the informal space of politics and facilitate access to resources to enable women to negotiate formal structures of power.

In this context the problematic posed by Darini is a necessary caution and opens up the possibility of an alternative way of seeing. She reopens the debate about the empowering value of the strategy of getting women into formal politics when politics are violent and polarised, arguing that women leaders like Chandrika Kumaratunga who came to politics with an alternative vision of an ethnic peace, inevitably became captive to the violent political forces and structures which thrust them into power in the first place. Of course it can be argued that you need a critical mass of 33 per cent to impact upon the masculinised structures of institutions and processes. However, as Darini goes on to explore, nationalist struggles, which drew in an overwhelming number of women, also entail their own closures, especially those imbued in an ultra-nationalist ideology. She reposes her faith in the structural emergence of patterns of empowerment and social transformation in the lives of women as a result of the unintended effects of conflict dislocation.

In a further twist to the subject of unintended consequences and conflict, in Nepal's Maoist insurgency, in the better developed Gorkha district a linkage seems to be discernible between the literacy campaigns for women and women joining the Maoists. Its parallel is the Sandinista revolution in Nicaragua, where, '. . . young women participated in the literacy campaign when they were thirteen and in the militia when they were fourteen'.[22]

Finally, it needs to be acknowledged why in our articulation of a women's peace politics, the resolution of the women's question (i.e., reworking of the unequal gender relations) assumes such importance as not only desirable but necessary. The basic premise is that the meaning for peace for women cannot be separated from the broader question of unequal relationships between women and men in all spheres of life. The narratives in these chronicles explore the linkage between political violence and rising violence in the home. Paula, in laying bare the paradox of the declining female:male sex ratio in the north-east in India, where the predominance of matri-lineal societies should have made for a higher status for women, links it with conflict and rising violence against women. Indeed, its full implications merit a much more extended analysis.

Understanding women and peace is to understand the experience of militarisation and political violence for women in terms of phys-ical, economic and cultural violence. Disempowered in peace time, in the time of conflict, a time of decision by arms, women are even more disadvantaged and less able to assert their rights and the rights of their children to entitlements. War magnifies the already existing gender inequalities of peace time. Peace politics is of central con-cern to all in unequal power relations. Peace is not envisaged as a return to the status quo. A just peace involves the reworking of gender status quo.

In the voices of the women negotiating conflict, the space for the women's question in democratic struggles remains an unresolved and contested one. For Kalpana Chakma of the Hill Women's Fed-eration in the CHT, the struggle for rights had also to do with women's rights. But for Chanmaya Jajo of the Naga Peoples Move-ment for Human Rights, 'women have deliberately avoided the woman–man confrontation due to the larger issues which have had to be faced unitedly by our people'. She quotes an indigenous sister from Colombia, 'our people's history has taught us that we can ill afford to pursue the luxury of gender justice for our communities as a whole. Men and women together need to fight against the sys-tem and not with each other'.[23]

Mapping Women and Conflict in South Asia

Mapping women and conflict in six of the hottest conflict situations in South Asia should be seen as only a beginning in honing a frame-work of analysis which may prove helpful in exploring a myriad women's experiences of organised politicised violence in the region. Waiting to be tapped is the experience of women activists in the *dalams* of the Peoples War Group in Andhra Pradesh, India,[24] women in caste and communal violence across India, Pakistan and Bangladesh, women's anti-militarism and anti-nuclear activism in Orissa, Bihar and Balochistan and cross-border mobilisation for peace between India and Pakistan.

This book has been built on the pioneering studies done by scholars like Kumari Jayawardene on women in nationalist struggles in the Third World.[25] Academics like Partha Chaterjee have turned over that material to produce critical insights into the closures inherent in the nationalist projects and the inevitable limits to women's empowerment not because of the priority of nationalist issues but because of the specific role assigned to women and the family in the nationalist project.[26] Regional studies of women in the nationalist struggles of the Quit Kashmir movement, the Nupi wars in the Northeast and in the revolutionary struggles in Telegana and Tebhaga[27] in India, provide a rich historical resource. Indeed the oral history project of the women in the Telegana movement is an inspirational innovative methodology for promoting an alternative reading of history, for making visible women's agency.[28]

Despite this, the relative barren landscape of a gender analysis of political violence in South Asia was highlighted by the dramatic impact made by the partition studies of Menon and Bhasin and Butalia. Till then, in the violence of partition, women had been visible only as gross statistical generalisations of abducted women (or rape victims of the partition of Pakistan and Bangladesh). Ritu Menon and Kamla Bhasin's study *Borders and Boundaries*[29] and Urvashi Butalia's work, *The Other Side of Silence*[30] provide rare insights into the lived experience of women caught in conflict and the gender politics of partition. Their analysis of the nationalist obsession with the recovery of the abducted women explores the politics of their bodies becoming the subjugated territory across which national and community boundaries were marked.

International feminist scholars like Brownmiller, Turpin and Copelon recognise that the scale and ethnically defined nature of rape in Bosnia is not unique. Historically the use in war of genocidal rape, i.e., aimed at destroying the racial distinctiveness of a people, is located in earlier incidents such as the mass rape of more than 200,000 Bengali women by Pakistani soldiers in the Bangladesh Liberation War in 1971.[31] Twenty-five years later, the Women's Action Forum of Pakistan in March 1996 formally apologised to the women of Bangladesh for the mass rape and humiliation of Bangladeshi women. However, there has been no corresponding acknowledgement of the mass rape in 1971 of 'Bihari' women (Urdu-speaking immigrants in East Pakistan) by Bangla militants.

Post independence, despite the escalation in ethnic armed conflicts and the growing discipline of women's studies, there have been relatively few systematic attempts to engage with a gender analysis of conflict. The occasional gendered study of violence indicated how unchartered the field was, e.g., Veena Das' essay on the anti-Sikh carnage in Delhi, Valli Kanapathipillai's analysis of 'The Survivor's Experience' and Malathi De Alwis on the Sinhala Mothers Front during the JVP insurrection in Sri Lanka. On the whole though, it was through the human rights discourse that women's experiences of political violence were made visible but that discourse is one of victimhood.

Early essays at documenting women's peace activism in the Nupi Lan[32] women's revolt in Manipur, north-east India, opened up a field of study which is still waiting for an author. In history, the Nupi Lan women's war of 1904 and that of the Meitei women of Manipur in 1939 remain only footnotes. Its modern incarnation is the women's struggle in the 1990s against human rights violations and excesses by the security forces. Black laws like the Armed Forces Special Powers Act turned Manipur into a garrisoned state with a ratio of one soldier to four civilians. Traditional forms of struggle were adopted like the *Meira Paibis* or the legendary torch-bearers of the Meitei community physically patrolling their neighbourhoods to keep at bay the security forces, and the infiltration of narcotics and alcohol.

All over the region there are pockets of spontaneous, sporadic and fledgling women initiatives to reduce the impact of violence and to build peace, initiatives which remain invisible, unrecognised and undervalued. In the Naga hills of Manipur, India, in Churachanpur district bordering Myanmar, the ferocity of internecine violence between two Kuki tribes Thadou and Paite, brought 5,000 women across the conflict divide out on the streets in 1995 to appeal for peace. They forced the village elders to broker a peace which still holds. In Assam, Bodo Women's Justice Forum has appealed to Santhal women to create a neutral space for a dialogue. In Orissa in India, women were in the forefront of the popular agitation against the setting up of a missile test site. In Bihar, women were over-whelmingly present in the struggle against a military firing test range. In Balochistan in Pakistan, women, men and children marched against the Kargil war. Women peace activists have taken the lead in voicing protests against the nuclear tests in the Chagai hills of the province, linking it with regional discrimination and denial of demo-cratic rights.

Women's groups have been in the forefront of the myriad peace initiatives against the militarisation of the subcontinent and the emer-gence of a national security state pathology. For it is women who have been the worst hit by the deprivation of economic resources from social sectors and the politics of hate which has fuelled the mutual rise of fundamentalist forces and heightened cultural vio-lence against women. It is therefore not surprising that women's groups have mobilised to support people-to-people initiatives like Pakistan India Peoples Forum for Peace and Democracy and the Pakistan Peace Coalition. The Forum is exceptional as its agenda conceptualises as interdependent the four themes of Kashmir, de-militarisation, governance and religious intolerance. Women have been conspicuously present at candlelight vigils for peace. They have innovated on the official India–Pakistan bus diplomacy (tarnished by Kargil) to launch a Women's Peace Bus initiative flagged off in March 2000 involving a reciprocal visit of Indian and Pakistani women talking peace.

However, the map of South Asia is also marked by the failure to build solidarities across issues of internal and external militarisation. This has weakened not only the peace movement but also women's peace activism both internally and across borders. National women's groups have been reluctant to forge solidarity even on a human rights plane with women in ethnic conflict situations, especially in pro-separatist national identity struggles like in Kashmir. The WAF initiative in Karachi stands out for its singularity.

Where there has been much more attention, research and solidarity has been in the area of women and communal violence in South Asia.[33] We have already alluded to the sexual violence against women in communal conflicts as women's bodies become markers of the boundaries of community identity. Moreover, women's testimonies of communal riots reveal the misogynous form communal violence takes and the predatory sexuality unleashed in conflict. Women's complicity in communal violence has also been insinuated in Surat in Gujarat, India, though fact finding reports have not been able to document it.[34] Equally, women across communities have built peace committees and helped each other in crises. For one powerless woman in Surat, political agency was expressed in her stubborn refusal to bear her husband's child, the child of a man she knew had raped the woman next door, i.e., a rapist's child.

In Ahmedabad, in Gujarat, India's most communalised state, despite the fact that model organisations like SEWA exist which have brought women of all communities together in income-generating schemes, in a riot situation women have only minimally succeeded in stemming the communal behaviour of the men. Some did try to keep their men home, help those in distress and keep joint vigils in mixed neighbourhoods,[35] but increasingly the communalising poison has ghettoised minds.[36]

An analysis of women's experiences of communal/ethnic conflict remains confined to the victimhood paradigm as in the case of the anti-Sikh 'riots' in Delhi in 1984. This is evident in Chakravarty and Haksar's record of testimonies of Sikh widows.[37] However, in an attempt to move away from victimhood, Veena Das' essay, 'Our Work to Cry: Your Work to Listen'[38] explores how the widows of the Delhi Sikh carnage took the symbols of mourning and pollution and gave it a political meaning. In defiance of the authorities, who wanted them to terminate their mourning, these women fashioned a language of protest against the utter injustice of their situation through prolonged mourning and the adoption of symbols of pollution and dirtiness. In a companion piece on the transformation of the social reality of Tamil women in the aftermath of the 1983 ethnic violence in Sri Lanka, Kanapathipillai[39] looks at the central role played by women in the process of reformulating their worlds as they learnt to operate bureaucratic and judicial systems. This alternative discourse was lightly touched, waiting to be defined.

Six South Asian War Chronicles

This volume is structured around six chronicles of women negotiating violent politics in their everyday life and women's agency for change and transformation in major conflict situations in South Asia. It is from the experiential plane that this inquiry was initiated into the questions: where are the women in South Asian conflicts, and what conditions motivate women's agency for peace and war. Indeed, as Deepa Ollapally, drawing a distinction between western and South Asian approaches notes, 'In South Asia theory may be viewed as being in the process of being built from bottom up rather than top down as has been the case in the west'.[40] This is an exploratory effort to develop within a comparative framework women's perspectives of conflict in the region. A comparative framework opens up the possibility of developing a generalised framework for analysing women's experience of conflict across political units and typologies of conflict in the region and beyond.

It is true that South Asian women are united by virtue of being women living in the poor underdeveloped post-colonial states of South Asia and labouring under oppressive patriarchal structures sanctioned by custom and religious orthodoxy. South Asian women share the common experience of the extremely low status of women in the region. But, it is true also that they are separated by caste, culture, ideology, religion, ethnicity and nationality. A comparative perspective guards against tendencies towards over-simplification and generalisation in what are diverse historical and cultural situations. Still, in the mosaic of women's experiences of conflict represented in the six chronicles, a pattern of generalisations can be picked out.

'Guns and *Burqa*: Women in the Kashmir Conflict' in this volume tracks the Kashmiri women's shifting and contextual construction of the legitimacy and illegitimacy of political violence, from women's mobilisation in popular struggle to turning their backs as militancy deteriorates into the politics of extremism. Looking at the many faces of Kashmiri women in conflict, it shows how women's political activism was rooted in their everyday concerns of managing survival, that is, 'stretched' roles. From the icon of the sorrowing mother who grieves in private but sacrifices her son for the cause, is the transformation of the mother as agency, who takes her private grief into public space thus politicising it, e.g., the Association of the Parents of the Disappeared. Motherhood is seen as available for mobilisation as resistance but also for co-optation in support of militarism and nationalism. The chapter explores the ambiguities inherent in women's negotiations with ethnic identity and nationality through the metaphor of 'some mother's son' in reaching across the Muslim–Pandit divide and the limitations of the space for an alternative response. It enters into the dynamics of how the self-identity of a community is constructed around its women and in particular women's bodies which become sites for reproducing a politically reconstructed community identity, in this case, an Islamised identity in denial of the liberalism of Kashmiriyat cultural identity. The essay reveals that the political leadership developed an instrumental relationship with women categorising them as martyrs' mothers or raped women and dismissing their activism as accidental and denying them agency.

In 'Ambivalent Empowerment: The Tragedy of Tamil Women in Conflict', Darini Rajasingham-Senanayake develops the provocative argument of unintended 'gains' from conflict and the need for the cultural legitimisation of those gains if women exploring new empowering roles are not to become double victims. She takes on the discourse of victimhood which frames the policy interventions of the human rights and humanitarian agencies. Focusing on the border villages and the camps for the internally displaced, Darini looks at the structural changes wrought by 18 years of violent conflict in displacing caste and gender hierarchies. Violent death and protracted conflict have opened up analogous spaces for agency and empowerment for women. At one end is the violent catapulting of women into high office, e.g., Chandrika Kumaratunge. Darini stresses the limits to women's empowerment through formal politics at a time of violence. Then there are the 'nationalist' women in the ranks of the LTTE and Sri Lankan military, whom the prevailing feminist discourse sees as captive to a patriarchal nationalist project. She warns that to deny the LTTE women agency is to further position them as victims. Finally, there is the social structural transformation wrought by protracted violence in the daily lives of thousands of invisible Tamil women who have become heads of households. Darini argues,

> The greater challenge to the status quo comes less from women in fatigues who might be asked to do desk jobs after the conflict, and more from the women who refuse to erase the red *pottu* (symbol of marriage) the unsung civilian women who daily struggle to sustain their families and themselves.

In 'Between Two Armed Patriarchies: Women in Assam and Nagaland,' Paula Banerjee argues that women denied formal political power negotiate their own spaces within and between opposing sets of belligerents, both representing patriarchal power. Taking up the theme that women are not without power in their non-public roles, Paula contrasts how the social situation in Nagaland has enabled women to use that power as authority in the public sphere but in Assam, the politico-cultural framework has been disabling. Women's activism in Nagaland has been supported by both the state and the Naga Ho Council whereas in Assam, Matri Manch type peace initiatives are blocked. In Nagaland, powerful women's groups for peace have emerged and been accepted as peace makers between warring communities. In Assam, sporadic and dispersed local-level initiatives in Assam have been more successful. Paula believes that the failure of Assamese women to transit to formal spaces of political power, has marginalised them. In the vacuum, young women have been attracted to militancy. While women militants in Assam and Nagaland are a study in contrast, there is a common experience of gendered politics as women are discriminated against in combat roles and food entitlements. Paula critiques the dominant images of victim and amazon to show how both embody agency and limitation of choice.

Anis Haroon's essay, '"They Use Us and Others Abuse Us": Women in the MQM Conflict', focuses on an experimental initiative to build solidarities with women trapped in the crossfire of political violence in Karachi. The rise of MQM saw the biggest mobilisation of women since independence but their activism was undervalued and women were denied institutional power. When the MQM leadership was forced underground, MQM used women as the reserve force at the office, in demonstrations, getting them to claim bodies and even burying the dead. But when the MQM was in power women activists were sent back home. It was the WAF's interaction with the MQM women which pushed the patriarchal leadership of the MQM to co-opt the women's question into its agenda to neutralise the competing pull of a secular mainstream women's organisation. Anis, a founder member of WAF, analyses the process of forging solidarities with women across class and ethnic divisions. Empathy and trust built on human rights violation and humanitarian need opened up an opportunity for a multi-ethnic across-class platform to talk about ethnic discrimination, violence and conflict. Through the voices of women she reveals the ambivalence and complicity of the women in whose basements were torture chambers. The MQM women's voices carry the burden of victimhood. The scope for agency is limited.

'Where There Are No Men: Women in the Maoist Insurgency in Nepal' by Shobha Gautam, Amrita Banskota and Rita Manchanda analyses the societal impact of the Maoist Peoples War. Whole villages in the remote mid-western hills of Nepal, the epicentre of the Peoples War, are without men. Left are the women, to confront the brutality of the police and feed and shelter the Maoists. The chapter contrasts the differentiated attitude towards armed struggle of the Maoist widows and the widows of the Maoist victims. It explores how women have negotiated a space without men, innovating a language of resistance, taking up non-traditional tasks like ploughing, stepping into the public space and forming all-women elected village development councils. Others have become guerrillas in the Peoples War. A third of the fighters are women in the Maoist strongholds. The women's question and in particular land rights for women is an integral part of the Maoist revolutionary programme. Is this one struggle in which the women's question has not been postponed till after the revolution? The essay analyses how the Peoples War ideology has created space for women to claim rights but the women joining the movement have also shaped that ideology. Two-thirds of the women in fatigues are from the Tibeto-Burman stock which is relatively less culturally oppressed than the upper-caste Hindus. But it is the liberating promise of the movement which has drawn in so many women even from the better developed Gorkha district.

In 'Women's Narratives from the Chittagong Hill Tracts', Meghna Guhathakurta constructs an alternative reading of the Jumma people's struggle through the voices of indigenous women and Bengali settlers. She explores how their lived experience of the institutionalised terror of army raids and their everday humiliation shaped their resistance and willingness to send their children to fight for the 'dignity' of self and community. She shows how in identity struggles, women internalise their personal humiliation and sexual violation as the humiliation of the community/nation. Its corollary is the use of rape as an instrument of war with one in 10 women being raped in the affected areas. Meghna locates the fierce rejection of mixed marriages in the 'exclusivist' politics of identity struggles with women's bodies becoming markers of community identity. Its extension is the politics of dress in an identity conflict. In her narrative of Shikha Chakma, whom her husband, a Bengali army officer, obliges to wear the traditional dress, Meghna shows how Shikha's dress marginalises her both in her husband's society and her own. The possibility of transcending the majority-minority divide is explored through the forging of a limited solidarity between the Hill Women's Federation and mainstream women's groups on the issue of rape but it does not extend to politics of ethnic discrimination. While civil society mobilisation for peace was a significant feature of the conflict, in the formal negotiations, groups like HWF were marginalised.

Exploring Hybrid Styles

The chronicles have been so laid out as to enable the reader to 'listen' to the voices of different women as they narrate their individual yet collective stories, harmonising their individual voices in a polyphony of other voices. The concern not to lose the authenticity of women speaking about their own experience has determined the nature of what becomes at times a string of narratives. While there is substantial accent on rigorous analysis, it is the empirical experience of these women which has driven the study. In most cases their names have been changed to protect privacy and safeguard their security.

This volume reflects a hybridity of styles in the treatment of the six chronicles, given the heterogenity of the professions of the contributors from academics to journalists, feminists to strategic study specialists. My own engagement with this project grew out of my interest in alternative peace discourses.

Notes

1. Broadly speaking, amidst the many feminisms, a feminist perspective is taken by those men and women who believe that most social systems discriminate against and oppress women and require fundamental restructuring. See Ingeborg Breines, Doroto Gierycz and Betty Reardon, eds, *Towards a Women's Agenda for a Culture of Peace*, UNESCO Publishing, Paris, 1999, p. 13; and Sara Ruddick, 'Women of Peace', in Lois A. Lorentzen and Jennifer Turpin, eds, *The Women and War Reader*, New York University Press, New York, 1998, p. 214.
2. Gender is a social category used here to talk of power relations between women and men as well as the roles they are socialised to play. This definition was accepted at the 'Women in the Aftermath of War and Armed Conflict' conference in Johannesburg, July 1999. See Meredeth Turshen's Report. Unpublished.
3. Verghese Koithara, *Society, State and Security: The Indian Experience*, Sage Publications, New Delhi, 1999. See also my paper 'Redefining and Feminizing Security: Women Making a Difference', presented at the seminar on 'Discourses on Human Security' organised by the Sustainable Development Policy Institute, Islamabad, 24–26 May 2000.
4. See Simona Sharoni for an analysis of the shifts in feminist theorising about

gender and war in 'Towards Feminist Theorizing in Conflict Resolution', September 1994, p. 7. Unpublished paper.
5. See Breines et al., *Towards a Women's Agenda*, n. 1.
6. Dan Smith, 'Women, War and Peace', in Breines et al., *Towards a Women's Agenda*, n. 1, pp. 69–70.
7. Kumari Jayawardene, *Feminism and Nationalism in the Third World*, Kali for Women, New Delhi, 1986.
8. Brigit Brock-Unte, *Feminist Perspectives on Peace and Peace Education*, Pergamon Press, New York, 1989.
9. R.W. Connell, 'Arms and the Man', paper presented at UNESCO meeting on 'Male Roles and Masculinities in the Perspective of a Culture of Peace', Oslo, September 1997. Unpublished.
10. For elaboration of the linkage between patriarchy and militarisation, see Anuradha Chenoy, 'Militarisation, Conflict and Women in South Asia', in Lorentzen and Turpin, *The Women and War Reader*, n. 1, pp. 101–10.
11. This was shared by Thandi Modise, a South African MP, at the 'Women, Violent Conflict and Peacebuilding: Global Perspectives' conference, organised by International Alert, London, 5–7 May 1999.
12. Comment made at a UN Working Group on Women and Armed Conflict preparatory meet for Beijing +5 meet. Also see Cynthia Cockburn, 'Gender, Armed Conflict and Political Violence', background paper presented to The World Bank, Washington, D.C., 10–11 June 1999.
13. Karren Warren and Duane L. Cady, 'Feminism and Peace: Seeing Connections', *Hypatia*, Vol. 9, No. 2, 1994, pp. 1–15.
14. Meredith Turshen and Clotilde Twagiramariya, eds, *What Women Do in Wartime: Gender and Conflict in Africa*, Zed Books, London, 1998.
15. Bernice Carrol, 'Feminism and Pacificism: Historical and Theoretical Connections', in Ruth Roach Pierson, ed., *Women and Peace*, Cromm Helm, Sydney, 1987.
16. Lecture notes of Nimalka Fernando for Human Rights Peace Studies Orientation Course, SAFHR, Kathmandu, 14 February 2000.
17. Validation of domestic activism as a legitimate mode of political activity in the Palestinian struggle is analysed in Monica E. Neugebauer, 'Domestic Activism and Nationalist Struggle', in Lorentzen and Turpin, *The Women and War Reader*, n. 1, pp. 177–83.
18. Malathi de Alwis, 'Motherhood as a Space of Protest', in Patricia Jeffrey and Amrita Basu, eds, *Appropriating Gender*, Routledge, New York, 1998, pp. 184–201.
19. Cynthia Enloe, *The Morning After: Sexual Politics at the End of the Cold War*, University of California Press, Berkeley, 1993, p. 250.
20. Statement made at the 'Women, Violent Conflict and Peacebuilding: Global Perspectives' conference, organised by International Alert, London, 5–7 May 1999.

40   *Rita Manchanda*

21. Virginia Woolf, *The Three Guineas*, Harbin·;er Books, New York, 1938.
22. Diana Mulinari, 'Broken Dreams in Nicaragua', in Lorentzen and Turpin, *The Women and War Reader*, n. 1, p. 160.
23. 'Indigenous Women: The Right to Voice', quoted by Chanmayo Jajo, in Report of the North East Regional Workshop on 'Women and Regional Histories', Guwahati, All India Coordinating Forum of Adivasi and Indigenous Peoples, 24–25 June 1999.
24. Sudesh Vaid, 'Breaking Fear's Silence', in Madhu Kishwar and Ruth Vanita, eds, *In Search of Answers: Indian Voices from Manushi*, Zed Books, London, 1984, pp. 233–53.
25. Jayawardene, *Feminism and Nationalism*, n. 7.
26. Partha Chaterjee, 'The Nationalist Resolution to the Women's Question', in Kumkum Sangari and Sudesh Vaid, eds, *Recasting Women: Essays in Colonial History*, Kali for Women, New Delhi, 1989.
27. Peter Custers, *Women in the Tebhaga Uprising, 1946–47*, Naya Prakashan, Calcutta, 1987.
28. Lalitha K., Vasantha Kannabiran, Rama Melkote, Uma Maheswari, Susie Tharu and Veena Shatrugana (Stree Shakti Sangathan), *We Were Making History: Life Stories of Women in the Telegana Peoples Struggle*, Kali for Women, New Delhi, 1998; and Vasantha Kannabiran and Lalitha K., 'The Magic Time: Women in the Telegana Peoples Struggle', in Sangari and Vaid, *Recasting Women*, n. 26, pp. 180–203.
29. Ritu Menon and Kamla Bhasin, *Borders and Boundaries: Women in India's Partition*, Kali for Women, New Delhi, 1998.
30. Urvashi Butalia, *The Other Side of Silence*, Oxford University Press, New Delhi, 1998.
31. Rhonda Copelon, 'Surfacing Gender: Reconceptualizing Crimes against Women in the Time of War', and Jennifer Turpin, 'Many Faces: Women Confronting War', in Lorentzen and Turpin, *The Women and War Reader*, n. 1, pp. 63–79 and 5–6 respectively. Also see Susan Brownmiller, *Against Our Will: Men, Women, and Rape*, Simon Schuster, New York, 1975, and 'Making Female Bodies the Battlefield', *Newsweek*, 4 January 1993, p. 37.
32. Jarjum Ete, 'Role of Women in the Economy and Environment of the North East India', Report of the North East Regional Workshop on 'Women and Regional Histories', All India Coordinating Forum of Adivasi and Indigenous Peoples, Guwahati, 24–25 June 1999, pp. 24–26; also Devaki Jain, 'Night Patrollers of Manipur', in Devaki Jain, *Women's Quest for Power: Five Indian Case Studies*, Vikas Publishing House, Sahibabad, 1980, pp. 219–68.
33. Sheba George, 'Aspects of Behaviour of State Machinery: Police & Judiciary ... Women's Experience and Women's Response', in Shirin Kudehedkar and Sabiha Al Issa, eds, *Violence Against Women*, Pencraft International, Delhi, 1998.

34. See 'Women and Communal Riots', Report of the Joint Delegation of Women's Organisations fact-finding team, Bhopal, Surat and Ahmedabad, 16–19 February 1993.
35. Mirai Chaterjee, 'Religion, Secularism and Organising Women Workers', in Kamla Bhasin, Ritu Menon and Nighat Said Khan, eds, *Against All Odds*, Kali for Women, New Delhi, 1994, pp. 105–16. Also Report of the Joint Delegation of Women's Organisations, n. 34.
36. See Report of All India Democratic Women's Association (AIDWA) Team Visit to Ahmedabad, 17–18 August 1999, in *Equality*, No. 23, September–October, pp. 23–26.
37. Uma Chakravarty and Nandita Haksar, *Delhi Riots*, Lancer, New Delhi, 1987.
38. Veena Das, 'Our Work to Cry, Your Work to Listen', in Veena Das, ed., *Mirrors of Violence: Communities, Riots and Survivors in South Asia*, Oxford University Press, New Delhi, 1986.
39. Valli Kanapathipillai, 'July 1983: The Survivors Experience', in Das, *Mirrors of Violence*, n. 38, p. 31.
40. Deepa Ollapally, 'Rethinking Gender and Security: Balancing Regional and Global Perspectives', paper presented at the WISCOMP Summer Symposium on Human Security in the Millennium, New Delhi, 21–26 August 2000.

2 Guns and *Burqa*:
Women in the Kashmir Conflict

RITA MANCHANDA

In the past 50 years, the colonial legacy of the unsettled territorial dispute over Jammu and Kashmir has driven India and Pakistan into three fullscale wars, local wars, proxy wars, low intensity wars and artillery duels on the Line of Control (LOC). For the international community, the Jammu and Kashmir conflict is a possible nuclear flashpoint. For the 1.2 billion people of the subcontinent, the 1999 war in the Kargil sector of Kashmir exposed how real the threat of a nuclear war could be as a consequence of the unsettled Kashmir dispute. But for the 13 million[1] people of undivided Jammu and Kashmir, what does it mean to live in a homeland whose destiny remains unsettled? What do the politics of the Kashmiri separatist nationalism struggle mean to the most disempowered members of its society, that is, the women?

The conservative stereotype that men make war while women wait at home, has been turned on its head in today's wars. Violent conflict in protracted low intensity wars by design intrudes into the home and family, to undermine the social fabric, psychologically demoralise the community and alienate the people from the militants. It is not incidental that in counter-insurgency operations women, the physical and social bearers of the community, become targets.

This chapter consciously explores the relevance of a women's perspective in analysing the last 10 years of violent conflict in Jammu and Kashmir. Is there a women's narrative of the Kashmir conflict which challenges the dominant binary stereotypes of nationalist and pro-separatist; soldier and militant; or grieving mother and dry eyed martyr's mother? In Kashmir, how did violence shape women's lived experience and responses and how did women forge survival strategies, new roles and new meanings in their lives? What new modes of action and codes of honour came into being, especially following the discourse of rape as a war crime? Can we see structural changes leading to an empowering shift in gender roles? In a highly militarised and masculinised struggle is there the possibility of space for women's agency for resistance and conflict transformation?

Problematique

Women in the Kashmir insurgency have been boxed into the human rights discourse of victimhood—as victims of direct violence, of rape as a weapon of war by the security forces and of indirect violence which has made them widows, half-widows of the disappeared and mothers of sons killed or orphaned. The conservative patriarchal ideology of the Kashmir struggle cast women as symbols—Grieving Mother, Martyr's Mother and Raped Woman. It developed an instrumental relationship with women as the frontline of the propaganda war over human rights violations by the Indian state and undervalued their activism, dismissing it as accidental. This chapter challenges the victimhood discourse to explore the many ways in which Kashmiri women confronted politicised violence and in the furnace of struggle shaped survival and resistance strategies. But where are the Kashmir women activists today? Politically marginalised. Their activism in the informal space of politics has been depoliticised, for, denied recognition (by men), they have been unable to translate it into authority in the formal sphere of politics.

In protracted conflict situations like Kashmir where the cultural space for women in the public sphere is highly restricted, women's political mobilisation has been manifested in domestic activism. In their everyday life, ordinary women forged survival strategies for their families and communities, they entered into negotiations of power with the security forces and the administration for the rescue and safety of their families. Their traditional roles as mothers and wives were 'stretched' as they emerged as agents of political resistance. The collapse of the divide between the public–private sphere following the societal upheaval attendant on conflict pushed women into negotiations of power in the public sphere. Put another way, the public sphere entered the private sphere as the management of survival became politicised. Indeed, the political mobilisation of the domestic sphere challenged the dichotomy between the domestic and public sphere of politics.

As the Kashmir conflict became more militarised, it also became more masculinised and both the space and recognition for women's contribution got undervalued and marginalised. After 10 years of violent conflict, the once highly visible women activists of the Dukhtarane Millat (Daughters of the Faith, DM) and the Muslim Khawateen Markaz (Council of Muslim Women, MKM) have virtually disappeared. Does it mean the eclipse of women's resistance and of women's agency? Women have innovated forms of resistance grounded in the cultural space of women, especially around mourning, for example, the Association of the Parents of the Disappeared (Kashmir's Mothers Front), which politicises the women's traditional *motherist* role by taking the private act of mourning into the public space. Women's ways of acting are increasingly challenging the notion of what political activity can be. In the experience of Kashmiri women negotiating conflict, can we pick out a pattern of women most active when the struggle is spontaneous and less structured, and marginalised when it becomes more hierarchically structured?[2]

This chapter looks through women's eyes at the war narrative of a nationalist struggle around a politicised 'Kashmiriyat' identity. While the dominant militant discourse is organised to direct community/individuals to violence, women have a more ambivalent and shifting understanding of the legitimacy or illegitimacy of violence[3] according to the evolution of armed struggle. The chapter questions why women are willing to embrace the construction of a self-identity which shrinks their space as women to enjoy rights, i.e., the veiling of Kashmiri women. In the nationalist discourse women's bodies are both the material and metaphoric markers of community identity. Conflict brings into heightened focus the ambiguities in Kashmiri women's negotiations with the public sphere of nationalist and ethnic identity politics, as reflected in the politics of veiling and reaching out across the religious divide.

The experience of violence has had structural implications for a shift in gender roles especially with the emergence of thousands of women-headed households. But armed conflict also reinforces sexist roles. It militarises manliness, makes a macho-misogynist of the soldier/militant and masculinises the struggle.[4] Men emasculated by a powerful armed enemy, hit back by reasserting control over women. The campaign to veil Kashmiri Muslim women reflects the reassertion of male control over their 'own' women.

Finally, the question remains, is there the possibility of women emerging as a constituency for fostering a politics of conflict transformation? Assuming that women's support is the necessary backbone of a protracted struggle, does the apparent distancing of Kashmiri women from armed struggle signal a decisive turning point? There is the risk of over-determining the 'findings', by the posing of the problematique, that is, investing into the research the search for women's agency for resistance and peace building. There is a need to be alert or at least, to acknowledge our desires and our politics in the 'discovery' of women's agency for resistance and peace building.

This chapter draws upon interviews with a wide range of Kashmiri women[5] conducted during 1998 and 1999. It reflects the ambiguities of a remembered reconstruction of their lived experience of how violence shaped their lives and responses and their current sense of fatigue and alienation. In recuperating women voices I laboured under the disadvantage of not speaking Kashmiri and having to work in English and Urdu. Moreover, learning to listen for silences in the words of women from a different culture made it even more difficult. I owe an enormous debt to the women who trusted me and spoke to me. Inevitably in the telling of their narrative, it has become more my narrative, reshaped through my mind, my prejudices and my politics.

Historical Prologue

In India, in the Kashmir valley and the hill districts girdling it, 1989–90 saw a popular upsurge for self-determination which brought women, men and children out on the streets raising the cry for *aazaadi* (independence). Within the mass popular protest was the undertow of a fledgling armed militancy. The Indian state retaliated with severe repression and military force. In the ensuing armed conflict, an estimated 60,000 people have been killed, more than 2,000 have 'disappeared' or are in illegal detention.[6] There are 15,000 widows and thousands of half-widows of the disappeared. A generation has grown up which has known nothing other than armed conflict. The social capital of Kashmir has been destroyed as multiple armed agencies are at large with little or no accountability. More than half-a-million people have been displaced.[7]

Kashmir has been turned into a garrisoned state with more than 300,000 army and security personnel inducted into the state for counter-insurgency operations.[8] Constitutionally guaranteed freedoms have been suspended under special laws like the Armed Forces Special Powers Act. In the last 10 years, popularly backed insurgency has morphed into the politics of armed extremism. Militancy has substantially retreated from Srinagar city and with it the ubiquitous security bunkers, the symbol of India at war with the people of Kashmir. However, it is in the villages on the hills in the border districts and on the strategic heights along the LOC that the battle for Kashmir is being waged with local and foreign militants and the regular armies of India and Pakistan. The people remain trapped, terrorised by multiple armed unaccountable agencies, at risk of being picked up, 'disappeared', illegally detained, tortured, raped and killed.

In 1996, the Indian government decided to revive democratic politics and people were pushed at gunpoint to vote. An elected state government took office with the security forces keeping at bay the militants but the political opportunity for the proverbial silent majority of fence sitters to begin building a peace, was frittered away. The democratically elected state government has not permitted the non-armed pro-separatist political groups to organise democratic public protest. Real power still rests with the security forces and the Pakistan-backed militants.

The people, caught between the savage repression of the Indian state and the extremism of militancy, are tired and disillusioned with armed struggle and resentful about having been used by Pakistan. But the fundamental sense of alienation from India remains. The Kargil war experience further reinforced it, as it was a war for territorial security with scant concern shown for citizens living in the territory. For the people of the valley, the dream of shaking off six centuries of foreign domination, of self-determination, is not spent. Popular support for the cause is there, though not for armed struggle. In a sense, the current phase of 'democratic politics' with the battle lines being held by the security forces on the one side and the militants on the other, is an interregnum in the unfinished agenda of the people's struggle.

The Dispute

India maintains that the territory of Jammu and Kashmir is an integral part of the country after the Hindu Raja of the princely state acceded to an independent India in 1947. Pakistan's claims on Kashmir are derived from the raison d'être of the founding of Pakistan as the homeland of the Muslims of the subcontinent. As such Jammu and Kashmir, a Muslim majority territory should join Pakistan. The territorial dispute of Kashmir has become the ideological battleground for the two nation theory of Hindus and Muslims being separate nations. India has made it the test case of its secularism, linking its fate with the survival of a pluralist Indian state, home to 120 million Muslims.

In the Kashmir wars, Pakistan wrested two-fifths of the territory of the former princely state. Jammu and Kashmir as the name suggests is not a homogenous entity. The Line of Control (ceasefire line of the 1971 war and recognised in the 1972 Simla agreement) divides Pakistan- and India-held Kashmir and by design or accident reflects the broad ethno-cultural divide. What is referred to as Kashmir and imbued with the cultural identity of Kashmiriyat is the valley and the surrounding hill districts.[9] This is the epicentre of the armed struggle.

India and Pakistan are committed through UN Resolutions to hold a plebiscite in their respective areas of Kashmir to enable the people to exercise their right of self-determination. Neither has done so. India insists that the people have exercised their democratic rights in the successive elections held in Jammu and Kashmir. The experience of rigged elections culminating in the blatant manipulation of the 1987 polls was an important catalyst in the upsurge of pro-separatist demands in 1989.

In India, despite constitutional guarantees upholding the separate status of Jammu and Kashmir in the Indian Union, there has been a systematic erosion of autonomy as a result of New Delhi's policies of intervention. For the Kashmiris it was a betrayal of the special status negotiated on its accession in 1947. Kashmiris trace their written history back a thousand years and claim their independence was compromised by the Mughals and the Dogra rulers. The princely state of Kashmir was singular in that, parallel to the 'Quit India' movement in British-ruled India, there was the Quit Kashmir movement against the Hindu Dogra Raja of the state. The founder of modern Kashmir, Sheikh Abdullah, in the 1930s and 1940s forged a united Muslim–Pandit (Hindu) front around the construct of a common Kashmiriyat identity shaped by Jammu and Kashmir's twin *rishi*–Sufi cultural heritage.

Islam came to Kashmir in the 12th century not as a religion of conquest but through itinerant Sufi mystics who brought it as a message of love. It knitted well with the older Kashmiri tradition of Hindu Shaivite *rishis* (saints). The Sufi Islam *pirs* too came to be styled as *rishis* and revered by both communities. Muslims account for 64 per cent of the population of Jammu and Kashmir but in the districts of the valley they comprise 96 per cent of the population. After accession to India the peculiar unfinished status of Jammu and Kashmir as a disputed territory fostered contradictory allegiances in Pandits and Muslims hinging on Kashmir's ultimate historic destiny, i.e., (*i*) union with Pakistan, (*ii*) integration within India, and (*iii*) independence.

Increasingly, Kashmir's autonomy and independent political leadership was sacrificed to the Indian state's territorial and ideological insecurities exacerbated by violent conflict with Pakistan centering on India's sole Muslim majority state, Jammu and Kashmir. Sheikh Abdullah was arrested and eventually co-opted, state politics corrupted and made captive to New Delhi's intrusive control. The watershed was the 1987 elections, when a loose coalition of political leaders, the Muslim United Front (MUF), challenged the ruling National Conference (NC). Massive poll rigging and violence against MUF drove its youthful supporters, disillusioned with democratic politics, across the border for arms training. Since then the Kashmiri people's defining identity, Kashmiriyat, has been politicised to serve a pro-separatist Islamic nationalist goal.

Mapping Kashmiri Women's Experience of Violence

Kashmiri women's experience of politicised violence has not been homogenous. The mapping of the space of Kashmiri women in the conflict can be analytically structured into three overlapping phases—(*i*) popular upsurge and public demonstrations, (*ii*) repression and armed struggle, and (*iii*) politics of armed struggle gives way to the politics of extremism and the side show of the politics of the Hurriyat and the revived democratic process.

Through these phases emerge different faces of women's agency. The first phase sees a public outburst of women's activism in the struggle for *aazaadi*. In the second phase as the struggle goes underground and is articulated through a mutually reinforcing cycle of violence and repression, women come out and enter into negotiations of power with the security forces for the survival of their families and their neighbourhoods. In the third phase, as militancy gets corrupted, women turn away from armed struggle. The social fabric of Kashmiri society is destroyed and multiple agencies spread terror. The despair over the spent dream of freedom and sacrifice is unable to transform itself into a beyond conflict politics of healing, reconstruction and accommodation in the space created by so-called democratic politics.

Popular Upsurge

The image of the Kashmir insurgency fixed in the world's eye is that of Kashmiri women militant in protest and loud in lament. In 1989–90 as the spirit of *aazaadi* swept over the valley, women were visible everywhere. Heavily swathed in *burqas* or in voluminous head scarves, mothers, wives and daughters came pouring out into the streets, their voices joining that of the men in the cry for *aazaadi*. As young men turned *mujahids* and went across the border with their *kafans* (winding sheets) wrapped around them, Muslim women came out of their homes, braving the blow of *lathis* (sticks) to demonstrate for freedom outside the UN office in Srinagar.

In January 1990, every evening as dusk fell and rivers of people flowed through the streets towards the mosques, women were in the forefront, their voices excitedly shouting, '*Marde mujahid jag zara abb, vaki shahadat ayah hai!*' (Oh, you holy fighters, rise and awake! The time of your martyrdom has come). The cry for freedom was encoded in the language of appeal to an Islamic, masculine and militarist stereotype. The populist heady discourse of the Kashmir struggle configured Kashmir's youth as holy fighters ready to die, and women ready to see their sons and husbands go off to fight and to martyrdom.

For Kashmiri Muslim women, coming out of their homes and neighbourhood into public spaces, the experience was an empowering one. 'Those days we used to all come out, in the evenings from our colonies and march together raising slogans. We believed that if we came out and demanded *aazaadi*, loud enough, we would get it,' recalled Nusrat Begum, a housewife, transformed into the wife of a political ideologue of the Jammu Kashmir Liberation Front (JKLF).

From schools and colleges came boys and young men, girls and young women, 15 to 30 years old, to plunge into the struggle.

Mothers and fathers lustily cheered them on. Rich traders of the city opened their doors and lavishly fed the demonstrators for *aazaadi*. At local weddings, women were eager to have a *mujahid* pointed out. They would break out into a *wanuwan*, the traditional Kashmiri song of celebration, intertwining couplets in praise of local *mujahids*. Mothers, sisters and aunts would bask in the glory of a *mujahid* relative who had gone across for training. Cutting across class, mothers, wives and daughters all came out to join the swelling processions which congregated nightly in the neighbourhood mosques. It was a time of innocence when they believed freedom was at hand. *Aazaadi* itself seemed to be all things to all people, to some an end to corruption, to another a seat in a medical college.[10]

Women's popular participation, if it was structured at all, found some organisational articulation through the Dukhtarane Millat and the Muslim Khawateen Markaz, both of which were originally inspired by Islamic social reform activism. Women seized the democratic space for popular protest. They would march to the UN office, out in front, shielding the men, braving *lathi* (cane) blows and teargas. Reports of excesses by the security forces would see them rush out to protest. If a boy was picked up, women from the neighbourhood would go to the security bunker, agitate and get him released. It was an activism rooted in their cultural role as mothers, wives and sisters.

Women's activism was most visible during this spontaneous phase of popular struggle. The ideologues massaging the populist groundswell, encouraged and even manipulated women's participation. Women were used to enforce the people's curfew. A magazine report[11] on women and the militancy described a woman heavily swathed in black, briskly ordering shopkeepers in Srinagar to down their shutters. Ten minutes later she steps into a waiting autorickshaw along with two other men. Behind her, the tall Life Insurance Corporation (LIC) building bursts into flames.

A familiar sight became the *burqa* or *chadar* shrouded activists of the MKM acting as guards or sounding an alert as the security forces approached, blocking their way in the narrow alleys and twisted staircases, to give time to the militants to escape.[12] Women swathed in *burqas* would smuggle out wanted militants, arms and explosives.

The then president of the MKM, 'Bhenji', shot into fame because of her dare-devil rescue of the badly wounded JKLF chief Hamid Sheikh, whom she rushed to hospital. Anjum Zamrood Habib, general secretary of the now largely defunct MKM, recalls how, 'We would visit jailed militants, take them shoes, a shirt, pajamas, cigarettes and collect funds to bail them out.' 'We did go for training in the use of guns, but we never used them,' Zamrood explained.

The symbol of the militant Kashmiri women was Asiyah Andrabi,[13] the leader of the Dukhtarane Millat. Asiyah's oration at the funerals of the 'martyred' was an integral part of the propaganda of the pro-separatist struggle to instill courage and solidarity amongst grieving and wavering mothers. The *burqa* brigade of the DM was ready to rush out at her call to join public demonstrations against excesses by the security forces, or in a zealous show of support for the Kashmiri people's right to choose their political destiny.

In a protracted low intensity conflict, the domestic activism of women is vital, for it is women who keep intact the fabric of the family and the community which enables the men to go on fighting. Women faltering in the support of the struggle would have seriously crippled the movement. There were hundreds of 'ordinary' women who organised food supply lines during the months of unbroken curfew. In 1991, there was uninterrupted curfew for 190 days. 'The men couldn't go out, it was too dangerous for them. It was the women who would go to see who had tea, who had sugar, who had rice,' explained Nusrat Begum. She described how once when people were injured during a demonstration in Sopore, they were brought to a hospital in Srinagar, 40 km away. 'We women got to hear of it and we went with food for them,' she said.

In situations of struggle, women's everyday activities of managing survival—from their reproductive role to their nurturing one— get politicised. The political action of ordinary women arises from their everyday reality, of affirming concern for the safety of their family and the sustenance of their community. The populist demands of the struggle created the social space for women to come out. For 'ordinary' women coming out of their homes and neighbourhoods and asserting themselves politically along with the men, was a liberating experience.

Mobilising Women: Motherhood, Nationalism and Militarism

As happens in pro-separatist or nationalist struggles elsewhere, appeals were made to Kashmiri women's allegiances as members of a specific ethnic or religious community. These allegiances were insidiously threaded with appeals that linked motherhood with nationalism and militarism.[14] In the Kashmir conflict, the propaganda ideologues of the armed struggle built up in story and song, the nobility of the self-sacrificing mother and the martyr's mother. Held up as an ideal was the mother who puts henna on the hands of her son and sends him off not to a bride but to fight a holy war; a martyr's mother who refuses to mourn at her son's funeral. Shafaq Sopori's poem below celebrates a mother who danced at the funeral of her son.

> We danced over burning flames
> Even the shadows danced, behind the doors,
> > behind the walls,
> In our frenzy, we broke all custom,
> > we broke all traditions.
> We danced over the withering flowers
> We set our tents on fire
> We danced to the music,
> The music of the caravan bells
> With love, we placed the dagger on our lips
> We danced over the carpet of flowers
> Was it a song or a melancholy lament,
> > Who knows?
> We never stopped dancing that entire night
> We mourned with moistened eyes
> We danced with an open heart,
> The candle, the smoke, the flame, the moth
> > and the gathering.
> For you we danced, we danced.

—Shafaq Sopori

Through such constructions of active consent, maternal voices of resistance to sons joining the militancy were hushed by the loud applause for the ultimate maternal sacrifice—the loss of a beloved son. Mothers of martyrs were given pride of place and the moral authority to access the powerful in the militancy. Funerals were made into public occasions for forging solidarities.

The myth-making of armed struggle demanded the validation of the binary stereotype of men fighting to protect their women and women's honour at risk from the enemy. It was promoted through the representation in the local media of the women who turned up at the legendary Afghan *mujahid* Akbar Bhai's funeral in Sopore. Despite the risk of firing by the security forces, a mother and daughter go out and join the funeral procession. The mother tells her son who is fearful for her safety that Akbar Bhai had stood between her and dishonour. 'If we're killed at his funeral, you will be able to hold your head high for our honour will no longer be at risk.'[15] The subtext of the mother's mockery of her non-militant son's cowardice is an integral part of the construct of what is the desired role for the mother and son in armed struggle. The imperative of defending the community is morally and existentially framed by the institutionalisation of memory/story in a particular manner.[16]

In the heightened political atmosphere of 1989–90, women, like the men, were mobilised. Jammu and Kashmir's peculiar 'unfinished' status as a disputed territory since 1947, intertwined with the historically reworked memory of a people with a unique Kashmiriyat identity living under the yoke of 'foreign rulers', has made for a highly politicised people. Kashmiris are weaned on a history of imprisoned Kashmir, betrayed by India. 'It's in our genes that we will get *aazaadi*. We've grown up on Kashmir being disputed and of Pakistan being our friend,' said Gazala Kyaz, a teacher at the Government College in Baramulla.

Moreover, survival demanded that 'ordinary' women develop the habit of listening to the news, reading or having read to them newspapers and being connected to the informal grapevine. 'We had to find out about strikes and curfews. We needed to know when there was a "crackdown" or where there was an explosion or crossfiring. Our children, our men were out there. We had to be alert about what the militants were saying about wearing burqas or who was being accused of being an informer. When we women met,

what we talked about were crackdowns, custodial deaths, disappearances and the new diktats of the militants,' explained Mishra Basheer,
a government schoolteacher from Sopore. 'Ordinary women', incorporated in their everyday language words like 'curfew', 'crackdown' and 'custodial deaths'.

Tradition of Political Activism

When the women came out into the streets, it was not the first time
that Kashmiri women had pushed their way into the public sphere
of politics. Their political activism tapped into an older vein of populist activity by ordinary women during the Quit Kashmir movement of the 1930s and 1940s. In the popular struggle against the rule
of Maharaja Hari Singh thousands of women came out in anti-
government demonstrations carrying babies and facing bullets.[17]
Later, during the Pakistan-backed attack by tribal raiders, educated
upper-class women and lower-class Kashmiri women formed a
women's militia. But despite the political activism of 'ordinary'
women, as the Kashmiri historian P.N. Bazaz observed, not one
came to prominence in formal politics.[18]

Many of the women freedom fighters of the Quit Kashmir movement of the 1930s and 1940s came from Maisuma, a rough lower
middle-class warren of a neighbourhood in the heart of Srinagar.
Maisuma was the centre of support for Sheikh Abdullah's campaign
to free Jammu and Kashmir from Dogra rule. Maisuma women were
in the forefront of demonstrations in support of Sheikh Abdullah's
National Conference party. The women's question was given great
importance in the manifesto of the National Conference, *Naya
Kashmir*. Subsequently, the Jammu and Kashmir Constitution guaranteed women equal opportunities in education, employment and
development. Universal franchise was recognised in 1951. However,
citizenship laws remained discriminatory. Under state notification
I-L/84, a woman citizen of the state marrying outside forfeits her
citizenship.

Fifty years later, the women of Maisuma still have a reputation
for being agitationists. A Central Reserve Police Force (CRPF) officer

on duty in Srinagar, described the routine confrontation between the women and the security forces as a regular cricket match with well worked out positions. 'They throw stones and we fire tear gas shells.' Maisuma is the home of many well-known militants, including the JKLF chief Yasin Malik. Names of an earlier generation of women freedom fighters like Aziz Thuj, Mukhta and Jan Ded are well known, but the women of Maisuma feel little sense of continuity with them. These historical legends fought for the National Conference, a party which is denounced by the people of Maisuma as betraying the people of Jammu and Kashmir to India.

Position of Women

Nationalist struggles demand that women be politically mobilised and the Kashmiri women's response both in the Quit Kashmir struggle and especially the *aazaadi* struggle of the 1990s was overwhelming, as they seized what was also a liberating opportunity. However, it should be mentioned that traditionally the Kashmiri woman has enjoyed more freedom than women in other parts of the country. According to a Kashmiri scholar in women's studies, Momin Jan, it was in the 14th century that *purdah* was imposed on Kashmiri society.[19] Excesses by Afghan rulers against Kashmiri women further drove more and more women inside. Even then, peasant and lower-class Kashmiri women opposed *purdah* as totally unrealistic for the working Kashmiri women. Uneducated, lower-class women continued to assert their right to freedom and expression. From the peasantry and the lower classes emerged revered women poets like Arnimal and Habba Khatoon who rose to be Queen. Kashmir alone has a woman saint-poet called Laleshwari by the Pandits and Lal Ded by the Muslims.

> *Whether they cook beef or mutton for dinner*
> *Lalla is destined to stay half hungry*

Lal Ded's couplet in its rustic simplicity represents the unequal situation of women in Kashmiri society. However, Kashmiri women then as now, did manage to hold their own in economic activities of agriculture, animal husbandry and handicrafts. A 1990s survey by the sociologist Bashir Dabla[20] found women without *purdah* working side by side with men as agricultural wage labourers. In the cities, women in the families of potters and milk and vegetable vendors, were constantly interacting with men. In the districts of Budgam and Baramulla, rural and urban, Dabla found there was social acceptability of women working outside the home. Literacy, however, remains abysmally low, at 16 per cent for women.

In Kashmir there has been a singular lack of secular women's organisations working for gender justice and social reform. All India women's organisations have been politically rejected in Kashmir. Social reform movements which emerged in the 1970s and 1980s in Kashmir, were imbued with an Islamic agenda. This fostered the emergence of fundamentalist women's organisations like the Dukhtarane Millat and the Muslim Khawateen Markaz. Women whom the *aazaadi* struggle was to politicise, like Asiyah Andrabi of the DM and Anjum Zamrood of the MKM came into politics through their involvement in promoting Islamic social reform. For Asiyah Andrabi, the defining identity of the Kashmiri women in the *aazaadi* struggle was the veiled Kashmiri woman.

Veiling of Kashmiri Women

Traditionally, women from the orthodox upper-class Syed families wore *burqas* to maintain their elite social status and their foreign origin. After the Quit Kashmir movement, educated upper-class women who come into public life, like Zainab Begum, Begum Zehan Abdulla, Mehbooba Ali Shah and Shyamala Mufti cast aside the *burqa*. Forty years later, it was Shyamala Mufti's niece, Asiyah Andrabi who launched the campaign to re-veil Kashmiri women.

The aggressive promotion of the valley as a tourist destination in the 1980s prompted an Islamic cultural backlash which targeted alcohol and the fashion conscious Kashmiri women. Moreover, the 1970s saw a mushrooming of Jamaat-i Islami schools with far reaching implications for the politicisation of Islam in Kashmir.

The political opposition front, the Muslim United Front which challenged the political mandate of the NC in the 1987 elections was an offshoot of this process. Its defeat manipulated through large-scale rigging was a catalyst in the popular uprising. The MUF's young supporters became the first batch of militants. The slogans of the *aazaadi* struggle raised by enthusiastic crowds of women and men as they marched nightly to the mosques were redolent of Islamic revivalism.

Fundamentalist militant groups like the Allah Tigers were determined to veil the unveiled Kashmiri woman.[21] In 1989, pamphlets were thrown in Srinagar's leading women's college, warning Muslim girls to wear *purdah* and Pandit (Hindu) girls to wear a *tikka*. Neerja Mattoo, a Kashmiri Pandit, who was then a senior teacher at the college, recalled, 'The students absolutely refused. As a protest, they insisted everyone would wear a *tikka*.' In the early days of militancy, there was still space for popular resistance to fundamentalist pressure to embrace a community identity that restricted women's autonomy and reinforced the communal markers of a differentiated Muslim and Hindu identity. This was before the mass exodus of the Kashmiri Pandits in 1990, which irretrievably communalised Kashmiri society.

Dire warnings appeared in the local press. The *Daily Aftab* on 13 June 1990, carried an appeal from the Allah Tigers warning against a lax attitude on *purdah*. But women continued to resist. Writing under a pseudonym, Saro Bano, in a letter to the editor in the daily *Al Safa*, questioned the legitimacy of linking the wearing of *burqa* with the struggle for freedom and vowed that she for one would never wear a *burqa* even if she was killed.[22]

Appeals were made to the Kashmiri Muslim woman's allegiance to an Islamic identity. But the *burqa* was not accepted by Kashmiri women as a symbol of the Kashmiri cultural ethos and struggle. However, as popular support for *aazaadi* surged, the injunctions of young *mujahids* on *purdah*, too, began to be heeded. The Kashmiri Pandit politician Khemlata Wakhlu, describes in her book, *Kashmir: Behind the White Curtain*, her shock at seeing four of her women political workers arrive at her house in flowing *burqas*. Parroting the notices in the local newspapers, they insisted *purdah* was necessary because Kashmiri women had become so bold and open. The women confided that the militants had given them a 'reprieve', till they could get their *burqas* stitched. 'Who had given you a reprieve?' Wakhlu asked. 'The *mujahids*. And the biggest *mujahid* is Khorsi's nephew,' she was told.[23] (Khorsi is the familiar abbreviation of the name of one of Khemlata Wakhlu's political workers.)

Women like Nayema Ahmed Majoor, a radio star and executive producer with Radio Kashmir, were under double pressure, to be veiled and to quit jobs denounced as un-Islamic. Nayema had colour thrown on her by the *purdah* crusaders. What amazed her was how people were swept up in a kind of blind faith that what the '*mujahids*' said was the voice of Allah. Even her otherwise non-conformist husband urged her to wear a *burqa*. Sabiha, a teacher in the elite Burn Hall school in Srinagar, took to wearing an *abaya* (a kind of loose-fitting buttoned overcoat), because young students would threaten a teacher who was not properly covered or had plucked her eyebrows.

The compulsory veiling of women seems to be integral to the defining of a politicised Islamic national identity as has been the experience in Sudan, Iran or Afghanistan. There were few veiled Palestinian women before the Intifada. Women in nationalist struggles are configured as embodying the community/nationality's distinct (superior) tradition and cultural identity. The graphic representation of women's subordination as symbolised in the veil, exposes the gendered nature of the process of constructing a nationalist identity.[24] Whether it is the political activism of Palestinian women during the Intifada or of Kashmiri women, in its wake is the pressure to push women back. The emphasis on *burqa* demonstrated an assertion by the men of the community of their control over their women, a protective control which had necessarily to be demonstrated given their sense of emasculation in the face of the armed might and humiliating treatment by the security forces and their resentment towards women's necessary activism.

In Kashmir, the *burqa*, which was expected to protect women, made them even more vulnerable to the security forces. It lent itself to subterfuge, as did the voluminous Kashmiri *phiren* (coat). Security forces were convinced that one in every three *burqa* clad persons was a militant. It was believed that the disguise was used when militants wanted to shift hideouts. Women wearing *burqas* suffered humiliation and sexual harassment as the security forces lifted their *burqa* to search for weapons and ammunition. As a result some militant groups decreed that women need not wear a *burqa*. But it was a brief reprieve.

Women's organisations like the DM and MKM were no less determined to veil the Kashmiri woman. The campaign came to a head in the *burqa* war[25] launched by the Dukhtarane Millat in 1992. For three months, students, working women and housewives who dared to venture out unveiled, were punished. Green colour was thrown on them. Even MKM activists like Zamrood did not escape and were coloured green. Asiyah insists that acid was never thrown. The campaign was withdrawn but not before it provoked a backlash. Hundreds of urban, middle-class Kashmiri women turned away from the movement. 'It was an experiment. Yes, it failed,' Asiyah admits. 'The Kashmiri woman has a deeply ingrained hostility to *purdah*, but when have I ever chopped and changed my politics, because the people didn't like it. I am a Muslim first,' she asserted.

Asiyah had grown up in a politicised, fundamentalist family. Her uncle was associated with Al-fatah, a militant group of the 1970s. Her brother is Dr Inayat Andrabi, who was head of the Jamaat-ul Tulba. For Asiyah, her political awakening took place when her brother blocked her from studying biochemistry in 'India' and by chance she stumbled upon the book *Khawateen ki Diloon Ki Batten*, which eulogised the heroics of women revolutionaries.

Asiyah's politics are inspired by the vision of creating a society in the image of the Prophet's time and the tenets of Islam. She is adamant that Jammu and Kashmir, a Muslim majority state should be united with Pakistan. 'I don't believe in secular politics, only Muslim politics,' she said. Asiyah herself always dresses in elegant dove grey *burqas*. For Asiyah, being a Muslim means that *purdah* is obligatory but it does not mean seclusion behind four walls. In the Prophet's time women in *burqa* were in business, in medicine and even in the battlefield. Asiyah claims that it never constrained her when in the early days of the struggle, she sat, comfortably, with the men in the Tehriq-i Hurriyat meetings.

Asiyah's *purdah* extremism severely undermined urban middle-class support for the movement. Abida, the elder sister of the JKLF chief, Yasin Malik, deeply regretted the way an extraneous element like the *burqa* campaign compromised the fight for *aazaadi*. 'It played into the hands of those who wished to make trouble for the movement,' Abida said. Abida's head was covered with a *dupatta* (scarf) Kashmiri style. She does not wear a *burqa*.

More women are wearing a *burqa* now than before the insurgency. There has been a hardening of the Islamic core of *aazaadi* politics and an Islamised construction of a Kashmiri identity. Women have become the visible sites for reproducing community/nationalist identity based on an Islamised Kashmiriyat identity. In understanding why Kashmiri women accepted that their primary identity was that of belonging to a particular community whose marker for women was *burqa* which circumscribed further their identity of self, there is need to look at how the discourse of a beleaguered community identity is constructed. In particular, the issue of sexual harassment and mass rape was used to foster alienation and hostility against the 'other' and pushed women to identify with their community identity.

But as we saw above, women were participants and not passive sites for reproducing a communal identity. This was most obviously reflected in their resistance to coercive veiling. But it was also discernible in women's ambivalent negotiations with the 'other', in this case the Kashmiri Pandit.

Women and the Communal Divide

When the popular movement for *aazaadi* first burst onto the public scene, its cultural expression took the form of Islamic revivalism. The diktat of the militant group Allah Tigers and the DM on *purdah*, sought to visibly enforce markers of the Pandit–Muslim divide. The JKLF, the dominant armed militant group of the time, wanted freedom from both India and Pakistan and espoused an independent Jammu and Kashmir for all Kashmiris, Muslims and Pandits. But the attacks on government functionaries, many of whom

were Pandits and the targeting of 'informers', again many of whom
were Pandits, fuelled fear and terror about a pogrom against Hindus.
Rumours spread like wildfire that Kashmiri Muslims were planning
to rape Kashmiri Pandit women.

The killing of Sarla Butt, a Kashmiri Pandit nurse working at the
Soura Medical Hospital, was used by the Pandit elders to spread
panic about the fate awaiting Kashmiri Pandit women. Sarla Butt
was raped and killed by the JKLF in 1990, apparently, because she
had passed on information about wounded militants in the hospital. She reportedly had JKLF scratched in blood on her naked
torso, according to Kashmiri Pandit sources.

Thousands of Kashmiri Pandits fled[26] on 19–20 January 1999, in
an exodus which is believed to have been encouraged by Governor
Jagmohan who had just taken control. Dr Shakti Raina, a leading
gynecologist in Srinagar, was one of the Pandits who fled. On 20
January at 4:00 a.m., she left her home with the daily army convoy
to Jammu. According to Dr Raina, her house in Sonewar, Srinagar
was the solitary house of a Hindu in the area. On 19 January, the
city was full of rumours about curfew being broken and an imminent anti-Pandit riot. Meanwhile, neighbours informed her that
she must join the colony people in the march for *aazaadi*. 'They
wanted me to act like a shield,' she feared. Seeking safety in the
home of a Muslim neighbour, she learnt her name had been taken
during a meeting at the local mosque. 'They urged me to leave. I
got into my car and with my mother and servant drove off,' she
said.

For Dr Raina there could be no choice other than Kashmir as an
integral part of India. 'I was identified with India. An independent
Kashmir, yes. But what did they mean by *aazaadi* except Pakistan,'
she said. The bitterness runs deep in Dr Raina, souring old friend-
ships. When the husband of a former colleague died, she wrote her
a letter of condolence. 'But there is no friendship left, no trust,' she
said bitterly. Her mirror image was Mariam Nizam, a schoolteacher
in Srinagar. 'They never told us they were leaving. Only 10 per cent
[Pandits] are left. They took everything and then filed false claims.
They made money,' she said. The poison of communal politics has
fed negative images of the Pandit abandoning his Muslim brethren

to the guns of the Indian state and the Muslim waiting to grab the property of his Pandit neighbour.

, A replay of the communalisation of Kashmir society can be seen in the border districts of Rajouri and Poonch in 1998. 'We do live together,' Shaheen Malik, a young college graduate from Poonch said. 'But last time when three Hindu "informers" were killed, the Hindus left because they didn't think that their Muslim neighbours would side with them. They left us alone in Surankot. If the army did something, it would be the Muslims who would suffer,' she said.

In the midst of communalisation there are those who have resisted like Neerja Mattoo, a highly respected former teacher of the women's college in Srinagar. Despite the fact that her husband, the conservator of forests, barely escaped an abduction attempt, the Mattoos stayed on in Srinagar. Unlike many of her co-religious brethren who are obliged to hide their Pandit identity as they live in Muslim neighbourhoods, she continues to wear a saree. She has armed security. But the real protection she has is the trust and love she enjoys as a Pandit who has not abandoned the valley, who represents the common Kashmiriyat cultural roots of the Pandits and the Muslims. Neerja Mattoo symbolises the possibility of a Kashmir where the two communities can live together beyond the bitterness of these 10 years of communalised violent politics.

Some Mother's Son

What has the communalisation of the struggle meant for women who grew up sharing common walls and foster mothered each other's children? They were being called upon in the name of a community identity to disown 'the other'. It was a process marked by a myriad mutinies. Women privileging their identity as women—as mother, wife and daughter—rushed out to save a boy from the neighbourhood who was being taken away. Mehran Meraj, the wife of a former militant recalled how in 1993 in Baramulla, when Border Security Force (BSF) jawans billeted at the Sheerwani College were taking away a young boy, all the neighbourhood women came out to protect him. 'A Kashmiri Panditain [Hindu] and a Sardarni [Sikh] also came out. All of us women came out. The boy was some mother's son,' she said. Nayema Ahmed Majoor, the executive with Radio Kashmir, described how in Srinagar in 1991, when militants were dragging away a local Hindu Pandit boy, first one woman and then dozens more from the locality rushed out and fell upon him to prevent him from being taken away. The men remained inside, the risks of being politically incorrect held them back, but not the women who spontaneously rushed out.

These Muslim Kashmiri women were foster mothers of Kashmiri Pandit sons, Kashmiri Pandit mothers were foster mothers of Kashmiri Muslim sons. There were common rituals at the time of birth, marriage and death. Language, food, dress and even names were the same reflecting a common ancestor. The cultural heritage was common. Lalla was equally revered as Lal Ded and Laleshwari. Khemlata Wakhlu recalled the common practice in Kashmir of shortening first names. An Abdul Gani would be called 'Ghana' and so would a Ganesh Das. It emphasised a common Kashmiri cultural identity.

However, as Wakhlu explains, relations between Kashmiri Muslims and Hindus were based on a peculiar love–hate syndrome. The Pandit minority, traditionally, had used their literacy skills to become the clerks of the ruling classes, while the Muslims depended on agriculture and handicrafts. The Kashmiri Pandits who were clerks and revenue officials of the government, were the visible face of the exploitative rule of the Dogra (Hindu) Rajas. Held back by the *maulvis*, the Muslims took to English education much later. Educated young Muslims, like Sheikh Abdullah, found themselves discriminated against. After 1947, with thousands getting modern education, the competition for jobs became acute and bitter. While Kashmiri Pandits took up jobs all over India, Kashmiri Muslim youth felt insecure about leaving Jammu and Kashmir. Employment in the state government was the only option.[27]

The exodus of the Pandits in 1990 played into the hands of the propagandists on both sides and people who had been socialised in a culture of interdependence were communalised. For every story of a Pandit boy being saved by the neighbourhood women spontaneously coming out, there were many more stories of Muslim neighbours watching while militants killed a Pandit boy. For every story of Muslims protecting the property of their Hindu neighbours, there were reports of arson and appropriation. Manipulated by the propaganda were the women and men of Kashmir, struggling as refugees or negotiating survival in a conflict ravaged homeland.

The crumbling of potential solidarities—of suffering women reaching out across the communal divide—is epitomised by the fact that for both Muslim and Pandit Kashmiri women, political activism was articulated through communal organisations like Dukhtarane Millat on the one side and the Daughters of Vitasta on the other. Dr Raina is a founder member of the Daughters of Vitasta, the women's wing of Panun Kashmir, which argues for a separate homeland for Kashmiri Pandits. She readily acknowledges that women are the worst sufferers in the conflict. At the National Conference of Kashmiri Pandits in Delhi in September 1993, the Daughters of Vitasta expressed their solidarity with 'all those Kashmiri women who have suffered gruesome human rights violations due to terrorism and the criminalisation of Kashmiri society'. But Dr Raina clarified, 'my heart goes out to the innocent women of Kashmir, not to the Dukhtarane Millat.'

Armed Militancy and Repression

Two events capture the contrasting character of the first and second phase of the lived experience of violent conflict in Kashmir. One, the surrender of the Indian state to the militants' demand for the release of the then Home Minister's kidnapped daughter had deluded the people into thinking that *aazaadi* could be won on the streets. Two, the Gaokadal massacre on 22 January 1990 was to demonstrate the force the Indian state could and would bring against the people of Kashmir. It took Kashmiris totally by surprise that the state hit back so hard. Street protests went underground, popular struggle gave way to hardcore armed militancy. The security forces cracked down, treating all Kashmiri Muslims, men, women and children as anti-nationals. A short story titled 'Terrorist', mocks at the absurdity of treating an entire people as suspects.[28]

*The security forces on patrol crossed the length of the lane. At the
other end stood young Shafiq, crying loudly, beseeching his mother,
Boba. An officer walked over to comfort the child. 'Son, do not be
afraid.' Boba interjected. 'He's not afraid. The silly fool, he wants
your gun. Whenever he sees a soldier he wants his gun.' The officer
recoiled, muttering, 'terrorist! scoundrel!' He walked briskly back, to
be among his own kind.*

—'Terrorist', a story by Akhtar Moiuddin

The militant was the boy next door. Someone who might casu-
ally walk into the house of a respected judge and be welcomed. The
militants were everywhere and seemingly in control of 'liberated
zones'. Ad hoc meetings with militants could be arranged at street
corners, in houseboats and in hospitals, planned meetings were announced in the Idgah and at the University with militants imposing
a cordon sanitaire in the heart of Srinagar. Popular support for the
'just political cause' was high.

Between Two Guns

The dominance of armed militancy and the state's repressive backlash severely reduced the public space for women to demonstrate
collective resistance. Moreover, as the struggle began to be articulated more and more through the gun, the early enthusiasm which
had attracted hundreds of women to organisations like the MKM
faded away. According to Zamrood, the present general secretary
of the MKM, many women drifted away because of MKM President Mohtarma Bakhtawar's strategy of identifying too closely with
JKLF militants.

For others like Nusrat Begum, the wife of a once prosperous
engineer turned senior ideologue of the JKLF, it was to be a personally painful and traumatic confrontation with the gun culture of
militancy. 'The gun played a role. It brought our just cause into the
newspapers and into the international forum,' she said. Her husband had never picked up a gun but that did not prevent him from
being arrested and tortured and the family to be constantly harassed.

Looking back over the last 10 years, she said with candour 'Initially, when the boys took to arms, many felt it was the correct thing to do. Later when they realised that the gun was not the way, it was too late. The boys would not listen.'

In the first flush of armed militancy, the dominant militant group was the JKLF. Its popular support base was, in many respects, the same as that which once backed the National Conference. The JKLF's cry was independence. There was public acquiescence in paying the tax levied by the JKLF, especially as its main funding source was the 50 per cent tax levied on all government development expenditure. There was a boycott on payment of tax to the state.

Shabnam Imroz, a schoolteacher in Anantnag, who is the wife of a senior JKLF leader, recalled that the monthly Rs 5 tax imposed by the JKLF, was paid willingly. However, as the militancy wore on and new groups made demands, there was resentment. When Shabnam was teaching at Mattan, she was obliged to pay Rs 100 to the Hizbul group active there. 'That was coercion,' she said. Later, it was at gunpoint that she fed eight *mujahids* of the Hizbul Mujahideen who knocked at her door in 1992. 'With JKLF, I have sympathy because of my husband but for the others, no.'

But even those not personally connected gave food, refuge and money. Zamrood, then an activist with the JKLF-affiliated MKM found that people were willing, in the beginning, to put up money for bail of detenus and to provide food. Women's support was manifest in their willingness to open the door to militants, to shelter and feed them. In 1992, when there were still 'liberated zones' in Srinagar, the Hizbul Mujahideen, a militant wing associated with the Jamaat-i Islami, held a firepower show, displaying Kalashnikovs and rockets. Women and children proudly posed in front for photo journalists.[29] It reflected the ground control held by the militants and popular support for the gun culture.

Already, however, the mushrooming of armed militant groups, often with no more than a dozen members, had brought into the lexicon of militancy, the phenomenon of the *naqli mujahid*. But in the early days, it was still possible to marginalise them. Top ranking political ideologues and leading militants publicly denounced excesses, extortion and abductions. Elders like the Jamaat-i Islami chief Syed Ali Shah Geelani, in public meetings urged, 'when you carry arms, you must have political goals.'[30]

Constructing the Legitimacy of Violence

In the militant discourse, there was much romanticism about the pro-people sensibility of the militants. Stories would be narrated about how militants would forgo an action to avoid civilian casualties. To alleviate the hardship of the 'people's curfew' imposed by the militants, the JKLF organised subsidised food distribution. In 'liberated zones', the militants' court delivered on-the-spot justice. Remnants of this 'people's justice', can still be seen in villages where the militants have ground control. In village Dewal Marg, Doda district in Jammu, Hizbul Mujahideen militants dispense justice. Traumatised by her in-laws, Fatima Bee approached them for justice and got it.[31] Militants reportedly intervened to persuade families to take back 'raped' women.

The state countered with propaganda about 'terrorists' deliberately striking in crowded places, thus provoking maximum civilian casualties in the 'crossfire' and using people as human shields. The propaganda war over human rights violations was as fierce as the armed struggle. Excessive and indiscriminate use of force by the security forces alienated the people and pushed them to support militancy. Human rights violations by the Indian state levered Kashmir back on the international agenda. However, the failure of the Kashmir human rights discourse to impact nationally reinforced the people's sense of alienation. In the lexicon of Kashmir counter-insurgency 'crossfire casualty' became a notorious euphemism for security forces firing at civilians in retaliation for a militant action against a bunker in the market-place. In particular, incidents of rape of Kashmiri women by the security forces generated mass revulsion and alienation.

In Kashmir, it was the human rights discourse which transformed the *matera dolorosa*, the stereotype of the sorrowing mother in conflict, to a mother who does not hold her son back, who encourages him to fight. Crackdown, torture, arrests, disappearances, killings and rape by the security forces fostered a psyche which made mothers shed their natural protective instinct and send their sons off to fight. If you were able-bodied and between 15 and 30 years of age you were sure to be picked up, arrested, tortured and maybe shot. Better then to fight. The list of martyrs increased. Women's support for acts of violence was threaded with ambivalence.

Jameela Gujjar of Bandipora was widowed on 28 April 1991. She accepted the death of her *mujahid* husband with stoicism. 'I knew my husband was a militant. I knew someday he would be killed. I grieve but I do not complain.'[32] The night he, a militant, was killed, six other male members of her family were killed. They were not militants. Jameela's mother-in-law managed to get a compensation of 6 lakh rupees for six men killed. Jameela can hope for no compensation. She has three young children to bring up. The stoicism gives way to rejection of violence when she confronts her responsibility—bringing up three children in a family without males—'Who wants all this killing?' No revenge burns inside her.

However, in the home of Fayaz in Baramulla, the spirit of revenge is strong. Fayaz, a local sports hero, had gone to play cricket in Sopore in 1990 when he went missing. His mother insists Fayaz had nothing to do with militancy. But his cousin Famida is full of grim determination in support of the struggle. 'Their blood should not be shed in vain. We are prepared for the worst.' Her son and daughter were clinging to her. Would she let her son join the movement and pick up a gun? 'Yes. Those who have been lost, killed or missing, were also someone's sons,' she said, unflinchingly. This was a refrain I picked up again at Baramulla Government College. Afshan Majoor, a teacher, was adamant, 'A mother, sister or son who has lost someone cannot give up. I will not stop my son, when he grows up,' she said.

Women speak defensively about militant killings, especially those in the early days before militancy got corrupted. Residual echoes of a distinction between illegitimate and legitimate violence can be picked up in the comment of Parveen Ahangar, the president of the Association of the Parents of the Disappeared, on the killing of fellow member Haleema Begum by unidentified gunmen. 'If the militants killed her she must have done something wrong, if the security forces. . .,' her voice trailed away. Was her comment guarded for fear of militant reprisal? Did it reflect a tacit acquiescence of 'justified' violence?

Impact of Violent Conflict

Everyday violence transformed women's lives. Women became indirect victims of the arrest, torture, disappearence and loss of loved ones. Also, women became direct victims of the physical violence of rape, kidnapping and murder. No house in the valley was left untouched, directly or indirectly from the protracted curfews, crackdowns, arson and generalised violence. 'It was to turn us all into [trauma] patients,' said Abida, the sister of the JKLF chief Yasin Malik. Post-traumatic stress (PTS) disorders have reached epidemic proportions among women and children. In an independent survey of the Government Mental Hospital in Srinagar in July–August 1999, Prabal Mahato found that PTS cases rose from 1,700 in 1990 to 17,000 in 1993 and to 30,000 in 1998.[33]

It is a truism of war that the most vulnerable sections of society—the women, children and the aged—bear the brunt of violent conflict situations. Violent conflict hits the social sectors of greatest need for women and their families. Health, education and welfare services are disrupted and undervalued as monies and energies are diverted to fight insurgency. Moreover, given women's reproductive role, the implications of generalised violence for women are gender specific. Dislocation in health services particularly hits maternal health and the survival of children, for example, as a result of disruption of immunisation schedules. Moreover, generalised violence results in women's reluctance to travel at night even if they have severe medical problems leading to a sharp increase in prenatal deaths.

Economic Violence

The disruption of armed conflict makes the socially assigned responsibility of women to feed and care for their families all the more difficult. Political violence sees fathers and sons withdraw, go underground and join the militants, women remain behind to manage the survival of the family. In Kashmir, after the first year of economic dislocation caused by violent upheaval, the economy of the state adapted rapidly, establishing direct market outlets for the valley's fruits, handicrafts, shawls and carpets in the rest of India. But in families which had lost male earning members, women and children were staring at sharp drops in income levels and even destitution. This is despite the fact that traditionally 50 per cent of the workforce in the handloom and handicraft sector in Kashmir are women. Also, Kashmir has a practice of women in the families of potters, milkmen and bakers working outside the home. But the rise of women-headed households was a new phenomenon.

With an estimated 60,000 men killed, there were thousands of widows and half-widows, the wives of more than 2,000 missing men. The insurgency left women vulnerable to male predatory violence and the worst kind of social and economic exploitation. Many widows and half-widows were dispossessed of their land. Women were often forced to turn to their maternal relatives[34] or seek employment in the homes of others as cleaning women, something unheard of before militancy. Educated middle-class widows took to new professions which had earlier been frowned upon, like nursing. But for illiterate women with children, the choice was stark—either they had to place their sons in an orphanage or a carpet weaving factory. There are said to be 30,000 orphans in Kashmir and virtually no support structure for them. The emergence of women-headed households did open up space for some power shifts in gender relations, new opportunities to learn skills and take control of their lives. But in Kashmir, cultural violence as symbolised in the veiling of Kashmiri women was used to limit the potential opportunities of reworking gender relations. Also, the experience of the gun culture was to destabilise interpersonal relations between generations, especially mothers and children.[35]

Generalised violence also drove many students to drop out of school or college. Girl students were especially vulnerable to sexual harassment from the security forces and at risk of abduction by the militants. Moreover, the loss of adult male earning members and the deterioration of income levels impacted upon the drop-out rate, especially for girls (Table 2.1).

TABLE 2.1
Drop-out Rate of Schoolgoing Children in Kashmir

Year	Class	Boys (%)	Girls (%)
1990–91	1–5	40	45
	6–8	20	53
1996–97	1–5	37	43
	6–8	17	52

Source: Mumtaz Soz, Director of Education, Jammu and Kashmir State Government, Srinagar, January 1999.

Cultural Violence

Cultural violence is the use of 'politicised' religion, tradition and custom which was most dramatically symbolised in the campaign to veil Kashmiri women. In violent conflict, cultural violence against women gets magnified. The promotion of macho values legitimises misogyny and a predatory construct of masculinity. Sexual violence against women by both the security forces and the militants is no accident of violent conflict and militarism. There is no information available to indicate whether engulfing violence in the public sphere has made Kashmiri men more violent at home; what is evident is that the gun culture turned topsyturvy the structure of social values in a society where elders and women were held in esteem. Before the insurgency, in the conservative and closed society of the valley, kidnapping, molestation and killing of women was rare. When Rubaiya Sayeed, the daughter of the then Union home minister was kidnapped in 1989, there was shock and disapproval.[36] Subsequently, women have been routinely abducted, raped, killed in crossfire or shelling and blown up in grenade explosions.

Rape as a Weapon of War

War-time sexual violence against women not only occurs but is a necessary aspect of conflict. History has demonstrated the link between war and the control of women's sexuality and reproduction. Through the rape of its women, communities are humiliated and men emasculated. Being young and pretty has little to do with becoming a victim of war-time rape. Rape and the sexual assault of women in situations of conflict, now, is recognised as a war crime. It is not a private crime, the ignoble act of an occasional soldier. Rape in conflict is neither incidental nor private. In Kashmir, both security forces and armed militants have systematically used rape as a weapon to punish, intimidate, coerce, humiliate or degrade.[37]

Mass rape of Kashmiri women by the security forces was first documented in the Chanpora (Srinagar) mass rape incident on 7 March 1990. In Chanpora, after a firing incident, there was a crackdown by the security forces. The men were called out and CRPF *jawans* (paramilitary) went inside the homes to search for militants and guns. The women inside were reportedly molested and raped. According to human rights investigations, mass rape began to be routinely used in search and cordon operations. Investigations into gang rape by the security forces in Pazipora (August 1990), Kunana Poshpara (February 1991), Chak Saidpora (October 1992), Theno Budpathery Kangan (September 1994) and Wavoosa in Srinagar (1997), establish rape as a collective form of punishment.[38] Eleven-year-old girls, pregnant women, to 60-year-old grandmother were raped. In raping them the security forces were punishing and humiliating the entire community. Rape was also used to target specific women accused of being militant sympathisers.

The security forces deny as 'wild' allegations of rape. Lieutenant General Krishan Pal, Commander 15th Corps, Srinagar, maintains that nine out of 10 rape allegations are false. 'You hear stories of molestation and custody killings every time any unit is effective against militants,' he said.[39] It is a fact that accusations of mass rape by the security forces have been used in a fierce propaganda offensive to indict the Indian government for human rights abuses in Kashmir. But it is also a fact that there is a pattern of impunity when it comes to rape. Investigations are more a cover up than an inquiry and those responsible are rarely, if ever, held to account.[40]

The most notorious is the Kunan Poshpara mass rape incident. On the night of 23 February 1991, in the village of Kunan Poshpara in the border district of Kupwara, 30 women were allegedly gang raped by an army unit of the 5th Rajputana Rifles during a search operation. The incident raised a storm over the human rights record of the army. It was widely splashed in the foreign media. Videos were made of the testimony of the raped women and sent all over the world. The number of women who claimed they had been raped, increased in every press report. The army's internal inquiry dismissed the accusation as 'malicious and untrue'. A police investigation was ordered but it never commenced.

In view of the international hue and cry, army officials requested a respected NGO, the Press Council, to investigate. The team looked at the evidence based on the medical examination of 32 women, done two to three weeks after the incident, and dismissed it. The team spent less than half-an-hour in the village, three months after the incident, and concluded that the allegation of mass rape was an 'invention', the charges 'totally unproven'. What convinced them was that some of the girls as they lined up to be interviewed, 'giggled' and seemed 'unashamed'.

Alluding to the increasing number of women who claimed to have been raped, the report said, 'Delayed reports of ever growing numbers would dilute family diffidence, stigma or shame. And there would be no stigma or shame if according to inside knowledge, the story was untrue but propagated for a cause.'[41] The statement returned to haunt team members when a Women's Initiative Report in 1994 revealed, 'No marriage has taken place in this village for three years. All girls raped and unraped are single.'[42]

For the army, Kunan Poshpara became a lesson to be taught in defence colleges on how to 'avoid manipulative human rights propaganda'. The army had exposed a 'massive hoax orchestrated by militant groups and their sympathisers. . . for re-inscribing Kashmir on the international agenda as a human rights issue', the Press Council report declared. But for the people of Jammu and Kashmir it signalled the pattern of impunity[43] on rape by the security forces. Those who reported rape or assisted in filing a complaint were intimidated. Medical practitioners were threatened. In November 1990, a surgeon in a hospital in Anantnag asked for a gynecologist to examine seven women who claimed they had been raped. He was picked up by the CRPF and detained for four days.[44]

As we shall discuss later, the rape of Kashmiri women by the security forces was located as an integral political event of the people's nationalist struggle, but the political leadership of the pro-separatist movement in publicly projecting rape as a war crime, failed at the same time, to politically challenge the patriarchal code of the 'dishonoured' women. That is, the rape of the women, from being located as an issue of family honour, became an issue located in the public sphere of national or community dishonour. Left unchallenged was rape as socially stigmatising the women in the private sphere of the family, or even more fundamentally, the construction of a discourse of sexual violation which privileges women's rights to their bodies. One social fallout of fear of sexual molestation and rape was that the marriage age for girls dropped.[45] Nayema Ahmed Majoor, the radio producer, confirmed that during a visit to Uri border district in 1998, she saw very young girls, barely past puberty, lining up outside a health camp for reproductive health. This trend of marrying girls off younger, was reinforced by the difficulty of finding suitable boys. Militancy has taken a toll of 60,000 lives, most of them young men. The others are in prison and if freed, crippled by electric shocks and made impotent. Many are unemployable having dropped out of school and college.

Women's Stretched Roles

Violent conflict saw the collapse of the divide between the public world of men and the private world of women. As men retreated because of their greater vulnerability to being picked up, tortured and arrested, women came out. It was mothers and wives who had never dreamt of leaving the shelter of their neighbourhoods, who went to the security camps, the detention centres and the courts in search of their men. Women 'stretched' their traditional roles as nurturers of their family and protectors of the community. Nusrat Begum had been a traditional middle-class housewife with two young children till her husband, a political ideologue of a militant group was picked up. Alone, she found her way to the Papa II interrogation centre and made them acknowledge her husband was detained there.

Such action by women in defence of their men is socially accepted as a legitimate extension of women's traditional roles. Within the structure of armed patriarchy, it is precisely as women that they have the right to access powerful men and to move them to compassion. But this practice also carried these ordinary women into the public sphere of negotiations of power with the security forces and the administration for the rescue and safety of their families. The stretched roles were grounded in women's traditional roles. It led Parveen Ahangar, an illiterate housewife, to found with her lawyer, Pervez Imroz, the Association of Parents of the Disappeared and forge a political strategy to demand collective justice.[46]

Parveen Ahangar is still looking for her 22-year-old son, Javed Ahangar who went missing in 1990. Like thousands of other parents, Parveen went to the hospital, the administration, the interrogation centres and the shrines of saints to try and find her son who was reportedly picked up by commandos of the national security guards. She wrote to the president of India and filed a *habeas corpus* petition in court. 'We [mothers] were going to the police and to the courts but getting nowhere. We would see each other waiting anxiously and share our individual grief. The idea of coming together emerged by itself. Alone nobody would listen to us but together we would be heard,' Parveen said. She turned women's weakness into strength. Demanding justice from a paternalistic state is an extension of the women's traditional mothering role. It disarmingly takes into public space the private act of mourning and politicises it.

Women's political activism flowed from their domestic concern of managing survival and protecting their families and was articulated in the cultural language of their everyday lives. Some like Mehbooba, the timid wife of a militant with Al-Jehad, evolved their own form of resistance in confronting the security forces. She recalled how on one of the many occasions when the security forces came calling late at night, she used her wits to keep them out. Hidden inside was her husband. 'Where is the lady police officer who should be with you?' Mehbooba taunted the BSF officer, 'You're too scared to go after the Afghans you say husband is with. Do you have courage only to threaten a woman alone and defenceless?' 'I saved him,' she said.

To keep militants at bay, women like the daughter of a wealthy Kashmiri businessman worked out their own survival strategy exploiting the ideology of *mujahids* to their advantage. 'At first when the militants knocked, we women being alone, were paralysed with terror,' she said. 'But later, when they knocked we told them that as good Muslim fighters, they had no right to come into a home when there were only women.'

Women Militants

There were Kashmiri women who stepped beyond the 'stretched roles' and emerged in the popular imagination as symbols of militant Kashmiri women. Media reports described women in Kashmir going in for arms training.[47] Zamrood of the MKM suggests that women did go for arms training although Samiya Noor, the current president of the MKM denies it. There is no convincing evidence to suggest that Kashmiri women were involved in direct militant action. The Kashmir conflict has not produced a woman *mujahid*. Asiyah Andrabi symbolises the militant Kashmiri woman, but she claims she has never picked up a gun. 'No, we never felt it was necessary, to pick up a gun, ourselves. Our menfolk are doing that work. If it should happen that our men weaken, you shall see a gun in our hands,' she said. In 1994, when the DM launched a campaign to resist sexual molestation, women armed themselves with knives.

Asiyah pragmatically argues, 'If all of us were to take up arms, our whole set-up would be destabilised. My husband is locked up. If I too were involved, what would happen to my child.' Asiyah's son was 5 months old when she was arrested and locked up for seven months. 'Many families have lost their men and women are obliged to become the breadwinners. What would happen, if women too jumped into the battlefield?' she asked. Were women *mujahids*, what answer would the widowed Jameela Gujjar have given her

10-year-old daughter who asked, 'Where has he [father] gone?' 'He has become a martyr.' 'Who will take care of us now?' 'I'm here, I'll take care of you,' Jameela reassured. 'You're not going to be martyred?' On 28 April 1991, all seven men in the family were shot dead by the security forces. Jameela has two daughters and a son to bring up in village Malagoan in Bandipora. They have land and animals, but no men. 'I have to bring up my children. If women become militants, what will happen to the children? Who will look after them? A woman cannot become a militant.'[48]

Kashmiri women have been couriers, aided in the escape of militants during a crackdown, kept quiet about hidden guns and even carried, knowingly and unknowingly, explosives. Asiyah, herself, was picked up under the Terrorist and Disruptive Activities Act in 1993, along with her husband, the intelligence chief of the Jamiat-ul Mujahedeen (JUM). He is still in jail for kidnapping and murder. The state accused her of being linked with the Pakistan intelligence agency, the ISI's network of funding and propaganda activities. Opposing her bail application the state alleged that she had sent some Kashmiri women to Pakistan for training in the handling of sophisticated arms and explosives.[49] Asiyah was released after seven months, but not before it was bruited about that she had become an Indian agent. Asiyah vehemently denies it. Six years later, although she is still watched, it is not clear whether her subterfuge style is a dramatic pose or a vital necessity.

Who then are these women who are said to have gone for training? Most of them turned out to be wives or relatives of well-known militants and were implicated more by familial association than actual complicity. Mehbooba was arrested in 1992 from Hyderpora in Srinagar along with her 10-day-old baby. She was accused of crossing over to Pakistan in November 1989 for training in subversion and handling of arms. She was the first woman to be accused of being a Pakistan-trained militant. There was a public outcry. Masses of women in Hyderpora came out to protest. They were caned, tear-gassed and fired upon. Mehbooba was released. Her husband, a prominent militant leader later told a local journalist on the telephone from his hideout that Mehbooba's arrest was aimed at putting pressure on him to surrender.[50]

In 1996, it seemed that the intelligence authorities had cracked the 'innocent' shell of the Kashmiri women. Farida Dar was arrested in Srinagar as a co-accused in the Lajpat Nagar, Delhi, bomb blast. Farooq Ahmed Khan, the principal accused in the case, identified her. Both were described by the Special Operations Group of the police, as important functionaries of the outlawed militant outfit Ikhwan-ul Muslimeen.[51] Farida's brother is Bilal Beg, the chief of the militant outfit and currently in Pakistan. Her neighbours say Farida's generous nature led her to provide refuge and sustenance to all, including her brother's militant friends. According to Farida's lawyer, her complicity in the case has yet to be established in court. A visit to her sister's home in Srinagar showed many treasured photographs of Bilal Beg. Evidently, the family still regards Bilal Beg as a hero, although both his sisters have suffered. The younger sister's husband, an Industrial Training Institute (IIT) employee, was picked up in 1997 and died under torture.

Had Kashmiri women become *mujahids*, it would have exposed them to the full repressive might of the security forces. Political activists like Zamrood who acknowledge that a few women did go for training in arms, said, 'It's a good thing they never picked up the gun. It would have legitimised women becoming the targets of the security forces.'

Politics of Extremism: Social Capital of Kashmir Destroyed

As militancy got corrupted, the political struggle for *aazaadi* morphed into the politics of extremism destroying in its wake the social capital of Kashmir. The face of militancy became the face of the renegade, the surrendered militant and the foreign militant. The moral conviction of fighting a 'just war' came unstuck. Also, as the Indian state dug in its heels, the people of the valley were forced to recognise that *aazaadi* could not be achieved by armed struggle. But power had passed into the hands of those who wielded the gun and had no other politics. Popular base groups like the JKLF moved away from armed struggle but the political platform of pro-separatist groups failed to emerge as a catalyst for a post-conflict politics.

Women whose support had provided the backbone to the struggle now turned their back on militancy. But its potential to be a turning point for conflict transformation was undermined by the undervaluation of women's activism and their marginalisation in the formal sphere of politics.

Militancy Gets Corrupted

The militant movement was subverted by a strategy of infiltration crafted by a former intelligence chief, who later became governor of Jammu and Kashmir, Girish Saxena. The security forces deliberately targeted the popularly backed JKLF and exploited inter-militant rivalry to weaken them. The pro-independence JKLF group was further hit as Pakistan shifted its material support away to groups like Hizbul Mujahideen which were committed to union with Pakistan. The ascendance of the Hizbul Mujahideen paved the way for extremist groups like the Harkat-ul Ansar spawned in the terrorist nurseries of the Afghan conflict. Kashmiri societal control over the militants, tenuous at best, was non-existent over these foreign militants. An extremist politics was taking over as demonstrated in the slew of arbitrary killings of highly respected human rights activists, journalists, educationists and professionals.

The gun put young 'militants' in charge. It was a devastating class equaliser. Overnight, it opened up for poor unemployed boys access to the leather jacket and boots culture and the power to extort, abduct and rape. A cook in a middle-class home picks up the gun and demands the daughter of the house in marriage. Middle-class mothers who had sheltered militants, even disguising them as sons-in-law discovered to their horror, that is exactly what they wanted to be, by force if necessary. Young middle-class girls swept away by the romance of militancy eloped with militants and found themselves widowed with little children. 'Command marriages' and elopements alienated middle-class support. The vocabulary of armed struggle became crowded with words like *naqli* or false *mujahid*, renegade *mujahid* and surrendered *mujahid*.

Ten years of conflict have brutalised the security forces, militants and Kashmiri society. It is in the border hill districts of Rajouri and Poonch, where the impact of militancy is more recent, that you feel the helplessness of people trapped between two guns—those of the corrupted militants and the security forces. 'When the militants ask for food and shelter, you don't say, no! They come with guns. If we refuse them, they call us *mukhbirs* [informers] and kill us. And then the army comes and beats us up for feeding the militants. They beat us and the army beats us,' said Sajjid, a student. Nineteen members of Sajjid's family in Saillon village near Poonch were hacked to death, including women and children. The Jammu and Kashmir State Human Rights Commission established it was a revenge killing by three 'surrendered' militants with the active help of the paramilitary forces.

Militancy, Abduction and Rape

Rape and atrocities against women have increased sharply as a culture of unaccountability has spread lawlessness in society. Gone is the forbearance once shown towards Kashmiri women. Official statistics record that 11 girls were abducted and murdered after 1993, 35 in 1994 and for the first half of 1995, there were 35 abductions of girls and women.[52] Many Muslim families fled the valley to escape their daughters being abducted.

Rape has become common, to coerce a marriage or to punish so called 'informers'. One of the first such instances was the killing of Sarla Butt, accused of being an informer. It took on a communal colouring and spread terror among the populace. A rumour gained ground that Kashmiri Pandit women were at risk of being raped by Kashmiri Muslims. In some cases women fell victim to being tarred as 'informers' out of desperation to get a loved one released. Shahina fell foul of the Ikhwan-ul Muslimeen because she sought the help of the BSF to get her brother released. The Ikhwan, hoping to recruit him, had kidnapped him. At a press conference arranged by the BSF, she explained that she was kidnapped, first by the JKLF and punished with 41 lashes and then by Ikhwan militants who repeatedly raped her. Shahina eventually joined the CRPF as a woman constable.[53] She claims that when she complained to Deputy

Commander Dr Haider, he merely released her with a warning not to contact the security forces.[54] Shahina was clearly on show to visiting journalists. Nonetheless, her account was corroborated by the experience of several other women. On occasion the leadership has chastised errant militants, but there is little evidence to show that top ranking militant or political leaders condemned rape by armed militants.

Security Forces Target *Mujahid* Families

As for the security forces, women relatives of *mujahids* became particular targets of intimidation and harassment. Their proximity to the militants was used to discredit their testimony and shirk responsibility for abuse. In July 1998, the media[55] reported the gang rape of Mehtaba and her two daughters by the security forces in the border district of Kupwara. Mehtaba was the sister of a JUM militant Sajjad who had been killed some time ago. Medical examination by Dr Bilkees at the district hospital confirmed rape. The state government promptly issued a denial. Dr Bilkees' testimony was discredited as there was a First Information Report (FIR) pending against her charging her with collusion with pro-separatist elements. She was accused of inciting Mehtaba's mother to make allegations of rape. The women were branded as 'known keeps of the militants'. The press statement claimed arms and ammunition belonging to Mehtaba's dead brother were recovered. However, the discrepancies in the state government's statement were pointed out by the seniormost district police officer.

Wives and sisters of militants have become soft targets to humiliate and pressurise militants into surrender. Bilal Beg, the head of the Ikhwan-ul Muslimeen, fled to Pakistan from where in 1996, he master minded bomb blasts in New Delhi and Dausa in Rajasthan. His elder sister Farida Dar was arrested and locked up in Tihar jail as a co-accused in the bomb blast conspiracy. Was she a militant or was her real crime that she was Bilal Beg's sister?

Whereas earlier, the security forces hesitated to physically attack the families of well-known pro-separatist leaders, the Special Task

Force (STF) of the Jammu and Kashmir Police seems to have no reservations. In October 1997 and again in 1998, the sisters of the JKLF chief Yasin Malik, were brutally beaten up. Abida and Ameena were staying in the family's modest two storeyed house in Maisuma. Yasin Malik was not at home the night when the STF jumped in through the window. 'No, our neighbours did not come to help us. If they could do this to us, what would they do to them. Everyone who has known us has suffered,' said Abida. As darkness falls, Abida's two small sons Ishfaq and Sohaib will not stay in their uncle's house and insist on going to their grandmother's. At night is when the security forces come.

Women Disillusioned

Wives of militants interviewed sounded disillusioned after 10 years of living through conflict. 'What is a *mujahid*?' 'Someone wanted to study medicine. He couldn't get in so he decided to cross the border for training to get guns,' Shabnam Imroz said. Her husband, a senior militant ideologue was arrested within two weeks of their marriage. He has been more in than out of jail and she has been bringing up her two daughters on a teacher's salary. 'What kind of freedom? We will never be free. No one believes anymore we'll get *aazaadi*. India will never leave us. Only more lives will be lost,' she said.

Yasin Malik's sisters have watched their brother, become a walking corpse as a result of torture in jail. They did not know when he went across for training. 'Yes, we would have tried to stop him. But he would not have listened,' Abida said. She is disillusioned with the role Pakistan has played in the Kashmir conflict. 'They use microphones, while we shed our blood,' she said. She rues the devastation that the gun culture has brought. 'We are caught between two guns,' she said. The result is that 'Kashmir is full of patients.'

Nusrat Begum, as mentioned earlier, is the wife of a senior political ideologue of the JKLF, once a prosperous engineer. As a result of his proximity to militancy, he has been tortured and jailed for a year and their house routinely raided by the police and the children threatened. Nusrat still believes in *aazaadi*, but through political negotiations. '*Aazaadi* can be achieved not through the gun, only through political talk', she says.

Activists like Anjum Zamrood, general secretary of the MKM, reject violence as a means to resolve anything. 'Guns achieve nothing—you can't talk to a man who is holding a gun at you and you at him. All that will happen is that both of you will be killed. And the problem will remain exactly where it was.'

The women quoted above were associated with the JKLF, which in 1994 gave up armed struggle and constituted a pro-separatist umbrella political organisation, the All Parties Hurriyat Conference. Many other women interviewed in 1998–99 also articulated an ambivalence, if not outright rejection of armed struggle. In the wake of savage repression by the Indian state and the corruption of militancy, women no longer willingly open their doors to the knock of a militant. *Naqli* or false *mujahids* have degraded the respect enjoyed by the *mujahid* and his family.

But there are no neutral spaces in a conflict where mothers have lost sons, wives husbands, children fathers and daughters have been raped. Can they turn their back on militancy? Mehbooba, the sister of top militant Bilal Beg, has watched her sister Farida hauled off to jail, her husband tortured and killed. Yet, in her family album, the photographs most proudly displayed by her two children are those of their uncle Bilal Beg in Pakistan. For every person who spoke of the futility of arms struggle there was another who passionately asserted that the sacrifices must not be in vain.

For Asiyah Andrabi, the necessity of armed struggle cannot be questioned. 'I would never say that the solution of Kashmir is possible only through politics. Militancy is necessary. We need to strengthen militancy. If the struggle is limited to political means, the problem of Kashmir will not go away for 200 years,' she says. Asiyah shrugs off evidence about the dwindling number of local militants. 'Many of the women in the DM have seen husbands martyred, children have seen their fathers killed. They've lost everything, how can they sit back? These children are asking their mothers, can't we grow up faster, so we can fight Hindustan?' she says. The security forces boast that at best, a militant can hope to last out for two years before he is captured or killed. Would Asiyah send her only son, now 6 years old, to fight? 'Inshallah! He is getting ready to fight, when he is older,' she says.

Asiyah's politics are speaking. But what of the thousands of 'ordinary' women? In Maisuma, the mother of Zahoor Hussain Gul sat beneath the prominently displayed photograph of her son flanked by two Afghans. The three had been killed a few months before in an encounter. After he was killed, Mobeena discovered that Zahoor had joined the Harakat-ul Ansar. He had previously been with the JKLF and since the group had moved away from armed struggle, had been working in a shop. Her third son sat near her, loudly declaiming the necessity of armed struggle. He wanted Islamic rule in Kashmir, which for him meant the right to say *namaz* seven times and for women to observe *purdah* as enjoined by the Quran. Mobeena had lost two of her sons, one killed and the other crippled by torture. Her youngest son was not a militant. Would she let him go? 'If one son has been martyred, then if another goes, what of it?' But Mobeena quickly added, she did not want him to join the armed struggle. 'Who will look after us old people?' Mobeena did not question the value of armed struggle. 'If India had listened to us, we wouldn't have picked up the gun. The army is forcing us to take up guns,' she said, parroting her son. Then she slipped in, 'we must guard against renegade militants.'

People were tired. But sons who had watched their fathers killed were growing up. Zamrood alluded to a report that the entire Class IX of a school in Kupwara district had crossed the border for training in arms. The report's authenticity was less important than what the persistence of such reports signalled in the makings of a discourse of a popularly backed armed struggle.

Targeting of Women

As militancy has become increasingly bereft of the politics of the people's struggle, Kashmir has become an open range for multiple agencies, armed and unaccountable. The local adjuncts of the security forces, the STF of the Jammu and Kashmir Police and the Special Police Officers, recruited from surrendered militants, have become the most dreaded force in Kashmir. 'For the Indian forces, it was difficult to recognise who was who, but these are Kashmiris,' shuddered Asiyah Andrabi.

Ironically, when militancy related incidents have become more focused on deadly duels between militants and security forces around the camps and police posts, women in the rural hill districts and even in Srinagar, are more at risk than ever before from the security forces, the STF, the pro-government militants, the *naqli mujahids* and the foreign *mujahids*. There is a new phenomenon of women being directly targeted and shot.

Victoria Scofield, in *Kashmir in Crossfire*[56] quotes a Kashmiri student narrating the story of his neighbour. The militants knocked at her door one night and asked for money. 'In the old days she would have asked them in and given them food. This time she refused and shut the door in their face. So they pushed the door in her face and shot her.'

From the border hill districts in Jammu division, the new terrain of spreading militancy, come reports of 'unidentified gunmen', a euphemism for security forces, surrendered militants, renegade militants and the *mujahids*, knocking at the door and shooting women at point-blank range. In the Surankot area of Poonch district on 28 August 1998 militants knocked at the door of Abdul Gani's house. No men were at home. They broke open the door and dragged out the two women inside. Latifa Bee and Khatija Bee were stood up against a wall and shot. Latifa died on the spot, Khatija was rushed to hospital. They were suspected to be informers.[57] Again in village Sailon, Poonch district, 19 Muslims, mostly women and little children were hacked to death by three Kashmiri SPOs (recruited surrendered militants) backed by a paramilitary army unit.

Three themes can be picked up in the above incidents. One, violent conflict has brutalised Kashmiri society as manifested in violence against women. Two, the incremental evidence is that women, alienated from a corrupted militancy, are turning their backs on the movement. With the moral justness of the armed struggle compromised, women are unwilling to provide refuge and support. Three, the branding of women as *mukhbirs* (informers) has laid them open to swift and brutal reprisals. The domination of militancy by renegade militants and foreign militants has made Kashmiri women who were beyond the pale of direct violence, a direct target.

Kashmiri Women as *Mukhbirs*

In the early years of militancy there were reports of women branded as informers being raped and killed. A woman who rushes to the security camp to rescue a son, a husband or a brother is at risk of being branded an informer as in the case of Shahina described earlier. What has changed is the substantial increase in the number of incidents in which women have been branded as informers and been punished with death, especially in areas like Rajouri, Poonch and Doda districts of Jammu, where militancy has more recently spread. A pattern seems to be emerging as in the killing of Masina Begum in Mahore area of Udhampur. She was dragged out of her home and shot dead. Police claimed she was killed on suspicion of being an informer. Apparently, three militants had entered her home and kidnapped her son, Majid. Maisina approached her brother, a member of the local Village Defence Committee. Armed, he chased the militants and freed the boy. The militants came back and killed Maisina Begum.[58]

According to a senior Kashmiri journalist, a suspicion has taken root in people's minds of women as informers. It has been reinforced by the image of *burqa* clad women going into the STF police camp near Bakshi stadium in the heart of Srinagar. They are women Central Intelligence Department (CID) or CRPF constables. But the *burqa* identity cloaks all women with suspicion as potential *mukhbirs* and imprints in the popular imagination the image of the Kashmiri women as informers. It is not that more women than men are becoming *mukhbirs*. As the social capital of Kashmir has been destroyed, more women and men are becoming informers. For destitute women it is a means of survival.

Army, BSF Camps: Rape and Prostitution

The security forces have settled into quasi-permanent encampments with the attendant evils of long-term occupation, including physically or economically enforced prostitution. Young girls going to school, collecting firewood or grazing sheep and goats, alone, in the border districts, are routinely sexually harassed. There have been many reports of girls who catch the eye of a local officer being called to army camps for interrogation. Often, to put pressure on recalcitrant girls, their relatives are tortured. In Saderkot village in Ganderbal district, we were able to investigate Hanifa's story.[59] Hanifa, a schoolgirl, claimed that her brother, Gulzar Ahmed Bhat, was blasted with explosives by the army because he refused to cooperate in procuring her for one of the officers at the army camp in Saderkot, Ganderbal district. Lt. Gen. Krishan Pal, the Commanding Officer in Kashmir, insists the villagers have 'rigged up a custodial death story'.

Pro-government Militants and the Special Task Force

In a culture of unaccountability, the most dreaded are the surrendered or pro-government militants. Surrendered militants, especially those recruited as Special Police Officers (SPOs), have been abducting and sexually exploiting girls. Villagers are intimidated from complaining as they are backed by the security forces. However, public outrage at the abduction of three girls by two taxi drivers in the Bandipora area in August 1998, forced the police to act and exposed a nexus between the two drivers and surrendered militants.[60]

The STF which is an offshoot of the Jammu and Kashmir Police, is regarded with much greater fear and dread than the paramilitary forces. Some of the worst excesses against civilians, and women in particular, have been at the hands of the STF. On 31 July 1998 at 11:00 p.m., the STF, led by a 'renegade militant' raided the house of Mehjooba in Maisuma (Srinagar) and accused her of hiding four guns. 'A rag was stuffed in my mouth and I was beaten and given electric shock treatment. Desperate, I told them the guns were hidden by the river. There were no guns. They held me down in the river till I was half dead. Brought back I was again beaten. I knew nothing to tell them,' she said. The incident made headlines in the media. Mehjooba and her family were threatened for making the incident public. They have disappeared.

Disillusionment with Political Leaders—The Hurriyat

Militant groups like the JKLF had given up armed struggle and forged a united political platform called the All Parties Hurriyat Conference in 1995. But the opportunity for the Hurriyat to emerge as the political voice of a people alienated from India and armed struggle foundered over the Hurriyat's lack of political unity and common vision beyond 'Quit India'. The Hurriyat leaders have been unable to disavow the extremist politics of armed struggle and move towards a beyond conflict political strategy. The Hurriyat leaders have squandered much of the popular goodwill they enjoyed. The Indian government's propaganda machinery has succeeded in tarnishing the image of the Hurriyat leaders by insinuating that while ordinary people made sacrifices, their sons went to study or work outside and while people's homes and properties were lost in arson attacks, these leaders built their houses and made money.

The Hurriyat's incapacity to adequately help the sufferers of conflict has further disillusioned supporters of the struggle. Parveen Ahangar, who founded the Association of the Parents of the Disappeared,[61] was particularly bitter at their failure to help parents of missing children. In 1996 the Hurriyat Conference did assist some 15 parents of the missing to plead their case in New Delhi. The Association was not involved. It was the failure of the Hurriyat to satisfactorily support the half-widows, orphans and mothers which pushed Parveen to found the Association. By and large, the political leaders in the Hurriyat have an instrumental relationship with the humanitarian story of the Kashmir conflict, manipulating it for propaganda purposes.

Anjum Zamrood of the MKM criticised the Hurriyat for having let down the widows of martyrs like Hilal Beg. He had been with the JKLF and allegedly crossed over to the government side. The 'unsuitable' marriage had been brokered by the JKLF chief, Yasin Malik. Hilal Beg's parents had thrown out his widow. She had appealed in vain to the JKLF for help. 'How much can the Hurriyat do,' defended a male political activist. Samiya Noor, the president of the MKM was injured on her spine in a *lathi* charge during the siege of the Hazratbal shrine. It was no use looking to the Hurriyat for the 0.5 million rupees needed for her operation, said Zamrood. It reflected the Hurriyat's failure to take the MKM's political activism seriously.

Political Challenge of Locating Rape

In the propaganda battle against the Indian state, women were projected as the front-line of the human rights story. Allegations of rape by the security forces were the main front of the propaganda war to crucify the Indian state's human rights record. Women were encouraged to give public testimony, videos were recorded and widely circulated. A Kashmiri academic, Hameeda Bano explained the enthusiasm with which women embraced the propaganda project of the militants. 'They [raped women] thought the whole of Kashmir had become one big family. That they would be forgiven. That there would be no social stigma as their suffering was in the cause of the movement.' They were to learn to their bitter cost—it made no difference.

The militant movement established an instrumental relationship with the women, whereby patriarchal relations were reinforced and the concept of the 'dishonoured' women, central to patriarchal ideology, was politically never challenged. Rape was dislocated from the status of being an event pertaining to family honour to become an event of concern to the armed struggle for national honour, i.e., it was located as a war crime in the public sphere. Left unchallenged was rape as socially stigmatising the women in the private sphere of the family.

The women of Kunan Poshpara were to find out that their innocent willingness to come forward and testify to rape left them socially ostracised. Kunan Poshpara became the village of raped women. A women's initiative team visited the village in 1994 and found no marriage had taken place in the last three years. Two husbands did agree to take their wives back at the intervention of militants and elders. One insisted that there be no conjugal relations, the other that he live in the city far away.[62] Asiyah Andrabi who went to Kunan Poshpara soon after the rape incident insists that some of the girls who were raped were married with great fanfare. Local journalist Ishfaq-ul Hassan who visited the village in 1997, confirmed some girls were married. Parents admitted, 'We married these girls out of compulsion rather than choice. We had to literally dispose of our girls as takers were few. . . . No outsider was willing to marry them.'[63] An *Indian Express* reporter who went to the village in 1998, found that 10 girls had grown past the age of marriage and 42 more could face a similar fate in the village of raped women.

The need for pro-separatist groups to take on the political challenge of raped women was raised by the MKM with the Hurriyat leadership in 1995. According to Zamrood, MKM proposed that militant leaders who had left armed struggle be persuaded to marry these girls to set an example. The idea was rejected. The instrumental relationship of the Hurriyat with the women victims of conflict was reflected in the conspicuous absence of women at the Hurriyat's hunger strike in Delhi, to spotlight the issue of rape as a weapon of war in 1998. Apparently, it had been so troublesome bringing along women in 1996, that the All Party Hurriyat Conference (APHC) decided against it. The issue was gender-based violence but Hurriyat leaders did not believe the presence of their women members was necessary. The MKM is a constituent member of the Hurriyat. At press conferences organised by the Hurriyat in the valley to protest against the increasing incidence of rape despite an elected government in the state, women are on show as silent victims.

Women have been used in the propaganda battle of the movement but not empowered with respect as contributing to the struggle beyond their traditional roles as self-sacrificing mothers and wives and as victims of rape. When politics gives way to armed struggle martial values are prized and women as reproducers of separatist nationalist identities are exalted but women's agency is marginalised and dismissed by an armed patriarchy.

Failure to Build Solidarities

The Kashmiri woman's voice has also been marginalised because of the incapacity to build solidarities with women's organisations, civil liberties and human rights groups in India. Reaching out comes up against the xenophobia of Kashmiri Muslim society reinforced by the conflict. Women, because they are excluded from 'politics', may see themselves as having less stake in defending correct political positions of the pro-separatist struggle. However, when the community's survival is at stake, women embrace the markers of identities of exclusion. The lack of local secular women's groups in Kashmir is both a historical development and symptomatic of the struggle. With the MKM and the DM articulating women's role in the conflict, any possibility of reaching out and building alliances, either with mirror organisations like the Daughters of Vitasta or with secular women's movements in the rest of the country, was undermined.

At the national level, women's groups, human rights organisations and civil liberties groups, with a few significant exceptions, have been reluctant to get involved in a pro-separatist struggle. The dominant narrative of national security has co-opted many in casting pro-independence Kashmiris as 'terrorists', while others have been alienated by the fundamentalist tendencies in the Kashmir movement. In these 10 years, there have been barely three to four independent women's initiatives to investigate the use of rape as an instrument of war in Kashmir.

It was thought that some space was opening up to strengthen women's activism in the informal sphere through building gender-based solidarities with women political leaders in the state and outside. In Jammu and Kashmir, the revival of the democratic process brought to power Mehbooba Mufti Sayed who as the leader of the Opposition was stridently raising the issue of human rights violations and the plight of a people trapped in violence. However, given the ambivalent if not hostile attitude of the people towards electoral politics in Jammu and Kashmir, hardly any of the cross-section of women interviewed recognised her as a possible ally. Her criticism of the violent excesses of the security agencies of the state against the people and especially women, was dismissed as political rhetoric.

Where Are the Women Activists?

When the popular movement for *aazaadi* burst into public space, women were visible everywhere. Ten years later, the most influential women's resistance group in the valley, the Dukhtarane Millat, has all but disappeared. Its leader, Asiyah Andrabi, has been reduced to more shadow than substance. The Muslim Khawateen Markaz,[64] with its boast of thousands of members spread in every district, has shrunk to a nominal organisation. The MKM is still one of the 32 constituent members of the Hurriyat but has no presence in its Executive Council.

The Dukhtarane Millat is not a formal member of the Hurriyat. In the early mobilisation for the *aazaadi* struggle Asiyah used to sit in the Council meetings of the Tehriq-i Hurriyat to coordinate the protest agenda. She insists that it is by choice that she now maintains a distance from the Hurriyat. 'It accommodates on its platform pro-independence groups. I don't want to share a platform from where you hear so many conflicting voices. We believe in Islamic politics, not secular politics,' she explained. Asiyah feels that her voice is still heard by the leadership, all of whom are men. But Hurriyat leaders are dismissive about the DM and Asiyah's relevance.

The DM continues to be politically visible through sporadic high profile activities of its members. During the run-up to the 1996 elections, when space opened up for political activity, DM women dressed in flowing *burqas* would suddenly hit the street with banners and rent the air with anti-India slogans till they were chased away with *lathis* and tear-gas. As the public space for struggle and resistance came under increasing pressure from the policing activities of the STF, the DM again withdrew. Activists of the DM still manage on occasion to strike out with a symbolic show of non-armed protest of 14 August, Pakistan's Independence Day. On the anniversary of the demolition of the Babri Masjid, 6 December, the DM supported the Hurriyat's call for a general strike which paralysed normal life in Kashmir.

In 1990, the MKM could call upon 2,000 activists in Srinagar alone. Ten years later the MKM's strength has whittled down to 10–20 activists in Srinagar, four-five in Anantnag, four in Baramulla and one in Jammu. In 1996, 'Bhenji' who so stridently led the MKM at its peak, has withdrawn from politics, bitter and betrayed. Anjum Zamrood described 'Bhenji' as a no-nonsense woman, unafraid to speak her mind to Hurriyat elders like A.S. Geelani. It did not endear her to them.

The Hurriyat leaders, all males, dismiss the value of women's sporadic and spontaneous actions in the informal space of politics, and have kept them out of the formal decision-making structures. Zamrood of the MKM is insistent that without women being present in decision-making bodies like the Hurriyat Executive Council, they can make no impact. She raised the issue with Geelani, the chairman of the Hurriyat Conference in May 1998 but got no response. When we posed the question to Geelani, he said it would expose women to unnecessary risk. They would be picked up, manhandled and arrested like other Hurriyat leaders. Shahbir Shah, who pulled out of the Hurriyat and founded his own Front, claims that one of the reasons he left was the women's question. It is a fact that he had deputed as spokesperson for his party, the Peoples League to the Human Rights Commission in Geneva, Hameeda Bano, a teacher at Srinagar University.

Association of the Parents of the Disappeared

The manner in which women's activism and in particular, organisations like MKM have been used and manipulated by the political patriarchs of the movement, may have something to do with the determination of organisations like Parents of the Disappeared to steer clear of co-optation by political groups. Praveen Ahangar, the president of the Association, is the sister of Mohtarma Bakhtawar, once the head of the MKM.

The Association's members are largely women. It is grounded in women's traditional mothering role, politicising the private act of suffering and grieving by taking it into public space. Sara Ruddick describes the strategy as one in which 'Women who act as women in public spaces transform the passions of attachment and loss into political action, transform the woman of sorrow from icon to agent.'[65] Initiatives like the Parents of the Disappeared or Mothers Fronts are innovative strategies uniquely available to 'disarmed' women to negotiate structures of power. They represent women taking responsibility for political action.

The Association was founded by a suffering mother, Parveen Ahangar, in 1996. It has about 300 members, largely from Srinagar. In the rural areas, women are much more vulnerable to intimidation. Five women did come from the border district of Uri to Srinagar to join 40 other mothers and wives to demand an investigation into disappearances at a press conference in September 1998. How real the risk is for these women was starkly demonstrated when Halima Begum, an active member of the Association, was shot dead with her son by unidentified gunmen a few days after the press conference in September 1998. Haleema was not at the press conference but Parveen is convinced that there is a link between Haleema's indefatigable search for her son and her killing. Parveen, however, is determined to carry on.

Their cry for justice is a brave one when the spreading rumours of reprisals from unaccountable multiple agencies, the security forces, surrendered militants and foreign militants have terrorised people into silence. It is a time when fathers are holding back complaints against the custodial deaths of sons and brothers are putting a cover on the gang rape of a sister. But these women are not ready to protect the living by turning their back on the struggle for justice and are demanding accountability from the system.

Can the Association of the Parents of the Disappeared, that is a human rights platform, become a catalyst—for the revival of civil society activism? So far the strength and limitation of the Parents of the Disappeared is its single agenda—justice for the missing. Whether it can be part of the regenerative process of rebuilding a beyond conflict politics of justice and peace is an open question. Also, there is a grave risk of sentimentalising mothers as anti-war agents, for the same mothers can be manipulated to raise sons to be soldiers. Unless the mothers develop a clear political position on non-violent ways of dealing with difference, that is, a political vision of peace, the sole identity of being suffering women is not enough. The experience of mobilisation strategies around motherhood is that they are vulnerable to co-optation by formal political groups as in the case of the Sri Lanka Mothers Front.

With Kashmiri women turning their back on armed struggle, an opening has been created to forge a beyond conflict politics. But Kashmiri women's agency has been marginalised in these 10 years of violent conflict. Women's lived experience as a resource and their survival strategies have been undervalued. The political patriarchs of the *aazaadi* struggle have had an instrumental relationship with Kashmiri women boxing them in the role of martyr's mother and raped woman, using them for propaganda purposes but denying their contribution to the struggle or providing space for their empowerment. In surviving conflict women have acquired power in the informal sphere but are unable to translate it into authority in the public space of formal politics. Their activism has been denied legitimacy. Moreover, as the struggle has become more militarised, it has also become more masculinised, squeezing the space for women's activism and recognition of its value.

Making the Kashmiri women's many-sided experience and response to conflict visible, that is, creating new roles and meanings—from icon to agency—may be a step towards getting women to be taken seriously, a vital necessity, if conflict transformation is to take place in Kashmir.

NOTES

1. According to the 1981 Census, the population of undivided Jammu and Kashmir is 13.5 million. i.e., the population of the state of Jammu and Kashmir in India is 8.3 million, 'Azad' Kashmir 2.2 million, Pakistan admin-

istered Northern Territories 1.0 million, refugees from Kashmir in Pakistan 1.5 million and expatriates in the UK 0.5 million.

2. For an analysis of women's activism in struggle along these lines, see Peter Custers, *Women in the Tebhaga Uprising, 1946-47*, Naya Prakashan, Calcutta, 1987.

3. For a development of the concept of the legitimacy and illegitimacy of violence, see Olivia Bennett, Jo Boxley and Kitty Warnock, *Arms to Fight, Arms to Protect: Women Speak Out About Conflict*, Panos, London, 1995, pp. 4-6.

4. Cynthia Enloe, 'All the Men Are in the Militias. All the Women Are Victims: The Politics of Masculinity and Femininity in Nationalist Wars', in Lois A. Lorentzen and J. Turpin, eds, *The Women and War Reader*, New York University Press, New York, 1998, pp. 53-60.

5. While the interviews were bunched together in 1998-99, I have also drawn upon the many trips I made to Kashmir as a journalist in these last 10 years. The names of people interviewed have been changed in most cases to protect their privacy and security.

6. The official figure of the number of persons killed in the violent conflict is 25,000. According to the Kashmir Awareness Bureau, the number of people killed in the last 10 years is 70,000. Human rights groups estimate that the figure is more than 60,000. Estimates of the number of people 'disappeared' varies from 800 to 2,000 including over 400 with respect to whose disappearance petitions were filed in the High Court. See also Amnesty International Report, India, "'If They Are Dead, Tell Us": Disappearances in Jammu and Kashmir', February 1999. AI Index ASA 20/02/99 (for circulation).

7. People displaced during the insurgency and the shelling in the border districts of Jammu and Kashmir on both sides of the LOC include an exodus of 200,000 Kashmiri Pandits, 70,000 Kashmiri Muslims to India and 120,000 to Pakistan and in Kargil and border districts, 35,000 in Pakistan and 100,000 in India.

8. On the basis of official statements and news reports, it is estimated that Army Corps XIV (Pathankot), XV (Srinagar) and XVI (Leh) are deployed in the state. Each Corps has three Divisions. According to an official release of the CRPF, 216 companies were deployed in Jammu and Kashmir in 1998 as cited in *The Hindu*, 31 December 1998. Official sources in 1999 state Border Security Force deployment in Jammu and Kashmir at 51 battalians (51,000). Rashtriya Rifles has 36 battalians deployed according to a figure quoted in *The Times of India*, 8 October 1997 and Jammu and Kashmir Police deployment in the state is 50,000 (*The Hindu*, 18 September 1998).

9. See B.G. Verghese, 'Autonomy, Restructuring and Peaceful Resolution in Jammu and Kashmir: An Agenda for the Future', in Kanti Bajpai, Dipankar

Banerjee, Amitabh Mattoo, Salman Khurshid, Arun Varma and B.G. Verghese, eds, *Jammu and Kashmir: An Agenda for the Future*, Delhi Policy Group, Delhi, March 1999, p. 51; and Tapan K. Bose, 'Kashmir: A Willing Suspension of Reason', *Himal*, May 1999, p. 15.

10. See Dipankar Banerjee, 'Internal Security in Jammu and Kashmir: An Agenda for the Future', p. 39. Also Khemlata Wakhlu and O.N. Wakhlu, *Kashmir: Behind the White Curtain, 1972–1991*, Konark, Delhi, 1992.

11. Sukhmani Singh, 'Velvet Gloves, Iron Hands', *Saturday Times, The Times of India*, 22 September 1990.

12. Harinder Baweja, 'Challenge of the Veil', *India Today*, 15 September 1991; and *Sunday Magazine*, 17–23 March 1991.

13. Shiraz Sidhva, 'Dukhtaran-e-Millat: Profile of a Militant Fundamentalist Women's Organisation', in Kâmla Bhasin, Ritu Menon and Nigat Said Khan, eds, *Against All Odds: Essays on Women, Religion and Development from India and Pakistan*, Kali for Women, New Delhi, 1994, pp. 123–31; and Rita Manchanda, 'Keepers of the Faith', *The Telegraph*, 14 March 1999; *India Today*, 15 September, 1991; 'J & K Govt opposes bail plea of Aisha', *The Times of India*, 15 February 1993.

14. Lorraine Bayard de Volo, 'Drafting Motherhood' (pp. 246–52), Nancy Scheper-Hughes, 'Maternal Thinking and the Politics of War' (pp. 227–33) and Malathi de Alwis, 'Moral Mothers and Stalwart Sons', pp. 257–64 in Lois A. Lorentzen and J. Turpin, eds, *The Women and War Reader*, New York University Press, New York, 1998.

15. Rita Manchanda, 'Who is Afraid of Foreign Mercenaries?', *Sunday Observer*, 2 September 1993.

16. I am indebted to Veena Das for explication of how the (Sikh) militant discourse was organised in order to direct individuals to violence. See Veena Das, *Critical Events*, Oxford University Press, Bombay, 1999.

17. For details, see Momin Jan, 'Women, Education and Social Change in Kashmir', Department of Sociology, Jamia Milla, New Delhi, 1993, unpublished Ph.D. thesis; and Madhvi Yasmin, 'Role of Women in the Freedom Struggle of Kashmir', in Md Yasin and Qaiyum Rafiq, eds, *History of the Freedom Struggle in Jammu and Kashmir*, Light and Life Publishers, New Delhi, 1980.

18. Prem Nath Bazaz, *Daughters of Vitasta: A History of Kashmiri Women from the Early Times to the Present*, Pamposh Publications, New Delhi, 1959.

19. Ibid. See also, Bashir Dabla, *Working Women in Kashmir*, Rawat Publishers, Jaipur, 1991.

20. See summary of the findings of a survey on 'Gender Discrimination in the Kashmir valley' by Dr Bashir Dabla, Khurshid-ul Islam, Kalpana Mehta, Maitraya Ghatak and Sundeep Nayak, reproduced in Balraj Puri, ed., *Occasional Papers on Human Rights*, July–August 1997. The survey however does not seem to factor in the impact of militancy in the otherwise valu-

able data on widow remarriage, abortion, wife beating, widow inheritance or women in the workplace.

21. In the 1980s a survey of educated working women found that while the majority approved the wearing of *burqa*, no one was wearing one. See Dabla, *Working Women in Kashmir*, n. 19; Jan, 'Women, Education, and Social Change in Kashmir', n. 17.

22. Committee for Initiative on Kashmir, 'Kashmir Imprisoned', New Delhi, June 1990.

23. Wakhlu and Wakhlu, *Kashmir: Behind the White Curtain*, n. 10.

24. See Rick Wilford and Robert Miller, eds, *Women, Ethnicity and Nationalism: The Politics of Transition*, Routledge, New York, 1998.

25. 'Operation Hijab', in *Mountain Valley Kashmir*, June 1992. See also Manchanda, 'Keepers of the Faith', n. 13.

26. According to the All India Kashmiri Pandits Conference, between September 1989 and March 1990, some 65,000 Hindus fled the valley. Thirty-two Kashmiri Pandits were killed in the valley during this period (68 Kashmiri Muslims were killed). See Committee for Initiative on Kashmir, 'India's Kashmir War', New Delhi, March 1990; and Jagmohan, *My Frozen Turbulence*, Allied Publishers, New Delhi, 1995.

27. Committee for Initiative on Kashmir, 'India's Kashmir War', n. 26, pp. 43–44. Taking 1987 as a benchmark, in terms of representation of Hindus and Muslims in government service, only 25 per cent Indian Administrative Service (IAS) officers were from the state and only 5 per cent were Muslims. In the category of gazetted officers, Hindus made up 51 per cent and Muslims 41 per cent and non-gazetted Hindus 38 per cent and Muslims 56 per cent. Twenty per cent of all employment in the state was in the government. On the eve of the Kashmir insurgency there were more than 0.1 million educated employed, including 3,000 postgraduates and 12,000 graduates and 18,000 technicians. See Wakhlu and Wakhlu, *Kashmir: Behind the White Curtain*, n. 10, p. 359.

28. 'Terrorist' was first published in Kashmiri. It was translated by Riaz Punjabi and reworked by me. Subsequently it was used in one of my articles for *The Hindu Sunday Magazine*, 8 November 1998.

29. Harinder Baweja, 'A Pox on Both Houses', *India Today*, March 1992.

30. Rita Manchanda, 'A Tale of Two Kashmirs', *Sunday Observer*, 12–18 July 1992.

31. *The Indian Express*, 15 June 1997.

32. Women's Testimonies from Kashmir, 'The Green of the Valley is Khaki', Women's Initiative 1994, Delhi, 1994.

33. Prabal Mahato, 'The Impact of Terrorism on Women and Children in Jammu and Kashmir'. Unpublished report, 1999.

34. Women's Initiative 1994 cites a figure of 11,000 widows and the Women's Fact Finding Commission Report 1997 cites 10,000 widows. *The Hindu*,

22 December 1998 quotes a survey by the Jammu and Kashmir Yateem Trust which estimates 15,000 orphans. See the report entitled, 'Impact of Conflict Situation on Children and Women in Kashmir' carried out by Bashir Dabla, Srinagar, 1998 and sponsored by Save the Children Fund (UK). Also see 'Kashmir Women Up Against Gender Discrimination', a summary of the findings of a UNICEF sponsored survey on Gender Discrimination in the Kashmir Valley conducted by Dabla et al., n. 20, edited by Balraj Puri, July-August 1997, no. 45–46.

35. See Dabla, 'Impact of Conflict Situation on Children and Women in Kashmir', n. 34.

36. For an account of the kidnapping of Rubaiya Sayeed, see Wakhlu and Wakhlu, *Kashmir: Behind the White Curtain*, n. 27. In June 1994 when militants made a bid to kidnap Yaseem, the daughter of the National Conference leader Ali Md Sagar, a crowd of 200 rushed out to stop them (*India Today*, 30 June 1994).

37. See Human Rights Watch, *Global Report on Women's Human Rights*, 'Rape in Kashmir', Oxford University Press, New Delhi, 1998.

38. See Committee for Initiative on Kashmir, 'Kashmir Imprisoned: A Report', July 1999, New Delhi; Human Rights Watch, *Global Report on Women's Human Rights*, n. 37; 'Women's Testimonies; Report on Theno Budapathery Gang Rape', in *Missive*, September 1994, Srinagar; and Women's Fact Finding Commission Probing into Army Atrocities on Women and Children in Kashmir, 'Wounded Valley . . . Shattered Souls', The Sixth Indian Peoples Tribunal Report, Mumbai, October 1997. The advent of an elected government has not seen a break in the pattern of rape as a weapon of war against the women of Kashmir. Hurriyat claims 18 women were raped between July 1996 and May 1997 by the security forces.

39. For details of my interview with Lt. Gen. Krishna Pal, see Rita Manchanda, 'Fact and Fiction', *Sunday Magazine*, 28 February–6 March 1999.

40. National Human Rights Commission (NHRC) claims about 20 per cent of the allegations of excesses by the security forces are baseless. Of 552 complaints received by the army from January 1990 to March 1997, 528 were found to be baseless. The investigations were carried out by the army (*The Hindu*, 29 April 1997). Also see Army Public Relations Office release, 'Human Rights Record of Army', undated; and Rita Manchanda, 'Defending Rights of Civil Society', *The Times of India*, 20 August 1997.

41. Press Council of India, 'Crisis and Credibility: Report of the Press Council of India, January–July', Lancer International, Paper No. 4, New Delhi, 1991, pp. 122–29. See my critique of Crisis and Credibility in *Economic and Political Weekly*, 15 August 1991.

42. Women's Testimonies, 'The Green of the Valley', n. 32, pp. 10–11.

43. The state government ordered inquiries into 87 incidents of rape, custodial killings and arson. None resulted in criminal prosecution (*Kashmir*

Times, 14 January 1993). In seven court martials held between April 1990 and July 1991 involving incidents of rape, deaths in custody, illegal detention and indiscriminate firing on civilians by the army, only one officer was dismissed, others had promotions postponed or were given displeasure notations on their personal file. See South Asia Human Rights Documentation Centre, 'Massacre in Sopore', Occasional Paper, 1993.

44. Human Rights Watch, *Global Report on Women's Rights*, n. 37.
45. In the urban areas, the average marriage age for girls was 22 to 25 after they had completed their education. See Women's Fact Finding Commission, n. 38.
46. Mothers Front and other such associations are a unique form of political protest by the disempowered. How powerful such protests can be is evident from the experience documented by Malathi De Alwis on the Sinhala Mothers Front in 'Motherhood as a Space for Protest', in Patricia Jeffrey and Amrita Basu, eds, *Appropriating Gender*, Routledge, New York, 1998.
47. Singh, 'Velvet Gloves, Iron Hands', n. 11.
48. Jameela's story is reported in Women's Testimonies, 'The Green of the Valley', n. 32, p. 17.
49. *The Times of India*, 15 February 1993.
50. *The Times of India*, 30 May 1992.
51. *The Indian Express*, 26 May 1996.
52. UNI report in *The Times of India*, 24 November 1995.
53. *The Times of India*, 4 February 1993.
54. *The Times of India*, 3 February 1993.
55. *See Kashmir Times*, 3 July 1998.
56. Victoria Scofield, *Kashmir in the Crossfire*, I.B. Taurius & Co., London, 1996, p. 267.
57. *Kashmir Times*, 28 August 1998.
58. *Kashmir Times*, 1 September 1998.
59. For details, see Manchanda, 'Fact and Fiction', n. 39.
60. *The Indian Express*, 29 August 1998.
61. See Amnesty International Report, India, 'If they Are Dead', n. 6; and also Rita Manchanda, 'My Son Hasn't Come Home', *The Telegraph*, 25 October 1998.
62. Women's Testimonies, 'The Green of the Valley', n. 32, p. 11.
63. See Ishfaq ul Hassan and Islah Mufti, 'Wounds Healed', in *Weekly Submission*, 2 July 1997; and Aasha Khosa, 'Stigma of Rape Cuts off J&K Village from Rest of the World', *The Indian Express*, 8 September 1998.
64. For details on Muslim Khawateen Markaz, see Women's Testimonies, 'The Green of the Valley', n. 32, pp. 23–24; and Tavleen Singh, *Tragedy of Errors*, Viking, New Delhi, 1995, pp. 194–95.
65. Sara Ruddick, 'Woman of Peace', in Lorentzen and Turpin, *The Women and War Reader*, n. 14.

3

Ambivalent Empowerment: The Tragedy of Tamil Women in Conflict

DARINI RAJASINGHAM-SENANAYAKE

> Women have come out strong during the war . . . they have stood out as
> individuals or as small groups exposing the atrocities and violations of
> dignity. . . . Women who in the midst of war pleaded and argued with
> the militants for their families and the whole nation . . . women's his-
> tory does have a triumph. There is powerlessness, disappointment and
> disillusion, but also hope. We have done it, a little bit.
> —*Rajini Thiranagama*, killed by the LTTE, Jaffna, 21 September 1989

Introduction

South Asian women it seems have greatness thrust upon them. They
are rarely born great though they may be born of great families,
and they rarely achieve greatness without great men. The phenomenon of women from powerful political dynasties becoming president or prime minister literally over the dead bodies of their husbands
and fathers is a telling reflection and indictment of the gendered
nature of political power and violence in the South Asian region.
For, while post-colonial South Asia has seen the highest regional
concentration of women heads of state and government in the

world—Benazir Bhutto in Pakistan, Khaleda Zia and Sheikh Hasina in Bangladesh, Sirimavo Bandaranaike and Chandrika Kumaratunga in Sri Lanka and Indira Gandhi in India—they are all widows and/or daughters of male presidents and prime ministers. These women in power have rarely succeeded in stemming the violent trends in South Asian politics or in chalking out an alternative vision and course for their conflicted countries. By and large even women heads of state who had an alternative secular vision of communal and ethnic peace, such as Chandrika Kumaratunga, have remained captive to the violent political forces, structures and processes that in the first instance thrust them to power.

Sri Lanka, with an 18-year-old armed conflict and its leading position in women's social indicators (literacy, health, education) in the South Asian region, has had more widowed heads of state/government and more widows contending for these posts than any of its larger neighbours. Family, motherhood and widowhood have been the symbols that women who sought political power, as well as women activists, have mobilised in their struggles for and ascent to political power in a country ravaged by multiple political conflicts and cycles of violence.

Whereas widowhood bears a stigma in Hindu and to a lesser extent Buddhist culture, it has been powerfully reconfigured by the Bandaranaikes (mother and daughter) in Sri Lanka, and other widows of presidents and party leaders such as Mrs Premadasa and Mrs Gamini Dissanayake. Notably, it was Chandrika Kumaratunga who took the unprecedented step among politicians of distancing herself from ethnic politics and Sinhala majoritarian chauvinism by calling for peace through justice for the minorities as a means to end the armed conflict between successive Sri Lankan governments and the Liberation Tigers of Tamil Eelam (LTTE) fighting for a separate state. But she has been unable to fulfil that promise, caught up in the violent game of political survival and unable to transcend it—a metaphor for women's ambivalent achievement in a period of social and political turmoil that has cast women in new roles in the subcontinent. Other widowed women such as Sarojini Yogeswaran of the moderate Tamil United Liberation Front (TULF) have not survived the violence. She became the first elected woman mayor in

1998 in the local government election in the northern capital Jaffna and soon after was shot dead by militants at her residence.

This chapter considers the changing shape of women's agency in the midst of armed conflict by exploring the new roles that women increasingly perform in their everyday activities in the north and east of the island where the armed conflict has been bitterly fought and has transformed social structures. Women from less politically powerful families than the Bandaranaikes have taken on many new and unaccustomed roles such as head of household and principal income generator mainly due to loss of male family members and displacement arising from the conflict. At the same time many women and girls have been rendered barely functional after suffering the violence of bombing, shelling, loss of family members, extended family fragmentation, and displacement. Moreover, due to the security situation and the perception and fact that men are more likely to be 'terrorists', civilian women from families affected by the armed conflict in the north-eastern war zones of the island have begun to play new public roles. Increasingly, women in the war zone deal with the authorities, from the government agent, to the military and the humanitarian aid agencies. They file documents, plead their cases and implement decisions in the private and public sphere in the presence or absence of their menfolk who are increasingly disempowered or have disappeared.

Women's agency, or to use a term more commonly found in development discourse, women's 'empowerment' in war or peace is not a zero sum game, achieved at the expense of men. War places different burdens on men. For it is men and boys who are mainly expected to fight and defend their nation, community, family and the honour of their women. Men are conscripted into paramilitaries to fight. Men and boys are more easily perceived as a security threat if they are of the wrong ethnic or religious community. They are also more likely to be killed. On the other hand, men who refuse to fight or who are forced to live off humanitarian aid in refugee camps suffer from feeling de-masculinated because they often cannot support their families and play the socially prescribed role of protector and breadwinner of the family. The result is low self-esteem and a sense of failure that might lead to suicidal tendencies among men and boys. Reports from those living in refugee camps indicate that alcoholism is high, as is increased domestic violence. Clearly, there is need for a systematic study of the impact of war and ensuing social and gender transformation on boys, men and the cultural construction of masculinity. However, this is not within the scope of this chapter, which mainly focuses on women's changing roles and lives in the armed conflict in the Tamil-dominated north-east of Sri Lanka.

Women's agency or empowerment is rarely unambivalent in war or peace. Likewise, as Patricia Jeffery has argued, 'agency is not wholly encompassed by political activism'.[1] But it would appear that too many South Asian women's initiatives have neglected the social structural transformations wrought by political violence. Rather, the overwhelming emphasis by women's groups as well as by women in relief and development continues to focus on bringing women into positions of political leadership and to foster women in governance. This is despite the fact that, in the recent South Asian picture of women's advancement women's rights seem, ironically, more likely to be advanced within an ethno-nationalist framework as has been the case with the Bharatiya Janata Party (BJP) women and the LTTE—an issue to which we will return.

This chapter suggests that the changes that war has wrought on women's lives and the social and cultural fabric of families and communities in the conflict zones might give us clues towards developing a creative strategy to enhance women's position and capacities for peace building in post-conflict societies. As such, I explore how conflict has opened up new spaces for women's agency and leadership within changing family and community structures, even as it has destroyed others, and placed a double burden on many. It is hence that I trace the transformations that the armed conflict in Sri Lanka has wrought on many civilian women in small but significant ways by thrusting them into positions of power and decision within their families and communities in war affected regions.

I start with the premise that conflict affects women differently, depending on religion, caste, class, ethnicity, location, political affiliation, etc. But conflict also reveals a certain commonality in women's experience. Women particularly experience gendered forms of violence, such as rape and the fear of rape, body searches and the fear of sexual violence, as well as the social stigma which dogs women who have been raped. Moreover, the fear of sexual violence that the situation of insecurity in armed conflict entails, limits and inhibits most women's mobility and hence their livelihoods, choices and realities. At the same time, women react differently to nationalist armed violence. Some like the women cadres of the LTTE, or the women cadres of the Sri Lanka Army and Air Force, have been radicalised in the process of taking up guns and weaponry for their respective nationalist struggles. Others have become political and social activists for peace, seeking to build alliances across ethnic, cultural and regional borders as, for example, through initiatives like the Mothers Front, Mothers and Daughters of Lanka, Mothers of the Disappeared, Women for Peace and Women's Coalition for Peace.

Gender Status Quo in War and Peace

The argument that 18 years of armed conflict might have resulted in the unintended empowerment of women (sometimes at the expense of their menfolk), is dangerous and disturbing for those of us who believe in and advocate the peaceful resolution of conflicts arising from social injustice. We still conceptualise peace as a return to things the way they used to be and this also includes, in the case of Tamil women, caste structures that buttress the (gender) status quo. For, after all, the gender hierarchy is one of the old established institutions of society, and as Partha Chatterjee notes of women in the colonial period, they are frequently constructed as the central purveyors of a community 'culture' and 'tradition', ironically enough, precisely at a time that their lives and social roles might be undergoing great transformations.[2] Chatterjee's argument pertains to the colonial and Indian nationalist construction of women. Moreover, as numerous feminist analyses have pointed out, in periods of violent nationalist conflict women are often constructed as the bearers of a threatened national culture, values and tradition. Hence, often a return to peace is indexed in the return to the traditional gender status quo—and even women revolutionaries are pushed back into the kitchen.

Social scientists, development workers, and activists have hesitated to address the issue of how social structural transformations wrought by long-term armed conflicts might have brought about desirable changes to entrenched social hierarchies and inequalities such as caste and gender. We have been wary of analysing the unintended transformations brought by war, of seeing positives in violence, lest we be branded 'war-mongers'. Yet for many women who have lost family members peace can never be a simple return to the past. Rather, peace necessarily constitutes a creative remaking of cultural meanings and agency—a third space between a familiar, often romanticised, past and the traumatic present.

Failure to conceptualise and assist the dynamic of social transformation in conflict and peace building might also impede recovery from traumatic experiences, particularly since women (and men), who have to take on new non-traditional roles as a result of conflict might suffer secondary victimisation arising from the new roles that they have to perform. This is particularly the case with a growing number of young Tamil women who have been widowed in the course of the armed conflict, and are challenging the conventional Hindu construct of the 'good woman' as one who is married and auspicious (*sumangali*). Increasingly, many young widows who have to go out to work to sustain young families are redefining the perception of widows and to a lesser extent, unmarried women, as inauspicious beings (*amangali*), by refusing to be socially and culturally marginalised and ostracised because they have lost husbands. But few of these women seem to have found a culturally appropriate language to articulate the transformations that they have experienced, and many feel ashamed, guilty and/or traumatised by their changed circumstances and the shift in gender roles arising from conflict.

This chapter also attempts to trace languages and patterns of empowerment in the generally tragic story of displaced Tamil women's lives towards recognising and promoting the positive changes to women's roles and lives wrought in conflict. The new spaces of cultural or ideological struggle opened by the social structural transformations engendered by long-term armed conflict, also empower the agents and ideologues of violence and recently invented nationalist 'tradition' which is often oppressive to women.

Sometimes for strategic reasons those of us who advocate peace have tended to exaggerate violence and seen it as an all-encompassing thing. Analysis has been the victim of such an approach to the study of violence, particularly gendered violence in war and peace. It is hence that this chapter attempts to rethink some of the gender dynamics of a return to peace by analysing women's new roles and the cultural frameworks that enable or disable them. For unless the cultural frameworks that denigrate women and especially widowed women, are challenged and transformed, women and men who are coping and trying to recover from the wounds of war will carry a double burden, rather than be empowered in the new roles thrust upon them.

This chapter seeks to chart the shifting terrain of women's ambivalent agency in armed conflict, the new spaces opened and the old spaces closed and the changing structure of gender relations in the war affected north-east of Sri Lanka. I explore the diversity and ambiguity of women's agency in the new roles that they have assumed and have had trust upon them over the course of 18 years of conflict in the north-east of the island.

The Framework

In the north and east of Sri Lanka the reality of war for women has been the loss of their menfolk, physical safety, psychological insecurity and a struggle for survival and sustaining the family. The social role for women of holding the family together, of caring for children, the sick and the elderly makes women the worst sufferers during conflict. In short, women labour under a double burden of keeping themselves and their families fed and sheltered while often assuming sole responsibility for the vulnerable and weak, the children, the elderly and the disabled. As a result women have crossed the private/public barriers to contend with the military, to compete in the market and to survive economically. In the process, many women who have been forced to take on various new roles within their families and communities during the years of armed conflict, have also gained greater self-confidence and decision-making power.

Over time women have gone through a process of transformation despite and because of the difficulty of taking on the added burden of traditionally male roles (head of household and principal income generator) following the loss of their menfolk and displacement.[3] Women have gained greater self-confidence, mobility and authority within their families and communities often at the expense of carrying a double burden. A backlash against women's changing roles and patterns of mobility is arguably one of the reasons for increased levels of violence against women.

The chapter examines (*i*) women engaged in peace and human rights work, and (*ii*) women who have had to take on new roles as heads of households. The second part of the chapter assesses the implications of women's transformed roles for humanitarian intervention and development work in war and peace time. The chapter also attempts to map militant and civilian women's agency in moments of violent social transformation and cultural change, to configure a more complex picture of women's agency, as well as their language of resistance and empowerment in conflict. It also takes a critical look at how the construct of the Sri Lankan woman as a double 'victim' of war, as well as caste, culture, and society in peace time might obscure and indeed impede women's agency and empowerment in conflicts.

I draw from ethnographic field research conducted during several fieldwork stints over a number of years between 1996 and 1999, among communities in the 'border areas', both cleared and uncleared areas as they have come to be termed in the media and popular culture. This border constitutes the shifting 'forward defence line' that demarcates land held by the Sri Lanka military and the LTTE. Land held by the military is referred to as 'cleared areas' while land controlled by the LTTE is termed 'uncleared'. Roughly, the border runs from the main eastern town of Batticaloa in the east, to Vavuniya at the centre, to Mannar in the west. It encompasses most of the eastern and north central provinces of the island which have experienced cycles of violent armed conflict, including repeated bombing and shelling of civilian populations.

My observations on displaced women are drawn from interviews conducted with women living in three different settings of displacement:

(i)   Welfare centres or refugee camps where people are housed in sheds, schools or structures constructed by the United Nations High Commission for Refugees (UNHCR) and other relief agencies working with the government.

(ii) Residents of border villages who have been displaced many times by the fighting, shelling and bombing, but chose to return to their villages rather than remain in refugee camps. These people live in constant fear of attack and displacement again, but since the majority are farmers they choose to return to their land.

(iii) New settlements in the border areas of the Vanni where the Sri Lanka government settles landless displaced families from the same province on a new plot of land. These new settlements are part of the rehabilitation and reconstruction programme in Vavuniya. In particular, I draw from interviews with young women heads of households in Siddambarapuram camp, which is located just outside the town of Vavunia in the north central province. This particular camp received a large number of displaced persons and families from Jaffna and the Vanni who had fled to India in the early 1990s and were subsequently repatriated. I also draw from interviews conducted with women heads of households in the new settlement scheme adjacent to Siddambarapuram camp.

Women as 'Victims' of War, Caste and Culture

The tendency to view women as 'victims' in armed conflict has been fuelled by a number of popular and specialist discourses concerning several brutal rapes committed by the Sri Lanka Army, as well as the Indian Peace Keeping Force (IPKF) when they controlled the conflict zones. Human rights discourse and humanitarian interventions have also significantly contributed to the tendency to view women as 'victims'. The various and systematic forms of violence that civilian women experience at the hands of armed combatants, whether state armies or paramilitary personnel, in situations of armed conflict and displacement were extensively documented and highlighted in the former Yugoslavia, Rwanda, and other parts of Africa and Asia. This process culminated in the UN resolution that established rape as a war crime and saw the appointment of Sri Lankan lawyer, Radhika Coomaraswamy as the first UN Special Rapporteur on Violence against Women in 1994.[4] Highlighting gross violations of women's bodies and lives in situations of conflict and displacement has been part of an important intervention by feminists and activists to promote women's rights as human rights internationally.

The focus on women as 'victims' of war and patriarchal culture has also arguably resulted in the elision of how long-term social upheaval might have also transformed women's often subordinate gender roles, lives and positions in non-obvious ways. At the same time, in secular feminist analysis women's political violence is often the uncomfortable black hole within which women's agency, because it is violent, is explained as a male patriarchal project. The claim is often made that women who enter new spaces as militants in nationalist armed struggles, such as the LTTE women, remain finally pawns and victims in the discourse of nationalist patriarchy, and it is hence that they are pushed back into the kitchen after the revolution/war.

Likewise, it is argued that civilian women who take on new roles such as heads of households, principal income generators and decision makers in the absence of their menfolk are in reality merely carrying a double burden. While there is little doubt that women in a war's interregnum carry a double burden, viewing women as merely victims of their culture, war and patriarchy elides women's agency in violence. Positioning women as victims might also mean that they are subject to secondary victimisation since victimhood also often entails carrying the burden of a social stigma. Women who are widowed and/or raped are particularly vulnerable to the double complex of a stigmatised victim.

But the construct of the Sri Lankan Tamil woman as 'victim' also draws from another genealogy. Anthropological, sociological and literary ethnography has tended to represent Tamil women as living within a highly patriarchal caste-ridden Hindu cultural ethos, particularly in comparison to Sinhala women whose lives are seen to be less circumscribed by caste ideologies and purity/pollution concepts and practices. The troubling figure of the LTTE woman soldier—the armed virgin—stands as one of the few highly problematic exceptions to the representation of Tamil women as victims.

Of course the representation of the Tamil woman in relation to caste and family is not entirely monochromatic in the anthropological literature which is split on the subject. Many anthropologists have also emphasised the strong matrilineal tendencies in Sri Lankan Tamil society, where women inherit property in the maternal line according to customary Thesawalami law and enjoy claims on natal families, in contrast to the rigidly patriarchal cultures of north India where patrilineal descent and inheritance is the norm.[5] Feminist ethnography, on the other hand, has emphasised the subordinate status of Tamil women in the Hindu caste structure, while frequently noting the split between the ideology of *Shakti* or female power as the primary generative force of the universe (also associated with the pantheon of powerful Hindu goddesses) and the reality of women's apparent powerlessness in everyday life.[6] Both schools emphasise the generally restrictive nature of the Sri Lankan Tamil Hindu caste system for women and often tend to see caste and gender relations as culturally rather than historically determined. By and large however, women have rarely been centred in debates on caste, and when they have been, they are more often than not constructed as victims rather than agents of culture.[7]

More recently, anthropologists have argued that colonialism permeated by British Victorian patriarchal culture eroded the status of women in south Indian societies which followed the matrilineal Dravidian kinship pattern, where property was passed down in the women's line, from mother to daughter. The practice usually indicates the relatively higher status of women in society. Anthropologist are now beginning to highlight how colonial legal systems might have eroded the rights and freedom that women had under

customary law, particularly in matrilineal societies, while emphasising the historically changing circumstances of family, kinship,
caste and gender relations. In this vein, this chapter explores how 18
years of armed conflict, displacement and humanitarian–relief–
development interventions might have altered the structure of the
family, caste, and rights and the gender status quo among communities in the border areas affected by the conflict.

Women as Nationalist Fighters and Victims

The figures of the LTTE woman soldier, the armed virgin, the
nationalist mother and/or queen of Sinhala legend who craved the
blood of Tamils, and women in the armed forces stand out as some
of the few problematic exceptions to the representation of women
as victims of war and their culture. Adele Ann,[8] wife of an LTTE
spokesman, and Peter Shalk have portrayed LTTE women as 'liberated'[9] and Radhika Coomaraswamy has described them as 'cogs in
the wheel' of the male leadership of the LTTE.[10] The reality of LTTE
women is probably somewhere in-between. For while they may
have broken out of the confines of their allotted domesticity and
taken on new roles as fighters, it is indeed arguable that they are
captive both to the patriarchal nationalist project of the LTTE leader
Prabhakaran and the history and experience of oppression by the
Sri Lankan military. However, to deny these Tamil nationalist
women their agency because they are nationalist is to once again
position them within the 'victim' complex, where the militant
woman is denied her agency and perceived to be acting out a patriarchal plot.

Arguably, the LTTE line on the woman question might have
evolved beyond the first phase of the nationalist struggle when LTTE
women seemed unable and unwilling to raise the question of gender
inequality lest they be accused of fostering division in the Eelam
nationalist cause. In the second phase of armed struggle in the 1990s
when the LTTE maintained a quasi-state in the 'uncleared areas',
non-combatant women played new roles, albeit in a highly war traumatised and transformed society. For in 1987 during an interview

with Dhanu (who subsequently assassinated Indian Prime Minister Rajiv Gandhi in a suicide attack) and Akhila (a senior woman cadre), at the LTTE headquarters in Jaffna, both impressed upon me that the most important liberation struggle was the struggle for Eelam and the liberation of the Tamil people. The woman problem would detract from focusing on the cause and hence could only be sorted out later.

Almost 12 years later in January 1999 on a visit to the LTTE-held 'uncleared area' near the north-eastern town of Trincomallee, I learned of the existence of a de facto LTTE policy on domestic violence. During a conversation with several members from a local community-based organisation (CBO) one young woman said that women who suffer domestic violence and are physically abused by their spouses now complain to the LTTE cadres who take appropriate action. At the first complaint, the abusive spouse is given a warning, on the second he is fined, and if there is a third complaint he might end up in the LTTE jail. There are also reports that women now sit in LTTE local courts and arbitrate local disputes in the 'uncleared areas'. What this suggests is that after the war, given the demographic as well as social changes that have occurred, if women are expected to return to the kitchen, rather than make policy on rehabilitation and reconstruction of the community, they might not do so willingly.

Since 1983 when Sri Lanka's ethnic conflict transmuted into a dirty war perpetrated by a number of armed forces and groups, civilian men and women in the border areas have lived amidst overlapping regimes of terrifying security. Between the major contenders in the war—the Sri Lanka government's military regime of passes and checkpoints and the LTTE's parallel security regime—civilian men and women also have to contend with the sub-regimes of several other armed groups—the Eelam People's Revolutionary Liberation Front (EPRLF-East coast) and Rafik group, People's Liberation Organisation of Tamil Eelam (PLOTE-Vanni), and the Eelam People's Democratic Party (EPDP-Jaffna). For 18 years of war has generated a number of armed paramilitary groups who seem intent only on retaining the power they wield at gun point. Many of these paramilitary groups which are bank rolled by the Sri Lanka government and work with the army to combat the LTTE maintain regimes of terror and torture in the areas they control. All these groups, comprising mainly youth, carry guns.

The paramilitary remains outside the authority and discipline structure of the government's armed forces, which are marginally better trained and better aware of humanitarian law. Thus, the paramilitary cadre tend to have a relatively freer reign than government forces to terrorise civilians, torture them, and extort money at gunpoint. At the national level, several leaders of paramilitary groups are installed as members of parliament and support the ruling government.[11] These groups have also developed systems of taxation of civilians by virtue of their control over the main transport routes, and the movement of persons and goods through an economy of terror, scarcity and fear. In the Sri Lankan conflict, the LTTE pioneered this system of taxation on the movement of goods and trafficking in persons. Since then, the army has resorted to similar practices. Where the army issues passes and identification papers, there is a high degree of corruption. Residents of high security areas complain of being asked to pay large sums of money to army personnel before they are issued with these papers.

Violence against women in this context consists of rape, trauma and disappeared persons, torture, assassination and the gendered politics of body searches at checkpoints usually conducted by armed youth who have been trained in the arts of terror, torture, and the degradation of their victims. Several instances of checkpoint rape by the Sri Lankan government's security forces have occurred, though rape has not been practised as a systematic policy for ethnic cleansing by any group in the conflict, unlike in Bosnia. Women suffer particularly from the poor security situation in the border areas. Their mobility and thus ability to go out to work is severely curtailed due to fear of body searches and checkpoint rape, not to mention anxiety about being caught in crossfire. Mothers are often fearful for their daughters' safety and sexual vulnerability and tend to confine them to the home or refugee camp. Simultaneously, a sexual service industry has developed in Anuradhapura area, where soldiers return from the conflict areas, with many homeless and displaced women engaging in prostitution.

The fear of checkpoint rape is a constraint on women's ability to move around and venture out of their immediate locale for work or any other purpose. Conditions are considerably worse for displaced women who are forced to live in refugee camps where privacy is minimal if not non-existent and levels of generalised violence, alcoholism and domestic violence are high.

Displacing Gender and Caste Hierarchies

Since the armed conflict commenced in Sri Lanka, the population of displaced people has fluctuated from half-a-million to 1.2 million, or between a tenth and a fifth of the country's population at various points in the conflict. At the end of December 1995, the Ministry of Rehabilitation and Reconstruction in Sri Lanka estimated that there were 1,017,181 internally displaced people in Sri Lanka while 140,000 were displaced overseas (some of the latter have sought asylum status). Figures of displaced persons are however controversial. The University Teachers for Human Rights, Jaffna, in 1993 estimated that half-a-million Tamils have become refugees overseas. The decennial census of Sri Lanka scheduled for 1991 was not taken due to the conflict. Estimates are that 78 per cent of the internally displaced are ethnically Tamils, 13 per cent are Muslims, and 8 per cent are Sinhalese.[12] Many displaced people, Tamils, Muslims and Sinhalese alike, fled the Sri Lankan army and LTTE brutalities.

Displacement and camp life also provided spaces for empowerment for several Tamil women who had taken on the role of the head of the household. In this section I outline some of the processes of transformation in the lives of young single and widowed women I met at the Siddambarapuram camp and in the adjacent new settlement scheme described above. Siddambarapuram was located a few miles outside Vavuniya, the largest town in the north central Vanni region. It was one of the oldest refugee camps and had received a large influx of refugees from the north. In many ways the facilities, location and environment/climatic conditions at that camp and the adjoining new settlements were exceptionally propitious.

The relative prosperity of the locale and its residents was evident in the fact that the market in the camp was a vibrant and happening place that had become a shopping centre for nearby old (*purana*) villagers as well.

At Siddambarapuram the sense of independence, empowerment and mobility of many women heads of household was tangible and remarkable in contrast to other women I met in camps in less propitious settings. This is explainable in terms of the camp's location close to the larger town of Vavuniya where women could find employment, particularly in the service sector. This is of course not an option for displaced women in other less conveniently located camps.

The Siddambarapuram camp was initially constructed as a transit camp by UNHCR for refugees returning to Jaffna from India in 1991, who were subsequently stranded when the conflict started again in what is known as the Second Eelam War. Many of the people in the camp had been resident there for more than five years. Several young Tamil widows whom I interviewed in the camp and the adjoining new settlements noted that while they had initially had a hard time adjusting to displacement, camp life and the burdens of caring for their young families, they had also gained freedom to work outside the household and increasingly enjoyed the role of being the head of the household and the principal decision maker.

Many women said that they had little desire to remarry, mainly due to anxiety that their children might not be well cared for by a second husband. Several women commented that previously their husbands would not permit them to work outside the household, even if they had done so prior to marriage. Of course one of the principal reasons for these women's newly found sense of control was the fact that they were able to find employment outside the household and the camp. Women in the service sector or in the NGO sectors had done best.

It is arguable that the erosion of caste ideology and practice particularly among the younger generation in the camps had contributed to women's mobility and sense of empowerment. For, except for the highly westernised Tamil women professionals, caste has historically provided the mainstay of the Hindu Tamil gender status

quo since caste identity often determines women's mobility. Seclusion, particularly among the high castes is a sign of high status. Unlike
in Jaffna where village settlement was caste and region based, in the
camp it was difficult to maintain social segregation, caste hierarchies, and purity pollution taboos for a number of reasons. This
is particularly true for members of the younger generation who
simply refused to adhere to caste inhibitions.

As one mother speaking about the disruption of caste hierarchies
in displacement observed,

> Because we are poor here as displaced people we only have two
> glasses to drink from, so when a visitor from another caste comes
> we have to use the same glass. Now my daughter, she refuses to
> care about maintaining separate utensils. She is friendly with boys
> we wouldn't consider at home. Everything is changing with the
> younger generation because they are growing up all mixed up
> because we are displaced and living on top of each other in a
> camp. . .

The mother went on to detail how it was difficult to keep girls and
boys separate in the camp situation. She thought that the freer
mingling of youth would mean that there would be more inter-
caste marriages and hence the erosion of caste. Presumably this also
means that girls had more of a choice over who might be their
partners.

The reconstitution of displaced families around who had lost male
kin curiously resonates with an older gender status quo—that of the
pre-colonial Dravidian matrilineal family and kinship system where
women remained with their natal families after marriage, and were
customarily entitled to lay claim on the resources of the matri-clan.
Hence, they enjoyed a relatively higher status, in comparison with
women in strictly patrilineal societies. For, as Bina Aggarwal has
pointed out in *A Field of One's Own*,[13] the existence of matrilineal
systems where matrilineal descent, matrilocal residence, and/or
bilateral inheritance is practised is usually an indicator of the
relatively higher status of women when compared to the status of
women in patrilineal groups. Similar observations concerning the

status of women in matrilineal communities have been made by anthropologists who have studied the Nayars of Kerala as well as the Sinhalas, Tamils and Muslims of the east coast of Sri Lanka where matrilineal inheritance is the norm.[14] These are also societies where social indicators have been consistently good, with high levels of female literacy, education and health care in South Asia.

During the colonial period in Sri Lanka, however, there was a general erosion of the matrilineal inheritance and bilateral descent practice, despite a general provision being made for the respect of customary common law for indigenous communities (Thesavallamai, Tamil customary law, Kandian Sinhala law as well as Muslim personal law). In the same period the modernising tendency towards the nuclear family enshrined in secular European, Dutch and British law also privileged male inheritance, thereby reducing the power of women within their families.

The switch from matrilineal, matrilocal, to virilocal forms of residence and inheritance, where women take only movable property to their affinal household may also be traced to various post-colonial land distribution schemes wherein title deeds for land were invested in male heads of household, with the injunction against the further division of land to prevent land fragmentation. It set a precedent for male inheritance of the entirety of the family's land. The result has been a tendency towards male primogeniture, with the eldest son inheriting the land and daughters being disinherited from land-ownership. Unfortunately, a similar pattern of title deeds being invested in male heads of households is still evident in the new settlements and land distribution schemes for landless displaced populations in Vavuniya under the rehabilitation and reconstruction project. In these projects it is only where the male head of household is presumed dead that title deeds are invested in women. Women whose husbands have left them or whose whereabouts cannot be ascertained, are not deemed eligible for land grants. Clearly, in the case of Tamil inheritance patterns customary practices are more liberal than those of post-colonial development practice.

What all of this indicates is the structure of cultural practices and the direction of changes in women's roles in situations of armed conflict. But while Tamil women have begun to play various unaccustomed public roles, for Muslim women the evidence from the war zones suggests that conflict has diminished their mobility in conflict zones and in the areas to which they have been displaced. Depending on the location of the camps and the resources the families had, some internally displaced Muslim women felt they had gained autonomy in their new situation but many more complained of greater segregation.

Rethinking Displacement and the Humanitarian Challenge

Currently there is growing recognition among those involved in humanitarian relief and rehabilitation work that women frequently bear the material and psychological brunt of armed conflict, and hence there is a need for gender sensitive relief and rehabilitation work. Yet few programmes have systematically explored how relief might aid recovery from individual trauma and social suffering, and facilitate women's empowerment in and through conflict. Thus many gender programmes organised by the government's relief and rehabilitation authority and non-governmental organisations (NGOs) still remain within conventional development thinking rather than attempting to work out *culturally* appropriate and effective strategies for women's empowerment in the context of the social transformations that have occurred over years of armed conflict and displacement.

Popular romanticisations of home as well as constructions of internally displaced people as victims like the victim discourse concerning women in conflict in the human rights field often obscure the realities of what living at home in conflict means. The Sinhala term, *anathagatha kattiya*, literally means 'the abandoned people', while the Tamil term *veedu attavargal* means 'people without a home'. However, there is growing evidence to suggest that despite the psycho-social traumas that displacement entails, long-term displacement has provided windows of opportunity for greater personal and group autonomy and experiments with identity and leadership for displaced people, particularly for women. Certainly this has been the case for many displaced Tamil women who have lost husbands and sons in the conflict.

It is time now for humanitarian relief efforts to be conceptualised in terms of (*i*) sustainability; (*ii*) maintaining local orders of
ethnic coexistence and empowerment between displaced people and
their local hosts; and (*iii*) empowerment of women within community and family structures dramatically different from the pre-conflict
situation. In Sri Lanka this is particularly necessary if the ethnic
conflict is not to spread to new areas where the displaced have found
refuge and are often perceived to be in competition with poor local
populations.

Many internally displaced women who have given up the dream
of return are in the paradoxical position of being materially and
psychologically displaced by humanitarian interventions and human
rights discourses and practices that define them as victims who need
to be returned to their original homelands for their protection and
for the restoration of national and international order and peace.[15]
The assumption of return is a fundamental premise of international,
national and NGO policies vis-à-vis internally displaced people. The
fact is that these policies might be contributing to prolonging the
conflict and be a cause of additional trauma for people who fled
their homes several years ago. This is particularly true of women
for whom restrictions on mobility are particular severe. Many of
these women may wish to settle in the place where they have found
refuge but they are being kept dependent on relief handouts rather
than being assisted to build new lives and livelihoods. Thus, ironically, relief might be prolonging the trauma of the very people it is
supposed to assist.

Under these circumstances, an approach which conceptualises
humanitarian work as part of a development continuum with
gender-sensitive post-conflict intervention is especially necessary in
instances where armed conflicts have lasted for several years with
communities experiencing cycles of war and peace and displacement.
Ironically, for some women the conflict has provided windows of
opportunity for greater personal and group autonomy and experiments with identity and leadership, for others there is only trauma.
Certainly this has been the case for many displaced Tamil women
who have lost husbands and sons in the conflict. It is hence important that relief aid should be conceptualised to sustain women's

empowerment and leadership roles within an altered family structure which was an outgrowth of protracted conflict.

Clearly, the process of a woman becoming head of the household is not transparent, unambivalent, or free of guilt, and this was
evident in the uncertainty felt by many young widows about whether
they should return home if and when the conflict ended. For them
displacement clearly constituted a space of ambivalence; a place of
regeneration and the hope for a future unfettered by the past loss
and trauma. They were also concerned that to return home would
mean a return to the pre-war caste and gender status quo. Of course,
anxiety about return was also related to qualms about personal security and trauma. Anxiety about return was clearest among young
women heads of households at Siddambarapuram, who had integrated into the local economy and those who had previously been
landless.

Recasting Widowhood: Return to Matri-focal Families

A generation of young Tamil war widows who have been displaced
to and in the border areas for many years seem to be increasingly
challenging conventional Hindu constructions of widowhood as a
negative and polluting condition which bars their participation in
many aspects of community life. Several young widows working in
Vavuniya town but resident in the camp displayed their sense of
independence by wearing the red *pottu*, the auspicious mark reserved
for the married Hindu women, despite being widows or women
whose husbands had abandoned them. Likewise in Batticaloa several
women who had lost husbands to death, displacement or family
fragmentation in the course of armed conflict and flight from bombing and shelling, increasingly refused to erase the signs of *sumangali*,
particularly the auspicious red *pottu* they wore when married. They
refused to be socially and culturally marginalised and ostracised
because they lacked husbands and children. Displacement, along
with fragmentation and reconstitution of families around women
in a conflict situation where men frequently have had to flee to
avoid being killed or inducted by the armed groups, appears to have

provided a space to redefine traditional Hindu Tamil perceptions of widows and single women as inauspicious beings.

Of course the demographic fact of a large number of young widows who are unwilling to take on the role of the traditional Hindu widow, who may not participate in auspicious social rituals such as wedding ceremonies and who are generally socially ostracised, facilitates the transformation of negative cultural patterns. But these young women's response to their changed circumstances marks the space for redefinition of what it means to be an unmarried or widowed woman in the more orthodox Hindu tradition. Consciously and unconsciously, they appear to be redefining conceptions of the 'good woman' as one who lives within the traditional confines of caste, kin group and village.

As they struggle with new gender roles and identities, many of these young widows also struggle to find a language and cultural idiom to speak of their changed roles. They refuse to wear the prescribed garb of widowhood and appear to break with the ideology of Kanaki (*Paththini*) the exemplary faithful wife and widow of Tamil mythology and ideology. Rather, they seem to evoke the signs of affinity with the *devadasi*—Kanaki's alter ego—who transcended conventional gender roles. She was the professional woman married to immortality for her talent and skill, most familiar to South Asian audiences in the name of the famed dancer and courtesan, Madhavi of the first century Tamil Hindu-Buddhist epic, *Sillapaddikaram*.

Yet with the exception of the young Tamil widows many of whom have found more freedom in the conflict, women still seem to lack a language to articulate this process of transformation and regeneration and clearly feel guilty about expressing their new found confidence. But one woman candidly told me, 'It is a relief now that he [her husband] is not with me. He used to drink and beat me up.' She worries about her personal safety and that of her children in the absence of her husband, particularly at night, but as for being left to fend for herself, she said that she any way had to support the children mainly on her own even when her husband was with her.

The victim ideology that pervades relief and rehabilitation as well as social health and trauma interventions for women in conflict

situations needs to be problematised especially as it may be internalised by some women with damaging consequences. Non-
combatant women who have found spaces of empowerment in the
conflict need sustained assistance to maintain their new found
mobility and independence in the face of sometimes virulently
nationalist assertions of patriarchal cultural tradition and practices
during the conflict and in the period of post-war reconstruction.
The return to peace should not mean a return to the pre-war gender
status quo. It follows that humanitarian and development interventions must creatively support and sustain positive changes in the
status of civilian women living in conflict.

Women in Political Conflict and Peace Building

To end then at the beginning—women political leaders seem to have
had little success in bringing about significant improvement in the
lives and position of women in the South Asian region or in building bridges across ethno-religious lines. However, they have mod-
erated the more extreme misogynist cultural practices in a region
where honour killings of women by their own family members for
defying the rules of whom 'one may or may not love' as Arundhathi
Roy puts it so evocatively, are increasing. This was arguably the
case with Pakistan under Benazir Bhutto, where the more negative
interpretations of Muslim Sharia law were not practised against
women, but became commonplace under Prime Minister Sharif,
notably when the banning of honour killing of women was brought
up in parliament. On the other hand, both the Indian and the Sri
Lankan record shows that without fundamental cultural and structural changes in society, the presence of women in leadership
positions and polity rarely results in the advancement of the position of women. Therefore, South Asian women activists are cam-
paigning for at least 33 per cent reservations for women in parliament
in order to begin changing the gender imbalances in politics and
society.

At the same time the case of Hindu women activists of the BJP in
India and women in the LTTE might indicate that for too long

pro-peace secular feminist analysis has denied nationalist women their agency and their place in the sun. For, ironically, it is arguable that the recent South Asian picture of women entering new public spaces in peace time as well as due to war indicates that women's agency and rights might be more effectively advanced within a nationalist framework as a result of the dominance of cultural nationalism in the region. In India and Sri Lanka it would appear that women's rights have been most systematically advanced within an ethno-nationalist framework. Of course there is the subtext of Hindu nationalist BJP women calling for a uniform civil code to enhance the rights of Muslim women vis-à-vis Muslim men, in a clearly ideologically biased manner. Similarly, Tamil women who dissent from the LTTE project have paid heavily and in some cases with their lives.[16]

At the same time secular women leaders like Chandrika Kumaratunga who try to transcend ethno-religious divides, fall prey less to patriarchal nationalism than the politics of survival in an increasingly violent political culture. Less high profile women also have had only limited success in reaching beyond their immediate circle to strike a common cord among the people at the national level. This is partly due to lack of access and control of political party machinery which dominates national political processes. On the one hand, many local women's organisations have done and continue to do important work to improve the condition of women and to build bridges across ethno-religious nationalist lines. Women's groups like the Suriya Women's Centre founded in Batticaloa, in the east of Sri Lanka in 1990 have been actively engaged in human rights work, advocacy and peace education. Several of the founder members of this group fled Jaffna after the LTTE killed one of their members, Rajini Thiranagama, a senior lecturer at the University of Jaffna for her outspoken stand on its human rights abuses. On the other hand, women's groups which had the potential to make an impact on national level politics such as the Mothers Front have been appropriated by traditional party politicians and armed militant groups. They have used women's contributions and support to achieve positions of power, but have rarely invested women with political power in the political process.[17]

Eighteen years of armed conflict and the culture of ethno-nationalist and political polarisation has also meant that activist women and secular women's groups have made little progress in peace building across ethnic lines. Though analyses of women's activism have sometimes privileged women's peace movements[18] most women's groups are mobilised by and large along ethnic lines with a few exceptions in Sri Lanka. The most powerful and oldest women's groups were in any case formed within a religious ethno-nationalist framework in opposition to colonialism, for example, the Young Women's Buddhist Association (YWBA). While such early women's organisations were more anti-colonial than ethno-nationalist, over the years they have become increasingly ethno-nationalist. Seva Vanitha which works for the bereaved families of armed forces personnel is explicitly nationalist.

When alliances across ethnic lines have been struck, it was over particular issues, such as the Mothers Front which came together to stop the disappearances of family members arising from military violence and state brutality. However, these organisations were subsequently coopted by a political party. By and large, it is arguable that this cooptation was largely due to the hostile ethno-nationalist climate in which secular women's groups operate and the reactive nature of the groups. The absence of a proactive vision for strategic action has made secular groups vulnerable to cooption. This was largely the case with the secular Colombo-based group, Women for Peace which emerged in 1983 after the ethnic riots and dissolved in 1997. It succumbed to the difficulties of working across ethnic lines in a time when the language of peace had been appropriated by a state intent on waging a 'war for peace'.

Clearly, there is a need to look elsewhere for women's agency and activism in armed conflict and peace building. Historically, the experience of women who took on various non-traditional gender roles in situations of social stress, conflict, war and revolution, has been to be 'pushed back into the kitchen after the revolution' as part of a return to everyday life.[19] Arguably, one of the primary reasons that the return to peace often meant a return to the gender status quo was the lack of social recognition and a culturally appropriate idiom to articulate, legitimate and support women's transformed roles and empowerment in the midst of conflict, trauma and social disruption.

This chapter then has attempted to distinguish between the kinds of transformations that have occurred by exploring their long-term impact. For social transformation to be sustained there needs to be cultural transformation, an acceptance of the legitimacy of women performing their new roles. And it is hence arguable that the greater threat and the greater challenge to the gender status quo come less from the women in fatigues who might be asked to do desk jobs after the conflict, and more from the women who refuse to erase the red *pottu*. It is the unsung civilian women who daily struggle to sustain their families and themselves who have the potential to be agents of structural social transformation.

Unlike in some conflict situations like Afghanistan where the situation of women has unambiguously deteriorated due to the war and the takeover by the Taliban, in Sri Lanka, the evidence suggests that despite many women's experience of traumatic violence and displacement, some changes to the gender status quo wrought by armed conflict might have empowered women whose freedom and mobility were restricted by partriarchal cultural mores, morality and convention in peace time. Several women who have faced the traumatic loss and scattering of family members due to displace-ment, conflict, and the breakdown of family structures have also assumed new roles which were thrust upon them as a result of the disruption of peace time community organisation, social structures and patriarchal values. But I do not wish to suggest that this is a general story which might be told of women living in conflict and displacement. Rather, this chapter has attempted to focus on some women's agency at moments when they seem most victimised, to excavate some hidden moments and routes of women's agency in the situation of conflict.

It is hence that this chapter has sought to develop an alternative framework for analysing women's agency and ambiguous empower-ment in conflict situations while analysing changing gender relations. This has meant exploring gender relations outside the scripted frames of nationalist women's mobilisation as well as gender analyses of women in politics. For it seems to me that the arena of politics proper in South Asia is violent space and process, where women politicians are stripped and humiliated, as has repeatedly occurred in election time in Sri Lankan politics in the last decade. In Sri Lanka, which celebrated 50 years of democracy and was considered a mature democracy with free, fair and non-violent elections until recently, the crisis is acute.

I have argued elsewhere that nationalist women and women combatants in nationalist struggles waged by groups like the LTTE, or the nationalist women in Ireland or Palestine, are imbricated in ultra-conservative 'nationalist constructions of women' and tend to subordinate their gender identities to the nationalist cause.[20] Suicide bombing is but the extreme version of this phenomenon which might, in Durkheimian terms, be glossed as altruistic suicide, when individual autonomy and personal agency is completely subsumed in the national cause. The question might well be raised as to whether women would be more given than men to altruistic suicide, given their socialisation in patriarchal Asian cultures where girl children and women are more often than not taught to put themselves second, and their male folk, family, and community honour first. Clearly, non-combatant women are differently imbricated in nationalist discourses, and the return to peace time which entails the reassertion of the gender status quo is as problematic for them as it is for combatant women, but for different reasons.

A multi-ethnic women's politics that crosses ethnic lines might be the best and last bulwark against growing ethnic chauvinism that is being built up by democratic politicians, intent on shoring up vote banks and personal power at the cost of national peace. Moreover, left liberal feminist positions that seek to transcend ethno-religious differences seem less likely to succeed in advancing women's rights than nationalist politics. Given that ethnic identity politics is increasingly coterminous with politics proper, it is arguable that women will have to forge new spaces for activism—outside the sphere of politics proper and by exploiting the social and cultural spaces that have thrust women into new roles. Violent deaths and armed conflict open up ambiguous spaces of agency and empowerment for women within their families and communities, that is for women who have not been directly implicated in the violence like the LTTE women.

The notion that wars disrupt social, political and gender hierarchies in unexpected ways and benefit marginal groups and individuals while obvious is yet unexplored. This lacuna in the understanding of conflict and its effects has much to do with the tendency to conceptualise peace as a return to pre-conflict normalcy of the gender status quo. Peace, we still think, constitutes a return to things the way they used to be; the certain certainties of familiar, older ways of being and doing. But to conceptualise peace thus, is another kind of (epistemic) violence. For women, wives and mothers who have lost a head of household or seen him 'disappear' in the violence, there can be no return to the old certainties of the nuclear family, headed by the father, the patriarch. For the war's widows, for those who have lived intimately with war, the changes wrought by 18 years of armed conflict in Sri Lanka are too deep, too complex, structural and fundamental. They force us to challenge our certain certainties about war and peace. In this context, peace is necessarily a third place divorced from the past, utopia perhaps, somewhere arguably between the old and the existing, the past and the present.

NOTES

1. Patricia Jeffrey, 'Agency, Activism and Agendas', in Patricia Jeffrey and Amrita Basu, eds, *Resisting the Sacred and Secular*, Kali for Women, New Delhi, 1999.
2. Partha Chatterjee, 'The Nationalist Resolution of the Women's Question', in Kumkum Sangari and Sudesh Vaid, eds, *Recasting Women: Essays in Colonial History*, Kali for Women, New Delhi, 1989, pp. 253–54.
3. Editor's note: According to the Department of Census and Statistics, profiling the changing role of women in Sri Lanka, in 1994, some 20 per cent were female headed households rising to 23 per cent by 1997.
4. See *Summary of the Fourth Report of the Special Rapporteur on Violence Against Women, Its Causes and Consequences*, UNHCR, Geneva, January 1998.
5. Susan Wadley, *The Powers of Tamil Women*, Manohar, New Delhi, 1991.
6. Selvy Thiruchandran, *Ideology, Class, Caste and Gender*, Vikas, Delhi, 1997.
7. Colonial evolutionary classifications of (primitive) societies presumed that fewer restrictions on women's freedom indicated a more primitive stage of civilisational advance.

8. Ann Adele, *Women Fighters of Liberation*, Publication Section, LTTE, Thasan Printers, Jaffna, 1993.

9. Peter Schalk, *Birds of Independence: On the Participation of Tamil Women in Armed Struggle*, December 1990.

10. Radhika Coomaraswamy, 'Women of the LTTE', *Frontline* (Chennai), 10 January 1997, pp. 61–64.

11. Many paramilitary groups have been trained by the state and have benefited from training in violence from various foreign sources including the Indian Peace Keeping Force (IPKF) as well as war experts from Israel and the US.

12. Mario Gomez, *Sri Lanka: State of Human Rights*, Law and Society Trust, Colombo, 1994.

13. Bina Aggarwal, *A Field of One's Own: Gender and Land Rights in South Asia*, Cambridge University Press, Cambridge, 1996.

14. Nur Yalman, *Under the Bo Tree*, University of California Press, Berkeley, 1971.

15. For those in the conflict regions, the right to set up residence in an area of one's choice and the right to movement is seriously restricted by the LTTE and the Government of Sri Lanka's security regimes. While the government restricts the movement of displaced Tamils southward, the LTTE will not permit Sinhalas to move or settle in the north. In fact, both the LTTE and the Sri Lanka government have used displaced persons as security shields or buffers during military campaigns. The Sri Lanka government's restrictions on the mobility of persons and their confinement to camps have other implications for youth and children. Militant groups which infiltrate camps have very little difficulty in recruiting new caders from deeply frustrated and resentful youth, men and women, girls and boys.

16. In Sri Lanka the debate over secular and personal law as it applies to women is somewhat different and it is arguable that customary law in the case of Tamil Thesawalami and Kandian Sinhala law is more favourable to women than is secular law on many matters. However this is not entirely the case for Muslim personal law in Sri Lanka.

17. Malathi De Alwis, 'Motherhood as a Space of Protest', in Jeffrey and Basu, *Resisting the Sacred and the Secular*, n. 1.

18. Kumudhini Samuel, 'Women's Activism and Peace Initiatives in Sri Lanka', paper presented at a conference organised by the Women in Conflict Zones Network on 'A Comparative Study of the Issues Faced by Women as a Result of Armed Conflict: Sri Lanka and the Post-Yugoslav States', Hendala, Sri Lanka.

19. Kumari Jayawardane, *Feminism and Nationalism in the Third World*, Kali for Women, New Delhi, 1986; and Cynthia Enloe, *Does Khaki Become You: The Militarisation of Women's Lives*, South End Press, London, 1983.

20. Darini Rajasingham-Senanayake, 'On Mediating Multiple Identities', in Margaret Schuler, ed., *From Basic Needs to Basic Rights*, Women, Law and Development, Washington, D.C., 1995.

4

Between Two Armed Patriarchies: Women in Assam and Nagaland

PAULA BANERJEE

Introduction

It was during the two great wars of the 20th century that for the first time in the modern era women's participation in armed conflict was institutionalised. Women were registered and sometimes conscripted. They were part of the regular army, led resistances and situated themselves at the centre of the militarised industrial economy. Small wonder then that historians of women treated these wars as watersheds in women's political experience.[1] By making gender a category in war, new questions emerged about women's participation in the public domain, which is largely controlled by men. In seeking answers to such questions it was revealed that although vulnerable to institutional power, women are not without power in their non-public roles and nor are they non-political beings. This necessitated a re-examination of women's involvement in all political conflicts not merely to understand how women negotiate in conflicts but also to understand the conflict itself. The same concerns make the present work necessary.

This chapter is on women's negotiations in state versus community conflicts in the two states of Assam and Nagaland in north-eastern India. The time span covered is the last 20 years. Assam, after several partitions, is still the largest state in the Northeast. In Nagaland the Government of India faces the longest running state vs. community conflict. The last 20 years have witnessed an escal- ation of the conflict to unprecedented levels. From the time of the first Pokhran test, the state has revised its national security policies leading to greater control over the peripheral areas. In rapid succes- sion Assam and Nagaland were brought within the realm of the Armed Forces Special Powers Act (amended in 1972) and the Na- tional Security Act (1980). This resulted in an intensification of the conflict in both areas. People became even more sympathetic to- wards secessionist groups and the situation became more violent.

There are a number of studies analysing conflicts in the North- east but none that discuss women's responses to these conflicts. This chapter explores the role of women in the conflict situations in Assam and Nagaland. It does not chronicle the lives of any Joan of Arcs in the region, if they exist. Rather, the focus is on ordinary women and their negotiations with conflict. Our assumption is that in con- flict women face two sets of belligerent institutionalised power, one composed of the state or majority community and the other of the rebel, and being strangers to such power, their vulnerability is in- creased. The chapter seeks to find out how women negotiate their own spaces within and between these two sets of opposing patri- archal power, in what ways they influence conflict and whether a re-examination of women's roles leads to a redefinition of the con- flict itself. In the process we hope to critique the two predominant images of women in conflict: the victim and the amazon.[2]

The Northeast

From its inception as Northeast India, the region has been an odd- ity. In ancient times this region was known as Prajyotisha, a power- ful kingdom with its capital at Pragjyotishpur, where lies the town of Guwahati today. Later it was also known as Kamrupa. The mod- ern process of nation building converted the region into Northeast India. But which North and whose East is it? This area can only be called the Northeast when viewed from mainland India. The people of the region find little, if any, legitimacy in that view.

To the outsider, in many ways, the region remains an enigma. Comprising seven states—Assam, Manipur, Tripura, Nagaland, Mizoram, Meghalaya and Arunachal Pradesh—and hundreds of indigenous peoples, the Northeast is attached to the mainland by a narrow corridor of foothills in north Bengal, about 80 km long, 33 km wide in the eastern side and 21 km on the west. This is the longest theatre of insurgency in India and it is from here that India's nation building process faced its first challenge. Yet, while conflicts in Kashmir and Punjab are internationalised, 'this region remained essentially a domestic Indian issue'.[3]

The People and Their Moorings

The Northeast is a region with 255,082 square km area and according to the 1991 Census has a population of 31.4 million. It accounts for 7 per cent of the total land surface and 3.72 per cent of the total population of India. Four foreign countries including China, Myanmar, Bangladesh and Bhutan flank the area. It is the only part of India that has no direct access to either the sea or the capital city of New Delhi for contact and trade.[4] While politically it remains within India, the region possesses its own geopolitical character different from the mainland. Soon after independence the region emerged as a hotbed for political movements. According to one analyst, the 'various movements in the Northeast have all to do with identity'.[5] Another suggests that ethnic assertion for identity in the Northeast is further complicated by the involvement of rival nation-states that have tried to 'fish in its troubled waters'.[6] One particularity remains its long-standing external linkages.

The north-eastern Indian states have historical and ethnic linkages with regions outside India. For example, many Nagas still refer to their own region as 'western Nagaland', while they call areas of Myanmar 'eastern Nagaland'. This has given rise to affinities with regions beyond the Indian frontiers, which has posed problems for the Indian nation-state making process.[7] In fact many of the tribes living here feel that they have more in common with other tribes living in the region who may be beyond the international boundary of India than with the Indian mainland of which they form a distant appendage. There may be some rationale in this feeling.

The Northeast is peopled by many different tribes. The more famous of them are the Kochs, Bhuyians, Kacharis, Ahoms, Kukis, Nagas, Bodos, etc. The British entered the region in A.D. 1826 during the Burmese invasions. Through the treaty of Yandaboo in 1826 they obtained political control over the region. Initially, they tried to rule the region indirectly through 'clients', though by the end of the century efforts were made to impose direct rule. The region was still considered as an 'excluded area' and throughout, British control remained 'shadowy' as described in a note prepared by Sir Robert Reid in 1941 on *The Future of the Present Excluded, Partially Excluded and Tribal Areas of Assam*. In it he wrote:

> Beyond the administered portion of the Sandiya and Balipara Frontier Tracts (but within the McMahon Line of 1914) and outside the ministered boundary of the Naga Hills and lying between the district and Burma is an immense tract of country over which we exercise, within the frontier of India though it be, only the most shadowy control.[8]

It was the British who clubbed some ethnic groups under the nomenclature Nagas. However, the hill areas remained excluded from all constitutional reforms until 1937. According to a famous historian of the region, the area was kept in seclusion as the under-administered museum specimen of the backward tracts.[9]

In the Khasi-Jayantia Hills reflections of modern political consciousness appeared earlier than the other hill areas. The formation of the Jayantia Durbar in 1900, the Khasi National Durbar in 1923 and the Khasi State Federation of 1934 are all examples of that consciousness. In Nagaland political activity based on colonial models can be traced to 1918 when the Naga Club was formed. Club membership was restricted to government officials and leading village headmen to discuss administrative problems. In 1929 they submitted to the Simon Commission a request to exclude their region from within the administrative framework of the Government of India. Their request was not granted but no punitive action was taken against them. However, a slightly different mode of request received drastically different treatment from the British. In 1937 some leaders in Aizawl put forward a demand for representation in the legislature for which they were imprisoned.[10] The British were not willing to accept the tribals as members of the political community of India. Among the nationalist leaders only Subhas Chandra Bose made any serious efforts to incorporate the tribal question within the nationalist agenda. He accepted Angami Zapu Phizo's demand for Naga autonomy and the Nagas collaborated with the Indian National Army. But the post-colonial India leadership inherited the British legacy of ignoring the demands of the tribal population.

It was under the auspices of the Government of India that efforts were made to Indianise and integrate the hill areas for the first time. This represented a sharp break from the late 19th century imperial politics. But the integrationist policy was also guided by a similar kind of chauvinism as was apparent in imperial policies. In 1947 several district-level tribal political organisations were formed. The Garo National Council was formed in March 1947. The Naga Hill District Tribal Council was officially sponsored in April 1946 which organised itself into the Naga National Council (NNC) within a year. In February 1947 it demanded an interim government for Nagaland for 10 years at the end of which the Nagas would be free to reconsider their political status. Phizo, who had lived for 17 years in Burma and had collaborated with the INA, was elected president of the NNC in 1949. He slowly built the case for Naga independence.[11]

Not every group in the Northeast called for independence. The Mizos under the Mizo Union urged for the consolidation of all Mizo areas into a single administrative unit. They also sought self-determination within Assam. Not only the Mizos but most of the hill tribes wanted some form of self-determination. There were other groups such as the Bodos who took advantage of the Government of India Act of 1935 and fought for the reserved seats for tribals in the plains. They extended their support to the Muslim League in 1940 to form the coalition government in Assam. In this way they tried to integrate themselves within the mainstream political system. Most groups therefore were politically reconciled to be under the Government of India. However, post-independence efforts to Indianise them came as a shock.

The independence of India brought forth an artificial boundary called the Radcliffe line. Enormous changes took place when delineating boundaries in Northeast India. From Assam, Sylhet was partitioned and handed over to East Pakistan. Tribes such as the Garos and Chakmas were divided among two or three countries. The Northeast was divided into three administrative units. Apart from Manipur and Tripura the rest were grouped under a larger Assam. But with an Assam consisting of over 100 tribes and over 300 spoken dialects, many more changes were inevitable due to the Nehruvian legacy of linguistic provinces.

Nagaland

The Nagas remained dissatisfied. After a prolonged struggle, in the early 1960s the Naga hill districts and the former Tuensang division of the North East Frontier Agency (NEFA) were constituted into a separate state called Nagaland. In 1972 by virtue of the North Eastern Area (Reorganisation) Act No. 81, Meghalaya was constituted and Mizoram and Arunachal Pradesh became Union Territories. In December 1986 Arunachal Pradesh and in February 1987 Mizoram were given statehood. There are observers who believe that some more states may be carved out of Assam.[12]

The diverse ethnic origins of the people in the Northeast, says Chintamani Panigrahi, 'naturally led to the growth of centrifugal forces'.[13] Many tribes resented the way efforts were made, initially, to Indianise and currently, to Hinduise the region. 'Keen to secure the integration of all sections of its population into the political mainstream the Indian state began its task of national consolidation . . . this step roused the spirit of tribes who perceived the state's action as an encroachment upon their rights and freedom.'[14] Even after achieving statehood Nagaland remained recalcitrant and the strongest opposition came from that region much to the chagrin of

New Delhi. The Sino-Indian border war and the subsequent shift in Indian regional ambitions led to further efforts to militarise the border and the periphery. When this caused a backlash the Border Security Forces were introduced. In the early 1970s the army moved into Nagaland and has remained in the region till date. By 1975 after a short span of president's rule, the Shillong Accord was signed with the insurgents.

The Shillong Accord proved to be a temporary settlement but it succeeded in splitting the NNC. In its place emerged the Nationalist Socialist Council of Nagaland (NSCN) which became the main insurgent group in the state. The NSCN split into two factions, one faction led by T.H. Muivah and Isak Swu (NSCN[IM]) and the other by Khaplang (NSCN[K]). The Khaplang faction gets its support from the Ao region of Mokokchung and the districts of Mon and parts of Tuensang. The rest of Nagaland is dominated by the Isak-Muivah faction. Since 1991 inter-factional conflict has escalated in Nagaland. The Nagas have also come in conflict with the Kukis of Nagaland and Manipur resulting in even bigger blood-baths. At different times the Nagas received support from China, Myanmar and Pakistan. The last feather in their cap was when the NSCN received international recognition in The Hague in 1992 and was admitted into the Unrepresented Nations and Peoples' Organisation.[15] Currently the NSCN (IM) faction has signed the third ceasefire with the Government of India but tensions persist.

Assam

The other long-standing problem in the Northeast relates to Assam. Independence established the primacy of Assam and the Assamese language in the region. This caused resentment among other groups living in the area. The impetuous drive by the Assamese to impose their language on the other groups living in the state 'activated fault lines along which it fractured politically to leave behind little Assam'. This shocked the Assamese. They suddenly felt vulnerable and the influx of Bangladeshi Muslim immigrants in the late 1960s and early 1970s did not help matters. Resentment against this in-migration caused the largest anti-foreigner protest movement in Assam in 1978–79. This movement was unique because of the unprecedented leadership role and support of students, both male and female. Following the protest movement the Asom Gana Parishad (AGP), or the political party formed out of the Assam Students' Union (ASU), got the chance to form the state legislative assembly. This did not help sustain peace. Many felt the AGP had betrayed the Assamese and dissident members of the former ASU formed an extremist organisation called the United Liberation Front of Assam (ULFA). This was a secessionist group.

For the last 18 years peace has eluded Assam although there is a growing apathy among the conflict torn Assamese against both the army and state as well as the extremist extortionists. Belief in the 'cause' however, remains strong. Other groups such as the Bodos, who have lived in the region for over 600 years and the Santhals, who were brought over from Chhota Nagpur as labourers in the tea estates in the mid-19th century have also begun to stake their claims for self-determination and autonomy.

The Northeast of India remains one of the most conflict prone zones of South Asia. There are over 15,000 Indian troops stationed in Assam and over 6,000 in Nagaland. If one includes the paramilitary which is working under a United Command, the number doubles. Conflicts in Assam and Nagaland exemplify the type of conflicts that plague the Northeast. It is Assam that first brought to national attention the issue of borders and its implications in governance. The anti-foreigner movement in Assam was the first of its kind and the present-day conflict is a continuation of the legacy of disputes not resolved by successive governments in New Delhi. In-migration remains one of the major causes of dissatisfaction of people living in the Northeast of India. The other cause of dissatisfaction as exemplified by the Naga conflict, stems from efforts of successive central governments to integrate a region which has for most of its remembered history been autonomous, and impose a state system that it considers alien.[16] The logic of the politics of state making within the Indian Union meant that once Nagaland became a state, other groups comprising a large number of people were encouraged to escalate violence in order to achieve statehood. And to further increase their numerical representation in certain areas, groups were even tempted to embark on what has come to be recognised as ethnic cleansing.

Analysts have recognised that the main issue in the Northeast is the question of identity. But what they have assumed is that this conflict is for the reassertion of the male identity in the Northeast. Other identities including the female identity are sometimes subsumed within the male voice or within questions of nationalism. But when conflicts over democratisation persist, faultlines appear which challenge this gendered view of identity. It is our quest to rediscover the feminine voice in this quest for identity, democracy and self-determination. This new voice may even redesign concepts of democracy, conflict and peace. It is not our intention to ghetto peace in the feminine realm or ghetto women within peace. Rather, we intend to analyse how women use issues of conflict and peace for greater equity between men and women in this quest for identity. For these purposes the indigenous societies of the Northeast make ideal test cases.

Paradox of Missing Women in the Northeast

Traditionally the Northeast is a region where there are a number of matrilineal tribes. The women constitute less than 48 per cent of the total population in the Northeast. The percentage of female literates is much higher here than the national average of 39.4 per cent. Before discussing women's responses to conflict we have tried to statistically analyse the situation of women in Assam and Nagaland through four indicators. They include: the male–female sex ratio, literacy among women, participation of women in formal politics and the right to inherit property. The Northeast poses a central paradox; its female–male sex ratio is decreasing, all the more surprising because of the matrilineal character of many of its societies. How far is violent conflict a factor?

The general trend is portrayed by Manipur where the ratio of women has declined from 1,015 to 1,000 men in 1961 to only 961 in 1991. Whereas in Mizoram in the same period it went from 1,009 women to 1,000 men, to 924 women only. Nagaland portrays a similar trend, i.e., from 933 women to 1,000 men to 890 in the same period. This is even more alarming because Nagaland has one of the highest growth rates. The decline is thus indicative of a situation that may be even worse than the one reflected in the abysmal Indian average of 929 women to every 1,000 men. In Assam, the sex ratio, although on the increase, is still less than the national average (Table 4.1).

TABLE 4.1
Northeast States: Selected Social Indicators

States	Literacy Rates 1991 %			Variation in Density of Population 1981 & 1991 (sq. km)		Comparative Shifts in Sex Ratio (1000 men) 1991* & 1961	
	Total	Male	Female	1991	1981	1991	1961
Assam	53.41	62.34	43.70	284	254	923	869
Meghalaya	48.26	51.57	44.78	78	60	954	937
Manipur	60.96	72.98	48.60	82	84	961	1015
Nagaland	61.30	66.07	55.72	73	47	690	933
Mizoram	81.23	84.06	78.09	33	23	924	1009
Tripura	60.39	70.08	50.01	262	196	945	832
Arunachal Pradesh	41.22	51.10	33.71	10	8	859	894

*Except Meghalaya figures which are from the 1981 Census data.
Source: Data collected from Statistical Handbook of Assam, 1990; Statistical Handbook of Nagaland, Kohima, 1997; Census Report, GOI, 1961; Census Report, GOI, 1981; and Census Report, GOI, 1991.

Putting it down to in-migration of men would be simplistic. One has to consider the ramifications of conflict. For example, in Nagaland, between 1991 and 1995, every year, at least 10 per cent more male children were born. No medical justification can be found which adequately explains this phenomenon. Further, given the total percentage of women in the population, the female death rate appears to be high. For example, in 1994 although there were 100,000 less women than men in Nagaland, 414 women died in rural areas and many violently, compared to 491 men.[17] In most conflict areas, such as Sri Lanka, the death rate of men is much higher but this is not true of Nagaland. This indicates that though many tribes in the

Northeast are matrilineal (implying a higher status of women) violence against women is on the rise.[18]

There are enormous regional variations in the sex ratio in the Northeast. For example, in Manipur there are 984 women for every 1,000 men in Bishnupur district but in Ukhrul district there are only 884 women. Ukhrul is more conflict ridden than Bishnupur, as it is the area of the Tangkul Nagas who are in conflict with NSCN (K). Even in Bishnupur the sex ratio was 992/1,000 in 1981 and 1,019/1,000 in 1951. Hence, we see a more adverse sex ratio in areas of greater conflict. There are other kinds of variations as well. In Nagaland there are 917 females to every 1,000 males in rural areas where women form the main agricultural labour force and only 759 women to 1,000 men in urban areas (1991 Census). Women labourers get more marginalised in the urban areas because of the growth rate and in-migration.

The percentage of female literates is much higher than the national average in the states of the Northeast (Tables 4.2 and 4.3). Especially in the predominantly Christian states of Mizoram and Nagaland, literacy among women is common. But there are massive regional variations.

TABLE 4.2
Comparative Study of Indian and Assamese Literacy Rates

	1971		1981		1991	
	Female	*Male*	*Female*	*Male*	*Female*	*Male*
India	18.44	39.51	24.88	46.71	39.42	63.86
Assam	18.62	44.28	22.31	42.96	43.70	62.34

Source: Data collected from Census Reports (GOI) of 1971, 1981 and 1991. Data for Assam is derived from Statistical Handbook of Assam, Government of Assam, Guwahati, 1997.

TABLE 4.3
Comparative Study of Literacy Rate of Rural and Urban Population in Assam

	Total Population			Rural Population			Urban Population		
	Total	*Female*	*Male*	*Total*	*Female*	*Male*	*Total*	*Female*	*Male*
Assam	52.89	43.70	62.34	49.32	39.19	58.66	79.39	73.32	84.37

Source: Data collected from Census 1991. Shows the discrepancy of literacy rate between rural and urban populations.

In the rural areas of Mon in Nagaland the female literacy rate is as low as 29 per cent whereas in urban areas like Kohima, it is over 61 per cent. In Assam the literacy rate is much lower among women. It is merely 43 per cent, although this is better than the national average. Among the tribal women it is even lower. Even among the Khasi and Jayantia women here it is only 17 per cent. This is significant because the Khasi-Garo and Jayantia women enjoy a special place in society. These tribes are matrilineal and property is inherited from mother to daughter, unlike the Nagas or the Ahoms. The children take their mother's name and the bridegroom traditionally lives with the bride's family. However, even among the Khasis the women are not the heads of the family. That position is reserved for the maternal uncle or the eldest brother. But much as 'the woman enjoys a high status yet she does not have any power or position in the political system. She is not entitled to attend the Durbars, be it at any level, village, territory or state. Politics was and is confined to men'. As for the Garos, although the women select their husbands and make them the *nokma*, or the head of the family, in reality this confers little authority. The *nokma* has no control over village politics.

Another feature of the Northeast, which is extremely apparent in Nagaland is the shattering and arduous condition in which the women are forced to survive. Women face increased poverty and the mortality rate is going up. One of the main reasons for the loss of livelihood is that people are being forced to give up *jhum* cultivation. An example from Nagaland shows that between 1981 and 1991 more than 4 per cent of the cultivators lost their lands and joined the ranks of the unemployed or non-workers. In the same region there are 178,974 male cultivators to 192,623 females.[19] So if the percentage of cultivators goes down it is largely women who are suffering. In many places women are the sole breadwinners but they are losing their sources of livelihood. 'All these [factors] have accelerated the process of impoverishment, inequality and hardships'.[20] Major victims of the deleterious phenomenon have been women. In addition, growing drug abuse and alcoholism have resulted in increasing violence against women. But perhaps the greatest problem confronting women in the Northeast is the increasing state vs.

community and community vs. community conflicts raging throughout the region.

Why Assam and Nagaland?

As has been stated earlier our research is based on the two states of
Assam and Nagaland. However, some of the conclusions have a
certain relevance that make them symptomatic of most people living in conflict areas in South Asia. We have tried to analyse the kind
of interventions that women make in conflicts in the Northeast.
There is a rationale behind selecting Assam and Nagaland. Assam is
still the largest state in the Northeast and Nagaland has the longest
history of state vs. community conflict in the region. In both conflicts there are evidences of involvement of powers hostile to India
so that we may address questions of citizenship and nationalism.
The state vs. community conflict is aggravated by inter-community
conflicts. Since the Northeast is composed of hill and plain lands we
have selected Assam which is predominately a plains region and
Nagaland which is a hill region. Although Assam is one of the oldest states of the Northeast, Nagaland is the first state to protest
against the Indian policy of state formation. Assam is a Hindu majority state and Nagaland has a Christian majority. Taken together
these are the two predominant religions practised in the region, although there is a sizeable Muslim population in Assam.

Even where gender indices are concerned Assam and Nagaland
present paradoxes that are symptomatic of the region. Nagaland
has the second best female literacy rate but its female–male sex ratio
ranks sixth in the region. In Assam female literacy is one of the
lowest in the region only ahead of Arunachal Pradesh but the sex
ratio is higher than Nagaland. This is again an oddity for in most
places where female literacy rate is high, as in Kerala, the female sex
ratio is favourable to women. A better educated female population
should result in less prejudice against women. The situation of
women in Assam and Nagaland overturns this assumption.

Although the literacy rate of women in Assam and Nagaland is
very different, as is their sex ratio, there is one common phenomenon

which plagues women in both areas and that is a lack of women's voice in formal politics. Due to this it is said that the women are generally unable to influence the course of the conflict. Yet they are its worst casualty. 'Be it acts of insurgents or raids of the security forces . . . women of perennially disturbed states suffer the most'.[21] Such views are also borne out by a study done under the auspices of the Tezpur District Mahila Samiti. In our project we have ventured to analyse the effects of conflict on women and study whether women affect conflict in the Northeast. Our major question is—although there is hardly any recognised space for women in formal politics, have they created any non-formal spaces for intervention? Have such non-formal spaces given them the occasion to negotiate their own space in conflict?

Our research gives us not only major insights into problems faced by women in conflicts but also reveals ways in which they negotiate their everyday lives and make different kinds of interventions. Women have been able to negotiate spaces in conflict in Assam and Nagaland. But the modes of such negotiations are numerous. Here we present a multiplicity of women's political voices in the region and the methods by which they negotiate in conflict. Such negotiations portray their immense creativity and perseverance and with the help of these qualities they try to redefine politics. Their success may be uncertain but the will is undoubted.

Women and Conflict in Assam

Assam has a long history of women's activism. In the second and the third decade of the 20th century, the first group of educated Assamese women such as Chandra Prava Saikiani, Hemaprava Das, Amalprava Das and Punyaprava Das joined hands with women from the elite families such as the Chaliha family from Sibsagar and the Agarwal family of Tezpur to form women's organisations. The Dibrugarh Mahila Samiti was the first women's organisation in Assam formed in 1915. The Assam Mahila Samiti followed in 1926. Women from undivided Assam participated in the nationalist movement in large numbers, especially during the Quit India Movement.

Many women gave their lives and others, such as Chandra Prava Saikiani accepted the ignominy of jail sentences, but continued working in underground movements. After independence the movement withered away. 'What remained was the fossilised shell without the original spirit in the Pradeshik Mahila Samiti, a conservative welfare oriented organisation'.[22]

It is in this context that the present women's movement in Assam assumes significance. In the wake of the International Women's Year in 1975 there were consolidated efforts to rejuvenate the women's movement in Assam. Old village Mahila Samitis were revived and new state-level organisations were formed. As a result of these efforts when ASU started its anti-foreigner agitations in 1978 a majority of educated women supported the movement. Towards the latter part of the movement there were attempts to give a cohesive shape to the women's response by forming local- and state-level co-ordination committees. But with the end of the movement these committees faded away. A few politically motivated women formed the women's wing of the AGP but the rest went back frustrated by the fact that their participation was never rewarded by giving women a voice in institutionalised politics.

Women's movements retained a sporadic and issue-based character. In both pre-independence and post-independence struggles, women were inspired by a sense of nationalism. But when the movement ended they found that they had not gained much. Against them worked not merely the state but also their own patriarchy which legitimised its actions by perpetrating the myth that Assamese women were not interested in politics. The nationalist paradigm was once again repeated here. Women continued to be marginalised in representational politics.[23]

One development however retained women at the centre stage of politics. Agitation over 'foreigners' in Assam continued and so did insurgency. Any debate on insurgency could not ignore women as they were the worst sufferers. Debates between the Government of India, the state of Assam and the insurgent groups revolved typically around the victimisation of women and children. Women found their fair share of space as victims on any reports on the conflict by any concerned groups. However, the role of a victim is not the only role that women endowed on themselves in this conflict situation in Assam. The interventions that women made are varied. The multiplicities of feminine responses break gender stereotypes and create new ones. In the process they also break the myth that women are not interested in political movements.

Attackers and Their Victims[24]

In places such as Nalbari, Lakhimpur or Sibsagar stories such as those of Tulumoni Devi or Tarulata Pegu are common. Tulumoni, the young wife of Harkanta Nath of Marigaon district, was raped on 24 April 1997, allegedly by the army, during a house-to-house combing operation for an ULFA activist. When eight of them entered Tulumoni's house they saw her alone with her 2-year-old child. They raped her and left her unconscious. Her child's screams brought in villagers who revived her. Her husband filed a case at Mikirkheta police station and was threatened by the army. In protest women from 40 villages took out a rally and submitted a memorandum to the Deputy Commissioner of Marigaon demanding a judicial enquiry. The Anchalik Mahila Sajagata Samiti also protested but nothing came of it.[25]

The cases of the women whom we will call Minoti Bala (21) and Nilima Bala (19), were a study in contrast of a victim and the makings of a militant. The two were from Sibsagar district. Their brother was suspected of ULFA connections. During a raid when they were home alone, the army gang raped them. The next day, the army came back and questioned Minoti; Nilima had managed to escape to the jungle. The army cordoned off the village and Minoti was tortured and raped to tell the whereabouts of her brother. Her father had already been killed by the army. When the army left her she was bruised all over and so traumatised, she lost her speech. For three days she was denied medical attention, till the army left. Nilima did not return. The villagers believed she was in an ULFA training camp.

We spoke to Nilima who had her face covered with a *dupatta*. She said that it should be the mission of all Assamese to liberate

Assam as it has become a colony. 'Assam is living under army rule which has imposed a reign of terror on the indigenous people. The people have lost their rights over land and resources but the army is unable to rob them of their dignity'. Nilima felt that over the last eight years crimes against women have increased, largely perpetrated by the state and the army. We asked her what attracted young women to militancy. She said if women live in villages they have no control over their fates but a militant woman can confront evil. If she dies she becomes a martyr. It is the love for a nation that prompts young women to join the insurgents, she said.

Nilima spoke of her tough life in the jungles. Even tougher is the training that young people receive in camps in Bangladesh and Bhutan. To go to these camps young people trek for days. Women are given a lighter training schedule but they are also given less rations. They are trained to handle firearms, to organise an ambush, make explosives and work as couriers. They also get some training in first-aid. After training, they come back to Assam and are given their briefs. We asked Nilima what kind of roles women play in insurgencies. An apathetic note crept into her voice. Even after extensive training, women are kept away from military action, she said. They play a supporting role. They send messages, help transport arms and pass on briefs from one village to another. Evidently, militancy is a gendered experience. Nilima, however, was proud that she unlike most women did participate in actions but refused to elaborate. Nilima knows that any time she may fall victim to army bullets. She is prepared for that eventuality. But she fears torture, worse still, she fears meeting the fate of a former colleague, Rashmi Bora who was killed by militants because she was suspected of spying for the army. Medical science however suggests that before that she may well succumb to ailments contracted in the jungle, including problems associated with malnutrition.[26] Is she a victim?

Nilima's may have been an exceptional life but a woman whom we will call Anjali Basumataray led a very ordinary life till she became the victim of militant crossfire. In the last decade she has lost three family members to militants. 'They were murdered by extremists', she told us quietly. One of the three, was her 12-year-old daughter, the other her husband. Unfortunately, her daughter was travelling with her father in the car. Anjali cannot accept her daughter's death as accidental. She feels her little girl was targeted by terrorists because she was her father's daughter and her father happened to be a politician. A hand grenade killed her before she could understand what the conflict was about. Anjali's husband was killed by a bullet from an AK-47. She can identify the people who killed him but she was unable to bring them to justice. They had telephoned to ask her her husband's whereabouts, and since she knew the callers she told them. She lives with the guilt that her indiscretion may have killed him. Her husband was shot on the road in broad daylight but the police could find no eyewitnesses. Not surprisingly Anjali is angrier with her friends than her enemies.

Her trials started after her husband's death. She received 0.1 million rupees as compensation and was asked to get on with her life. With few savings and two small daughters to look after, she got a job as a teacher. What haunted her most was the loneliness. No one visited her for fear of angering the terrorists. The normal support networks for Indian widows were missing in her case as, being aided by the state, she was a marked woman. No one wanted to befriend her let alone offer help. Other than her own immediate family, everyone avoided her. But Anjali feels she is fortunate since she lives in the city and not in a village. In the villages, she said, 'people's lives are plagued by three inexorable evils—the army, the flood and the terrorists'. Their cattle are slaughtered at will by the terrorists and their homes forcibly made into hideouts and shelters. When the army comes to know of this their bodies become the bargaining chip. The army directly targets women and the terrorists do so indirectly. When they kill a man the woman has to look after the children. Indirectly it is the woman who is punished.

Anjali is bitter about the indiscriminate killings by some terrorist groups. When questioned whether women were specially targeted, she felt that when the movement began women were very much respected. She maintained women are victimised and targeted; not all women, but largely political women are constantly harassed. The militants feel these women are greater transgressors than men. Anjali, however, still retains respect for 'the cause'. She remains convinced that the anti-foreigner movement started with the right ideals. She believes that the Assamese are becoming marginalised in Assam. So when the movement started she participated. But the original ideals of the movement have changed. The movement has lost much of its legitimacy because the participants are more interested in individual gain. All the extremist groups such as ULFA and the Bodo Security Force (BdSF), belong to the same network. They get their training in the same camps, money through similar means and arms from the same dealers. Anjali was hopeful peace would prevail as the common people were tired of the highhanded attitude of extremist groups.

Anjali said that the death of her husband has made her a stronger person. Shorn of any support she has learned to live on her own terms. She feels that the women's movement has failed in Assam since it could do nothing for women such as her. Even now women do not inherit parental property. Losing her husband and daughter has made Anjali appreciate peace. She said the people in Assam now just want to get on with their lives. Anjali is at present closely associated with a SULFA (surrendered militant co-opted by the state). Has she compromised for survival? Is she no more than a victim?

Unsettled Are the Well Settled

Bani Devi is a highly educated teacher at a university. She participated in the first phase of the 'Assam for the Assamese' movement in 1978. But today the movement holds no appeal for her. She said she still believes in its ideals but has been disillusioned by the experience of four of her female students who joined the movement. They had joined after some of their friends were raped in police custody. They were taken to camps and trained. Initially 'it meant special boots, special jeans and lots of money'. But then came the hardships. Two of them came back with kidney and liver failure. The third wanted to come back to her family but was not allowed to by the leaders. She probably knew too much. Further, even her family was not keen to take her back. If she came back they would not be able to get her married. There may be adulation for these young 'nationalists' but as returnees there was no glamour. In fact their rehabilitation is a problem. A man could easily become a SULFA and create a space for himself in society. But for women it is much more difficult. In such situations the families often eulogise them but do not want them to return and live with them.

In urban areas the insurgents get their staunchest support from women between the ages of 15 and 19, says Bani Devi. Even if these women do not join the movement they often act as fund raisers. In the process they are exploited by extortionists. These young girls are spurred on by idealism but their exploiters are not. In the villages, she says, it works differently. Often women are forced to support the insurgents but in cities there is a different kind of coercion. Women from poor backgrounds are promised economic advantages if they join the movement. Sometimes it works as a lure for young impoverished widows.

Bani Devi no longer feels safe in her everyday life. The lumpenisation of the movement not only pains her but has made her extremely scared. She spoke of a neighbour, a businessman who was ultimately eliminated because his father-in-law was a senior police officer. The increasing incidents of violence compelled her to initiate some form of a peace movement. She and her colleagues in the university organised a workshop on this theme. After the North Lakhimpur army rapes of minor girls, she and her friends tried to organise a women's rally for peace in 1991. When the news of the rally spread she started getting anonymous threatening notes. She disregarded them. Other friends too were severely warned. After their rally a young male volunteer was so badly beaten up by unknown assailants that he was maimed for life. The police was of little help. In the face of such opposition she could not continue her initiative. She is convinced that no belligerent group in Assam wants peace. She feels that peace is largely a woman's agenda. But women who are convinced that peace can be negotiated are actively discouraged, warned and threatened. She is scared that her pacifist views may make her a target. Neither her class, social status or education gives her any security.

The wife of a leading businessman, whom we will call Nivedita, feels no less insecure. Initially, she was very sympathetic to the movement in 1978. But corruption has corroded the movement from inside, alienating people. Ever since her husband's business took off, there were constant demands from insurgent groups for money. Her husband is a Marwari, an outsider, although his family has been living in Assam for over 50 years. Nivedita is Assamese but that has not helped her husband much. She has had to send her daughters to school outside the state. She did not want them to grow up with a sense of persecution. She cannot even take her daughters out in the evening because the curfew is on. Her movements are totally restricted. She feels that there are no winners in this situation. After the sacrifices women made for the movement, they have not even gained the right to live with dignity. Her only hope is that women have not given up. They may not be able to organise a mass movement, but in their own way they continue to protest. Such protest may be sporadic but its frequency is increasing.

Where Are the Women in Assam Politics?

In Assam the female to male sex ratio presents an improvement over the 1981 figures. The female literacy rate has also shown a marked improvement between 1971 and 1991. It went up from a mere 18.6 per cent to 43.70 per cent. But there are other figures that are problematic. In the last 18 years there has been no woman representative from Assam to the Lok Sabha. In the 'top 100 government posts of the state, there are only three female officers'.[27] Eminent women in Assam show concern over these trends. Santwana Bordoloi, who is a doctor, a movie director and a social worker is of the opinion that in Assamese politics women do not have adequate scope of advancement. She perceives this as a major problem of Assamese politics. A woman politician such as Mridula Saharia, who was the chairperson of the State Commission for Women in 1994 and 1995 shares the same view. Renu Debi, who was the previous director of the Women's Studies Research Centre in Guwahati University, feels that in these perilous times women politicians might have improved the quality of Assamese politics. Another woman politician, who prefers to remain anonymous, said that urban, educated young women know that there is hardly any possibility of women assuming leadership roles in politics. She said that in the anti-foreigner movement women participated in large numbers and contributed to its success. But after the AGP formed the government they felt cheated because their efforts did not translate into more representation for women. They got no recognition for their participation. Extremist groups try to recruit young women, where formal politics denies them that space.

The other area where women are losing out is in the workforce. Technological advancement in agriculture has proved problematic for women because now the machines do the traditional female labour of weeding, harvesting, carrying and husking. Further, for security reasons women cannot be in the fields unless it is in full daylight. In the industrial sectors too women are being marginalised due to technological advancement and due to conflict. For example, in the last two decades in the textile industry total employment has remained stagnant. But the absolute number of female workers recruited is decreasing with a corresponding increase in the employment of the male workers. Moreover, the system of employing workers in three shifts is being increasingly practised in factories and the average number of workers is increasing in the third shift where women workers are not allowed.[28] The justification given is that the general destabilisation of the region makes it impossible to employ women in night shifts as that may affect their security needs. But by not employing women it has not become a safer place for them to live in, rather it has added to their further marginalisation.

Most of our women respondents in Assam complained that they were being denied a voice in public affairs and so they supported the formation of the Assam State Commission for Women. The Commission came into existence on 25 January 1994. It was set up to investigate matters relating to constitutional safeguards and other laws, and take up violations with appropriate authorities. It was to call for special studies or investigations into specific problems of discrimination and atrocities against women and undertake promotional and educational research to ensure representation for women in all spheres and identify factors responsible for impeding their advancement.[29] The Commission, however, has steered clear of questions regarding political representation and political decision making. As for issues relating to conflict, insurgencies and conflict resolutions, they have held only one seminar. In the seminar it was acknowledged that terrorism 'sprouts from frustrations both political and social', but very little was said on how women deal with it or what kind of interventions they make.[30] The Commission can barely organise rallies to protest against atrocities on women let alone make any positive interventions for peace, said a spokesperson of the human rights organisation, Manav Adhikar Sangram Samiti (MASS).

When questioned, Dr Shahnaz Rehman, a former member of the Commission, and a lawyer by profession agreed that this has been a lacuna. The Commission does not even have rehabilitation programmes for women who have been tortured and raped. In our discussions some of these women spoke about their deep sense of guilt and shame. Such emotions increase their trauma and create marital discord. Often they also have to bear the onus of responsibility if the male members in their families get hurt while trying to protect them. There are no government agencies to help them and very few public charitable organisations are able to work in these situations. What the Commission fails to see is that income generation programmes cannot help women when their life, liberty and dignity is threatened.

One research intervention in the area of traumatised women has been initiated by the Leiden University of Holland. They are working with women who are victims of violence in villages in western Assam. Their deduction is that the women get terribly depressed after their trauma. Sometimes rape victims are used by the belligerents as showcases. But once they derive optimum political benefit from them, they soon forget these women. The women are then at best ignored, or at worst persecuted by society. Ultimately they are stigmatised as any other rape victim. They find it very difficult to adjust to their families. In such situations they sometimes choose the jungle, and at other times a martyr's death. Such deaths are not just protests against violence but also against patriarchal social norms that deny an equitable social space to women.[31]

Women in Assam find themselves marginalised in the processes of decision making. They have no space in formal politics. To make any intervention for peace they negotiate spaces elsewhere. Such efforts to negotiate some small spaces for peace are portrayed in the activities of the Kasturba Gandhi National Memorial Trust (KGNM), Anchalik Mahila Samitis and other organisations like Sajagata Samiti. The Kasturba Trust is by now well known in Assam since they send their *sevikas* to riot-affected areas in remote places such as Kokrajhar and Bangaigaon districts to offer help and negotiate peace between the Santhals and the Bodos. They have established two important centres near the border areas in Dhubri and Cachar districts.[32] Since they feel that borders need particular attention if peace is to be maintained in the region they have sent their *Santi Sainiks* there. The Trust has also created the Stri Shakti Jagaran Manch in which they make a sincere effort to bring together women from warring groups to rediscover their commanalties.

'In today's problematic situation in Assam only the mothers can unify the splintered groups and bring peace to the region.'[33] Shakuntala Chowdhury who has been a trustee of the KGNM since 1946, frankly admits that their relief work is more successful than their efforts to bring about peace. That is why the KGNM has established a special commemorative day in honour of Kasturba Gandhi on 22 February. On that day various human rights groups address people from the same stage used by the Trust and propagate peace. One of the reasons why the KGNM has not been able to sustain its peace-making efforts is because of its inability to attract younger women. There is a definite tilt towards middle-aged and older women. Younger women find themselves marginalised.

There have also been a number of other interventions for peace but these were issue based. After army atrocities in Nalbari and North Lakhimpur in 1989 and 1991 Mahila Samitis (women's groups) formed and the Matri Manch which is now defunct. A one-time spokesperson of the Manch told us that it was formed to protest against atrocities on women and debate on modes of achieving peace. In her experience the worst atrocities were committed by security personnel. But she felt that extremist groups were also callous about the problems of women. Once a case gets media attention they help the families. But after a while their sympathy changes to indifference. She felt that no organisation can survive without the patronage of the powers-that-be. After the initial success of the Manch, it could not sustain itself since institutionalised power groups did not support it. These groups had their own dialogues on conflict resolution and the Matri Manch intervention was not something they wished to tolerate. Men in Assam still have problems accepting any initiative from women especially relating to the public sphere.

Some women have been more successful in forming groups to protest against atrocities, as for example, the Anchalik Mahila Sajagata Samiti and the Chapar Anchalik Mahila Samiti. These organisations are able to marshal about 40 to 50 women, and sometimes more in a matter of hours. These women can be housewives, agricultural labourers or students. But whenever there are atrocities against women in their area, they congregate and organise protest marches. They may not be able to sustain these protests and organise mass movements but they do not give up. These '10 day protests', are becoming permanent fixtures on the political scene. It is through these initiatives that women are trying to appropriate public spaces.

Other than the Assamese women, the Bodo women too have been organising themselves. The Bodo movement for self-determination leading to the formation of the militant BdSF has witnessed tremendous violence. It has been reported that in the Bodo Autonomous Council (BAC) areas the BdSF has demanded huge sums of money from the non-Bodos. In this community vs. community conflict we found that the women remain the worst sufferers. In this situation as well, women's interventions for peace have taken the form of sporadic protests against violence. Peace interventions of the Matri Manch variety that challenge male domination of the public sphere do not get support from the patriarchal political leadership. Localised protests and demonstrations have a better chance of being sustained.

In our conversations with some women from the B. Baruah College we found that there is recognition that parties contesting for power are only paying lip service to women's empowerment. In any peace process initiated by these political forces, women are ignored. Women, however, dominate the sporadic, non-formal efforts for peace, if not always in the leadership, then at least in sheer numbers. In Guwahati, women organised the first convention of Northeast Women for Peace and Progress between 17 and 20 December 1997. More than 1,500 women from 100 tribes met in this convention. This was not a one-time affair and the latest one in the series was organised in February 1999. The spirit of the participants is portrayed by a Ms Magdalene from Kokrajhar who asked 'In my place which has witnessed some of the worst incidents of human suffering, I want to build up a culture of peace. But how?'[34] Most often women are divided into hostile positions according to their family/community affiliations. However, more women are realising that they have to define peace in their own terms. To make positive interventions they either have to appropriate spaces in politics so that they can have a voice in the peace-making process or they can convert their non-formal space into a legitimate space for peace. This is what they are hoping to do through local-level protest demonstrations.

The case of Assam portrays that it is possible for women to negotiate for peace. They are the natural constituency to do so. Like Mairead Corrigan and Betty Williams in Ireland they have also formed peace groups and demonstrated against violence. Where they failed was in assuming the dominant voice. Their movements were largely sporadic and dispersed because it is in the non-formal space that women are strongest. When the public sphere is divided into formal and non-formal spaces then the non-formal space is relegated to women. Women in Assam have taken advantage of that space to begin what are known as the '10 day' peace movements. But in doing so they sometimes create their own closures. Because of the very nature of these spaces their efforts remain local rather than national. However, any attempt to acquire a dominant voice brings them in confrontation with institutionalised patriarchal power. But negotiate they must because it is through negotiations that women in Assam have successfully confronted and in few instances mitigated their subordinate status and the politics of violence. The localised protest movements are their chosen mode of negotiation.

Women and Conflict in Nagaland

Any discussion on Nagaland should first begin with a description of who the Nagas are. The Nagas comprise 40 tribes living between the Chindwin and the Brahmaputra plains. The commonly known tribes are Angami, Rengma, Ao, Tangkhul and Phom. The term Naga was coined by the British. Nagaland, the 16th state of India, is bounded by Assam in the west, Myanmar in the east, Arunachal Pradesh in the north and Manipur in the south. Nagaland is the theatre of the longest civil war in India.

To make a generalised statement about the status of women in Nagaland is extremely difficult. Different tribal groups have set different standards for women. The status of a newly married Angami girl may be different from an Ao girl. The Angami mother can be a matriarch but a Phom mother may not be. In some tribes the women get a share of the parental property but among most Naga tribes they do not. Only recently Naga women's organisations have demanded the right to inherit property but as yet they have had little success.[35] But in some folklore women are considered guardians of family land. The Poumai's have one such folk tale where a woman named Khe Ngaonii inspired her brother to reclaim their family land. At the end of the story it was stated: 'Now the time has come for each and every Naga Women to be intelligent, informative, alert and concern [sic] for our land'.[36] In recent times this folk tale is being told and retold, as it is being used to push for women's right to land and also to culturally legitimise women's involvement in the informal and formal space of politics.

The Nagas are patrilineal, tracing descent from the father. Naga women are sometimes given immovable property as gifts. Clans are headed by men although some women wield a lot of influence as consorts. Women in Nagaland have taken to education with great fervour. There is also an increase in the number of professional women. Yet political parties and representational politics are still dominated by the men. According to one observer, 'participation of women in decision making body has been a taboo for women since time immemorial'.[37] There are no women in traditional village councils and only two women in the city council of Kohima but one of them is the first female chairperson. The women are not elected members but nominated by the governor. Women are marginalised in political decision making not only by the state, but as we shall examine below, by the rebel groups as well. The two most important rebel groups are the NSCN factions, none of which are led by women. Phizo's daughter heads an almost defunct faction of the NNC, which is of little consequence in Naga politics.

Victors and Vanquished

I went around taking photos of the cadres. And I spotted an innocent face in the drilling crowd. I looked at her face and decided to take a close-up of her. After the drill I spoke to her. Amy Ngullie (20) was doing her B.A. from Wokha College when she gave up her studies to join the NSCN in April last. What made her choose the jungle over college? 'I wanted to serve my own people for our cause,' revealed Amy.[38]

When we questioned some of our respondents we got similar answers. Unlike in Assam no one talked of the lure of a glamourised life as a reason for joining the insurgent movement. Amenla, who is a college student at Kohima said she intends to join the insurgents after her education is complete. I asked her why she wants to finish her education if she intends to live in the jungles. She said that education is important even within rebel groups' power structures. She also intends to be fully prepared to join in the nation building process once the 'war' is over and Nagaland achieves 'independence'. Many of Amenla's friends, though not so categorical about their sympathies feel that the insurgents are largely nationalists who are devoting their lives to the cause of liberation. The response of the Naga women was not surprising because of its content but because it cut across generations. A respondent from the Bara Basti in Khonoma, over a glass of gooseberry juice, said that people do complain when the NSCN groups ask for money. They feel that instead of six pigs a year they should give only four pigs.

But they understand why it is important to support these groups. 'Without pressure from the NSCNs the Government of India will not send any developmental packages to Nagaland. Rather they would give it to the Kukis,' she said.

On a cold January evening we met an outstanding woman in Dimapur. She belonged to the first generation of militant women. She held an important position in the women's wing of NNC. I will call her Mrs Mou. She was a pioneer in the youth wing of NNC and had joined her father and brothers in the struggle for liberation. She said the Women's Federation of the Naga Students' Council (NSC) and later NNC started as a peace mission. But atrocities against women forced the Women's Federation to arm themselves in self-defence. In the beginning, NNC refused to give women military training. But when some women members who had to take shelter in a church were raped by the army, women demanded combat training and the NNC leadership agreed. In fact, Mrs Mou had participated in combat actions and even led a number of ambushes. That was how she met her present husband, a general in the NNC. I asked her how her natal family had accepted her unusual role. Mrs Mou simply said that as a woman it was her duty to protect her home. The Indian army was violating that. Hence she took up arms against the army. She never hurt civilians.

Describing her life as a militant, Mrs Mou said she had to get up at three in the morning, finish her cooking before sunrise as smoke from the *chullah* would otherwise give away her hideout. After eating she might train new recruits or write and study reports. If an army raid was imminent she had to warn the *basti* (settlement). Usually, the army raided at night. If they got information of a raid, young men would be warned to slip away to the jungles. She raised money for family members of her recruits, especially for the elderly and the widows. But the last work was tricky because if the army came to know that some family was getting aid from the militants that would be the end of that family. Mrs Mou told us how the army picked up her own uncle and his son on similar charges. Later, they were found dead. Even in the midst of such a difficult life Mrs Mou found time to say her daily prayers as she was a devout Christian.

For Mrs Mou the decisive year was 1964 when the 'Indian government promised so much but gave us increased oppression'. She has no regrets that she has led a life of violence. Today, although, she does not get along with the leadership of NSCN factions she still believes that they have the right ideals. 'They care more for Nagaland than India ever will.' When I suggested that they could carry on their protest through representational politics, Mrs Mou said the Nagas do not understand or care about Indian politics. They have their own political systems, which the Government of India should respect. The regrets she did have were: one, after a life long effort for peace with honour, she was unable to see it, probably in her lifetime; and two, she regrets not having a child because she devoted her youth to the cause. Her greatest achievement—'I am still alive'. I left what for me was a surreal world unresolved in my mind whether I had met a victor or a vanquished.

Quest for Peace

One of the outstanding features of the Naga women's peace interventions is the multiplicity of peace groups. Although we shall largely focus on the Naga Mothers Association and the rival Watsu Mongdung, dotted all over the area are a myriad other initiatives aimed at reducing the impact of violence on the lives of people and to build a peace with honour.

Naga Mothers Association

The NMA is the best known group with its headquarters in the largely Angami city of Kohima. It came into existence on 14 February 1984, with a preamble that stated, 'Naga mothers of Nagaland shall express the need of conscientising citizens toward more responsible living and human development through the voluntary organisation of the Naga Mothers Association'.[39] Membership of NMA is open to any adult Naga woman irrespective of whether she is married or single. Members can join through the women's organisations of their own tribes. There are 10 office-bearers including a president, three vice presidents and a secretary, all of whom are elected for a term of four years. The organisation aims at upholding womanhood, human rights and human values. It encourages human development through education, is involved in efforts to eradicate social evils and economic exploitation, and works for peace and progress.

From its inception, the NMA has rendered valuable service for the cause of peace. Through activities like successfully lobbying with the government and the Nagaland Students Federation (NSF) over an age limit for jobs and pensions, the NMA was able to build credibility for its peace work. In October 1994, NMA formed a Peace Team to do something about the deteriorating political situation. Their theme was 'Shed No More Blood'. The NMA peace workers initiated dialogues with the 'undergrounds' (militant factions, self-styled as 'national workers') and the state government to arrest violence and bloodshed. They organised public rallies with religious leaders to appeal for peace. The NMA spoke against killings not only by the army but also by the militants. In a pamphlet released on 25 May 1995, representatives of NMA wrote that 'the way in which our society is being run whether by the over ground government or the underground government, has become simply intolerable'. The NMA appealed to both parties to stop the killings. 'The assassinated man may be a husband, a father, a son, or a brother. His whole family is shattered by his violent liquidation no matter what reasons his liquidators choose to give for snuffing out his life.' Each year on 12 May, Mother's Day, NMA renews its appeal for peace.

Once the 1997 ceasefire agreement had been negotiated between the Indian government and the dominant armed Naga group, the NSCN(IM), the Naga Mothers Association was in the forefront of strengthening the peace process. In support of the ceasefire, a four-member peace team of the NMA and the Naga Women's Union of Manipur (NWUM), trekked across the border into Myanmar to the headquarters of the NSCN Kaphlang faction to appeal to him to at least talk with the NSCN(IM) faction. Whenever the ceasefire

has come under strain, the NMA and NWUM along with representatives of the Naga Hoho (the traditional parliament of the Naga
people) and the church, have mobilised together in support of the
ceasefire. In September 2000, as the peace process came under increasing strain, the president of the NMA, Ms Neidonuo Angami
and the president of the NWUM, Dr Gina Shangkham appealed to
the Indian Prime Minister A.B. Vajpayee and the chairman of the
NSCN(IM) to heed their cry of peace and sustain the peace process.

All throughout the current round of peace talks since 1997, NMA
and other civil society groups in Nagaland have played a critical
role in keeping the two protagonists in the negotiating process, the
Indian government and the NSCN(IM), accountable to the Naga
people's desire for peace. This democratisation of the peace process
has been vital in pushing it forward in difficult moments. In February 2000, representatives of the NMA and the NWUM along with
the Naga Students Federation, the Naga Tribal Councils and the
Naga Peoples Movement for Human Rights, visited Delhi to lobby
with civil society groups to strengthen the peace process.

Apart from protesting against violence, the NMA works to fight
drug abuse and alcoholism as an integral part of the struggle of the
Naga peoples to take responsibility for their political, economic
and social rights. The NMA president, Neidonuo claimed that it is
the tacit policy of the government to allow free flow of drugs and
alcohol which has greatly affected the lives of the Naga people.[40]
While speaking to a representative of the NMA we asked why the
organisation concerns itself with such activities when it was formed
as a forum for peace. The Naga mothers realised, she explained,
that one of the main causes for the conflict related to the chronic
underdevelopment of the people. In trying to address that, the NMA
has ventured into developmental problems and has had enormous
success. But success has its own price and sometimes the members
are threatened by drug peddlers because they are trying to stop
their business. The NMA leadership remains unruffled by this opposition. The success of the NMA can be measured by the extent
to which large groups of women have accepted them as their voice
of protest. NMA rallies are always well attended by different tribal
groups.

Watsu Mongdung

Watsu Mongdung catapulted into fame as a result of its campaign for justice against the mass rape of women in Mokokchung by the security forces. On 27 December 1997 in Mokokchung town (a stronghold of the Nationalist Socialist Council of Nagalim, Kaphlang faction, or NSCN[K]), 10 members of the Assam Rifles and 16 members of the Manipur Light Infantry (MLI) entered the town and allegedly raped the women and set fire to the buildings there. The Naga Human Rights Commission asked the Watsu Mongdung to investigate and identify the victims. A special committee formed by the Watsu Mongdung identified eight victims and with their help reconstructed the incident. As no other social organisation wanted to get involved, Watsu Mongdung decided to litigate on behalf of the rape victims. The case is still pending.

Watsu Mongdung began as an initiative of the church in Mokokchung. The town and its adjoining areas are under the control of the Khaplang faction. The NSCN(K) is not one of the parties that agreed to the ceasefire. Although Watsu Mongdung has one of its offices in Kohima it is largely a Mokokchung-based organisation, which is formed by the Ao women. The organisation was formed to recreate interest in traditional socio-cultural values and to help women maintain their traditional identity and promote self-reliance. The organisation is meant for all Naga women over the age of 18. Initially it was formed out of the women's wing of the church but slowly it acquired an identity of its own.

Watsu Mongdung's activities were initially directed at aiding families where there were no male members or those who had no resources. Slowly it went into issues of women's rights. They would discuss folk tales of women who were great strategists and organise street plays based on stories of women's valour and other legends. They would intervene in social disputes such as disputes over property. Their community centre has become a place where Ao women can come together and rediscover their self-identity.

From 1994, Watsu Mongdung appropriated a new role for themselves; they started mediating between the people of Mokokchung and the army. In cases of rape and sexual harassment, they helped women file cases against the security forces. In 1997 they took up the case of the rape of minors and formed a United Naga Women's Forum to protest against such incidents. They tried to mobilise social groups in Mokokchung town to dialogue on peace. When there have been indiscriminate arrests they have spoken to the army and put pressure on them to release the civilians. Once during a combing operation in Mokokchung when the army wanted to separate the men and women, they refused to be separated since they feared that the army would kill the men. Ultimately the army had to interrogate both men and women together and then released most of them. When *bastis* (settlements) were burnt down they went in with aid. They carry out relief work during calamities, man-made or otherwise.

There are other women's groups such as the Tangkhul Shanao Long (TSL) which operate both in Nagaland and Manipur. The TSL is active in Ukhrul district and has branches in all the Tangkhul Naga villages. In July 1997 after an ambush by the NSCN(IM) the Assam Rifles went on a rampage in Ukhrul town beating up the men, including schoolteachers. People were so traumatised that life came to a standstill in Ukhrul town. The TSL not only spoke to the army and convinced them to release over 40 civilians but also tried to instil confidence among the people of the town and its adjoining villages. They helped the people of the area to return to normal life by requesting the shopkeepers to open their shops. They appealed to the stranded people to go back home which brought back some semblance of normalcy in the town.

It is a common occurrence for women to go on protest marches against army operations, as for example, marches by the Angami Women's Organisation. In August 1996 they staged several silent protest marches in the town of Kohima. There are other women who have strongly protested against killing of civilians by gun wielding maniacs who take the law in their hands.[41] Thus, the Naga women are not afraid of making political statements for peace. But they have problems in working together. The rivalries between different groups get translated into women's issues. The Ao and the Angamis have a traditional rivalry. The Watsu Mongdung, which is an organisation of Ao women and the NMA, which is largely made up of

Angami women, have problems in working together. An observer of these two organisations traces the problems back to an incident where an Ao woman, arrested by the police for drug peddling, was taken into custody by the NMA which tried her according to Angami common law. Some members of the Watsu Mongdung are convinced of her innocence. Others feel that even if she was guilty she should have been tried according to Ao common law. This inability to work together sometimes affects the extent of interventions that women are able to make.

In Nagaland the sense of tradition among women is very strong. Therefore, any interventions that women as a group make are an extension of what they perceive as their identity. When they make statements on human rights they do it feeling they are protecting their own people. Sometimes the state is able to use the women's traditional peacemaking role for statist purposes. For example, the Government of India is successful in mobilising support for the NMA for their ceasefire with the NSCN(IM), which has its strongholds in the same geographical region and has affiliations among the same tribal groups. But they are unable to interest them in representational politics that does not follow the traditions of the indigenous people. Even with a literacy rate over 55 per cent women do not enter party politics.

The activities of the NMA and other groups demonstrate that women are asserting themselves in public roles. They know how to negotiate their own space, which is a space for peace in conflict. Women activists in Nagaland have also given peace a broader and a more equitable definition. They are not satisfied with only organising protest marches or making statements in defence of human rights. They have also taken up development issues such as working for de-addiction among the youth and doing community services such as looking after the sick and the aged. But they do not like getting embroiled in party politics, which they feel, would be contrary to what they perceive as their traditional role. Their shunning of elections is a protest statement against Indian statism. They feel the battle is for self-determination and thus they should do nothing that in any way challenges their identity as indigenous people.

I have spoken to more than 30 women in the city of Kohima alone who had postgraduate degrees and tried to engage them in a debate over the issue of 33 per cent representation for women. Over 80 per cent replied that they were not interested in Indian elections and about 75 per cent stated that they did not believe in quotas, as in their tradition there is no place for such quotas. To the Nagas, questions of nationalism are imbibed within this battle for self-determination. The women can make their traditional role flexible but they do not want to change it. Efforts to change their traditional role can be misinterpreted as a loss of faith in their tradition. The women themselves become the testing ground for cultural self-determinism. Their personal becomes political. Thus, it becomes imperative for them to retain their tribal identity much like the Islamic identity of the Turkish women in Germany.

The church is the place where the Naga people congregate. Sadly enough the church has not become a common platform for unifying the Nagas. Their tribal identity overshadows their religious identity. Their interventions for peace often get stymied between their multiple identities and restrict their ability to find a common voice. However, this in no way should make us underestimate their peace-making ability. The number of peace groups initiated by Naga women bears testimony to that.

Conflict and Women: Some Observations

When I started this study my enquiry was around the posit: are women in conflict situations able to transcend their social subordination and make interventions? If they do make interventions then are those interventions for war or for peace? Do their interventions lead to empowerment or social change? At best the answers remain tentative. Because for every woman in a conflict situation there is a personal answer and a moment of choice. That being said, it is also possible to make some general observations about women's responses based on their gendered experiences that create their own political realities.[42]

The multiplicity of women's responses to conflict in Assam and Nagaland proves that women are not inherently pacifist. There are a number of women who are convinced that the only way to achieve self-determination is through armed conflict. Although women are less in number than men among rebel groups still their representation is sizeable. These groups generally attract young women because they make special appeals to youth. There are numerous examples where one or more of the rebel groups address young people through the media so that they may attract their attention.[43] There is perhaps another reason for it. Neither formal politics nor peace groups make any appeal to younger women. The leadership is invariably in the hands of middle-aged women and younger women remain on the margins. Rebel groups give space to these women. Further, life in the jungles is too tough for older women but that is not to say that older women do not support these groups. They provide other kinds of support. They may incite young people within their families to join the rebels. Their tacit support helps men to move away and go to the jungles. Sometimes they may act as couriers for messages but not for arms. Generally young women carry arms from one place to another in baskets of grains or vegetables or in baby baskets which they carry as backpacks.

Even among rebel groups the duties of men and women vary. Usually men take up arms and women play supporting roles. Life for women in these groups is tough. Women seldom rise to the position of commander. When they do they usually lead the women's wing. Some women are commissioned for their skills as nurses. In Nagaland education is valued in these groups. Both men and women need to be educated for further advancement. These groups are part of the society and their value system reflects the same social values. As expected, equity for women is usually not a priority and women's issues receive importance only when some political advantage is to be derived from it. The leadership can be as ruthless to women as to men. Transgressions lead to severe reprisals. But women joining these groups are looked upon as nationalists within their own communities and as such feared and respected. Abuse within these groups is never reported and we do not know whether it exists. Since these groups fight for self-determination and since that is based on their cultural exclusivity they are extremely strong on tradition, even the unsavoury aspects of it. Without challenging it openly women try negotiating spaces within it. Just like in other nationalist movements, women do not challenge the concept of the state. Rather they debate over who should form the state. They fight for their own patriarchy to do it and hope that they will negotiate their own space within it after the war is won.

Further, the unusual circumstances of women's lives within rebel groups lead to a reinterpretation of their traditional roles. When they leave domestic surroundings it gives them mobility, notoriety and independence. They become soldiers, prisoners and martyrs; none of these roles fell to their lot before. Their non-traditional roles have then to be legitimised so that these can be accepted within the patriarchal structure. In a society like Assam or Nagaland where avenues for the women's public leadership role is restricted this kind of freedom requires a reinterpretation of history and tradition. New myths are sometimes created based on women's valour where their actions are interpreted as supporting patriarchy and not as working against it. Women appropriate these myths to make interventions in the public domain. But for that freedom they pay a price and sometimes that price can be severe. They may end up betraying their belief or being betrayed by it. In such situations it becomes impossible to determine whether they are victimisers or the vanquished.

Interventions for peace are largely undertaken by women. Since this falls within their traditional scope of action they do it without fear of stigmatisation and also innovate within the parameters of that tradition. In the process this becomes their training ground for the public realm and it is through these forums that they acquire leadership roles in public spaces. The case of Ms Abeiu assumes importance in this context. She became a member of NMA and was then nominated member of the town committee of Kohima. When the previous chairperson retired she competed for that post and became the first woman chairperson much to the chagrin of many men. She has achieved fame as an efficient administrator. She is aware that her role is not an extension of the traditional role of Naga women. But she interprets her interventions as extensions of the work that women do best. For example, her first public action was aimed at cleaning up the town and emphasising the importance of personal hygiene. Only later did she get involved in legal literacy campaigns and human rights awareness programmes. First, she intervened on personal (women) issues and then she entered the political realm. Women are aware that as individuals if they want to make interventions in institutionalised power politics they will be thwarted. So they negotiate and creatively expand their spaces of intervention.

Few women such as Phizo's niece, Rano Shaiza are able to take advantage of institutionalised politics and make their voices heard. But even she had to pay a great price. Her husband was killed and so were three other family members. Her background and lineage influenced her decision to stand for elections. As Phizo's niece, she had been jailed many times and was a well-known public personality. Further, she married into a family where most men were involved in politics. Her husband was a politician and so were her brothers-in-law. But even as a politician she could not make interventions in the conflict because her's was a solitary voice. Most other women however, stay away from party politics. They consider the electoral process alien to their own tradition. Also, they use non-involvement in politics as a mode of protest against Indian state-centrism. The failure of the state to make representational politics more women-friendly, makes women more amenable to the demands being made on them by non-state actors in the game of power, i.e., rebel groups (and civil society peace groups).

Women recognise that they can become important actors for peace because it is within the traditional, patriarchal definition of their roles. But the state has failed to support their leadership in peace processes at the local community or national level. This has worked to the detriment of not only women but the peace process itself. It should be emphasised that not all women may choose to play a role in reconciliation. Stereotypical association of women with peace and the care ethic should be avoided as it is contradicted by the existence of militant women in the Northeast. However, these observations do not diminish the importance and potential of women to achieve a sustainable—and from a gender perspective—

just peace. The fact that women can work for an equitable peace can be gleaned from the way they rediscover and innovate on traditional forms of conflict resolution and use it for the cause of human rights.

One of the greatest motivations for women to work for the resolution of conflict is because in times of conflict they are the natural victims. In Nagaland and Assam women work as agricultural labourers. During combing operations their work suffers. Sometimes farms are burnt and women face joblessness. In a conflict situation there are no normal times. The hours in which the women may remain in the open get drastically reduced. Further, in times of social dislocation and crisis it becomes the sole responsibility of the women to take care of family. Women in the Northeast are no exception to that thumb rule. During conflict they face desertion, molestation and isolation. Even in cities constant checks and frisking by the police lead to an unnatural life. It rests on the women to bring back normalcy as men are more vulnerable to police 'encounters'. Most women in the Northeast agree that it is in their own interest to work towards peace-making. But when peace itself appears inequitable and contrary to what women perceive to be in their self-interest they become strong bases of support for insurgent groups.

After studying women in conflict situations in Assam and Nagaland we can make some tentative generalisations. As some women pointed out, the self-interest of their own larger groups is expressed as national interest. To a Naga, often the nation is the Angami community or the state of Nagaland. The same is true for the Assamese. Their sense of alienation from the Indian state is great. They feel that people administering from distant Delhi have no conception of what they in the margins want. But there is a difference in the attitude of the Assamese and the Naga women towards conflict.

Most of our respondents in Assam portrayed an apathy towards insurgency which they associated with further criminalisation of society. They still believe that there should be protest against continuous exploitation of their resources by non-Assamese people to the detriment of the daughters and sons of the soil. But some of the insurgent groups, they believe, have lost their focus. They have become exploiters instead of resisting exploitation. They have mixed feelings about the conflict. Many believe that it is because of these groups that they have come into national focus. But others question that if the rebels are nationalists then why are their actions proving to be detrimental to the economy of Assam. The exploitation in both towns and villages is increasing. Women in urban areas in Assam are losing faith in gun-wielding insurgents. In the rural areas however, women are putting up with the demands of militant groups because in these areas they have faced the maximum brunt of army repression. They may have mixed feelings about the insurgents but they are unanimous in condemning army action. Educated women in Assam realise that none of the groups fighting for power is doing so for the cause of women. There is a growing loss of faith in the patriarchal power structures, whether they are state-centric or non-state.

In Nagaland women still retain faith in the actions of the insurgents. They say that they would prefer to give these groups less in terms of food or money but they believe that they have no alternative but to support them. Their trust in the movement for independent Nagaland remains unshaken. They would like to have peace but not at the cost of what they perceive as their independence. They believe that the insurgents are nationalists. Some of them may not be truthful to the national cause but most of them are. They understand that women may be in an unequal position in society but for the cause of nationalism they prefer to keep quiet and negotiate spaces of empowerment rather than make their protest known. One of the reasons for their support of their own power structure may also be the absence of strict social hierarchy between the genders among most of the Naga groups. They perceive the Indian power structures as more hierarchical. The ability of the Naga leaders to manipulate the concept of nationalism has made the women more supportive to their cause. To most Naga women the Indian terms for peace are unacceptable. But one problem remains. For Naga women to make positive interventions in this situation they have to undertake concerted action. But strong allegiance to their tribal groups can work against their greater unity and ability to achieve peace on their own terms.

A comparison of the situation in Assam and Nagaland shows us that women, as agents of interventions, do not operate independent of social value systems. When they perceive a conflict as 'just' they support it. In the case of Nagaland, women are convinced that the Indian state is unjustly trying to integrate people and communities which were historically autonomous. They perceive that the kind of integration favoured by the state will lead to an erosion of their own identity and self-determination. In such a situation women may make interventions for either conflict or peace but never against the ideals of their people. The Nagas have developed a national character whose existence is based on separation from the Indian nation. They are fighting for their own nation. What motivates them is a sense of nationalism.

As rebels or as human rights activists or peace workers, the women find themselves in the mainstream of the struggle for self-determination. In this struggle they do not feel marginalised. The state is therefore unable to appropriate them. The women make interventions as nationalists. They want peace but not at the cost of the autonomy of their people. Their disregard for the Indian electoral system does not portray their marginalisation in public space but rather the mainstream character of their intervention, in support of the self-determination of the Naga peoples. By not participating in the electoral process they emphasise their disregard for a system of governance established by the Indian state. The action of the women has increased the sustainability of the Naga protest.

For women in Assam the case is different. Although they believe in the original cause for the struggle, they feel betrayed by their patriarchy. This sense of betrayal has resulted from two factors. The cause for which these women were fighting was not to separate themselves from the Indian state but to acquire greater space within it so that they may make their voices heard in governance. But once their own leadership decided to compromise, the women found their own space even more compromised. Women were marginalised in governance and their ability to make their voices heard decreased. Further, after the rebels became the state, the character of the state changed. It was no longer an alien institution. So women opposing it could not be looked upon as nationalist. There remained a group of rebels but their protest was perforce against their own people who were now the state. This undermined their ability to become the voice of the Assamese as a whole. Also, women were unable to acquire leadership roles even among these rebel groups. Further, the actions of the rebels against the state led to the victimisation of many Assamese women.

The criminalisation of some rebel groups has led to further loss of face. Women are getting marginalised and alienated from the public space. Thus, whereas in 1978 more than 75 per cent of women participated in the movement, today there are precious few. Even if women do not openly protest, they are no longer active supporters of conflict. There is general disenchantment with the conflict at least in the urban areas of Assam where women are trying to protest against conflict which is also a protest against their marginalisation. The increased number of peace rallies by women in the urban areas is an indication of this trend.

In certain ways women in Nagaland have been more successful in their efforts to form peace groups than their counterparts in Assam. This is not because they are *naturally* more peaceful or because they have achieved greater political power. It is because Naga peace groups such as Watsu Mongdung and NMA have defined peace differently. They have associated peace with justice and development. Hence they have been able to survive for a longer period and rally more diverse groups to their cause. They have also made inroads in institutionalised politics and have created a space for themselves in political negotiations. Naga women were able to survive as a group because they were willing to creatively change their tactics when the situation demanded. The NMA took up health issues, social issues of de-addiction, etc., while addressing political problems. Their social functions added to their legitimacy which they used for political purposes. Further, the Assamese 'cause' is based on exclusion but the different Naga tribes can fall back on their Naga nationality based on a Naga identity. Although sometimes their specific tribal identities work against their unity, they can still rally around the 'cause' of an independent Nagaland.

Another reason for Naga women to be able to intervene in conflict more successfully is that they have integrated themselves within the larger political movement sponsored by the Naga Hohos. Women's interventions become more effective in democratic situations. The Naga Hohos have made an effort to give women a space and voice within the larger mobilisation for peace. So the NMA and such other groups do not have to fight the Hohos which are predominantly male groups for survival. But in Assam the women find themselves in constant opposition to groups led by men. Hence it becomes extremely difficult for women to sustain their movements for peace. The Nagas have realised that the women have a special role to play in peace movements. Thus they make efforts to include the feminine voice. In this context it is important to mention that when women talk of peace they do not do so against their cause. Ceasefire to them is a strategy for survival until further negotiations. They believe that once they achieve victory in their political struggle their victimisation will end. History proves that victory does not automatically end the marginalisation of women. But discourses in peace can help women appropriate their share of the political voice as is portrayed by women's groups in Nagaland.

NOTES

1. For a discussion on the watershed theme, see Joan W. Scott, 'Rewriting History', in Margaret Randolph Higonnet, Jane Jenson, Sonya Michel and Margaret Collins, eds, *Behind the Lines: Gender and the Two World Wars*, Yale University Press, New Haven, 1987.

2. Hardly any secondary literature is available on women in conflict in the Northeast. In fact very little has been done on women in conflict in South Asia. Only recently an effort was made to study gender as a category in partition. In studies on women's situation in conflict in the Third World the theme of victimisation predominates. The other popular theme is the biography of extraordinary women such as Funmilayo Ransome-Kuti in Nigeria or Doria Shafik in Egypt. Here an effort is made to move away from either of these two themes and discuss ordinary women who are caught in conflict. Some of them may emerge as extraordinary as a result of their experiences. But neither the leaders of the community nor the victims of violence are the focus of the study. Their voices are heard only when they mix with many other voices of women living in conflict.

3. Subir Bhaumik, *Insurgent Crossfire in Northeast India*, Lancer, New Delhi, 1996, p. 41.

4. Joyshanker Hazarika, *Geopolitics of North East India: A Strategical Study*, Gyan Publishing House, New Delhi, 1996, p. 1.

5. B.G. Verghese, *India's Northeast Resurgent: Ethnicity, Insurgency, Governance and Development*, Konark, Delhi, 1996, pp. 280–311.

6. Bhaumik, *Insurgent Crossfire*, n. 3, p. 40.

7. Paula Banerjee and Lipi Ghosh, 'Towards a Shared Vision: The Border Between India, Myanmar and Bangladesh', *The Journal of North East*, Vol. 22, No. 2, October 1998, pp. 1–4.

8. Sir Robert Reid, *History of the Frontier Areas Bordering Assam, From 1883–1941*, Shillong, 1942, p. 295.

9. Amalendu Guha, *Planter Raj to Swaraj*, People's Publishing House, Guwahati, 1977, p. 320.

10. R.N. Prasad, 'Evolution of Party Politics in Mizoram', *North Eastern Affairs*, Vol. 2, Annual, 1973, p. 47.

11. S. Chaube, *Hill Politics in North East India*, Orient Longman, New Delhi, 1973, pp. 69–70 and 140–45.

12. According to B.G. Verghese, the Bodo Autonomous Council (BAC) areas may soon become a state.

13. *Ananda Bazar Patrika*, 16 October 1994, pp. 5 (i)–(ii).

14. Tiplut Nongbri, 'Ethnicity and Political Activism in North East: Tribal Identity and State Policy', in P.S. Datta, ed., *The North East and the Indian State: Paradoxes of a Periphery*, Vikas, New Delhi, 1995, p. 54.

15. A. Sunil Achay, 'Insurgency in Nagaland', in Datta, *The North-East and the Indian State*, n. 14, p. 227.

16. S.M. Krishnatry, 'The Return of Peace', *North-East Sun*, 28 November 1996.

17. *Statistical Handbook of Nagaland, 1997*, Directorate of Economics and Statistics, Government of Nagaland, Kohima.

18. Surya Kumar, 'The Battered Half', *North East Sun*, 15–31 July 1996.

19. *Statistical Handbook of Nagaland, 1997*, n. 17.

20. 'Women in the Hills', *Himalaya Today*, September–November 1997.

21. Kumar, 'The Battered Half', n. 18.

22. Aparna Mahanta, 'Problems of the Women's Movement in Assam', *North-Eastern Politics*, Vol. 1, No. 2, February 1990, pp. 11–12.

23. Kunja Medhi and Anuradha Datta, 'Constraints of Women in Political Participation: A Case Study of Assam', in Renu Debi, ed., *Women of Assam*, Omsons Publications, New Delhi, 1994, pp. 73–80.

24. The actual names of the respondents are not given for security reasons. Only actual names of those women leaders who have been interviewed and who have gone on record with similar assertions appear.

25. 'Rape: The Hatred Weapon of Indian Armed Forces', A Report of the Manab Adhikar Sangram Samiti (MASS), Guwahati, August 1998.

26. We could not find Nilima after two days. From our informants we heard that Nilima was in town for treatment. She has severe gynaecological and

stomach problems. She suffers from ulcer and other kinds of problems associated with malnutrition. She cannot undertake long-term treatments for fear of capture. She could not be admitted to a hospital due to fear of exposure.

27. Krishna Das, 'Better Half Who?', *North-East Sun*, Vol. 3, No. 1, 1-14 August 1997.
28. Rabindra K. Choudhury, 'Work Participation and Economic Status of Women', in Debi, *Women of Assam*, n. 23, pp. 38-55.
29. *First Annual Report 1994-95*, The State Commission for Women, Assam, Guwahati, 1995.
30. Mridula Saharia, address on the occasion of convention on the 'Role of Women in Preventing Terrorism and Violation of Human Rights on the Present Day Society', Chairperson, Assam State Commission for Women, Guwahati, December 1995.
31. Interview with Dr A. Richter, 8 December 1998, The Hague.
32. Nava Thakuria, 'Women Awareness by KGNM Trust', *North-East Sun*, Vol. 2, No. 8, 1996, p. 16.
33. Shakuntala Chowdhury in an interview on 27 December 1998.
34. 'Women for Peace', *North-East Sun*, Vol. 3, No. 12, 15-31 January 1998.
35. The Mayon women have raised such a demand. Interview with Gina Shangkham, President, Mayon Sanuw Ruwrkheh, 11 September 1999, Dhulikhel, Nepal.
36. Text of the folk tale narrated by Elizabeth in the 4th assembly of Naga Women's Union of Manipur in 1997 at Tamenglong. Reprinted in *Raisurung*, Fourth Issue, 1998, published by Naga Women's Union of Manipur, Imphal.
37. K.S. Paul Leo, 'Naga Women and Human Rights', *Raisurang*, Fourth Issue, 1998, published by Naga Women's Union of Manipur, Imphal, p. 14.
38. Excerpt of an interview by Deepak Dewan, Political Editor, *North-East Sun*, Vol. 3, No. 16, 15-31 March 1998.
39. *Constitution of the Naga Mothers Association*, Reprinted in Kohima, 1992.
40. Statement made at the Northeast Regional Workshop on 'Women & Regional Histories', Guwahati, 24-25 June 1999.
41. Monalisa Changkija, 'Of Rights Violations', *North-East Sun*, 15-31 October 1997, p. 27.
42. Susan Geiger has spoken of gendered experiences leading to 'situationally specific economic, social, cultural, national, and racial/ethnic realities', in 'What's So Feminist about Doing Women's Oral History?', in Cheryl Johnson-Odim and Margaret Strobel, eds, *Expanding the Boundaries of Women's History: Essays on Women in the Third World*, Indiana University Press, Indianapolis, 1992, p. 306. I posit that all these realities are political realities as gendered experience is essentially a political experience.
43. *North-East Herald*, 26 January 1999, p. 1.

ANIS HAROON

Introduction

In Pakistan, the province of Sindh has in the last couple of decades
seen what is the equivalent of an armed conflict situation with cycles
of widespread violence on a massive scale. At its peak in 1995, Karachi
alone saw 2,095 people killed. The participants in this conflict have
been the state, the government, political parties, as well as groups/
mafias and individuals with their own agendas and axes to grind. As
the violence spread, it became increasingly difficult to identify the
actors and issues.

The conflict is symptomatic of a gradual process of fragmentation of Pakistani society, the effects of which culminated in violence, first in Karachi, and then all over Sindh. The roots of the
violence lie in a history of deep-seated, real and perceived dissatisfaction and injustices.

The group most heavily involved in armed conflict has been the
Muttahida Qaumi Movement (MQM), the Urdu-speaking immigrants from India who make up the largest section of the population in Karachi. The state, in collusion with the political party in
power, has used its machinery to crush the forces opposing the government in power.

In this conflict women have been the hardest hit—used by their own groups and abused by the rest. The effects of the MQM conflict have changed the lives of women and society as a whole. Women have been exploited and repressed by all the groups involved, be it the state, the government in power, political parties, religious bigots or so-called nationalist forces. They have been used or abused, as the situation demanded, and eventually dumped.

This chapter analyses an initiative by the Women's Action Forum (WAF) to break the isolation of the MQM women trapped in violence and explore the possibility of bringing women from different, even opposing, communities together on a neutral platform. When a woman gets caught up in a national or ethnic identity conflict, is it possible for her to still see herself as a woman, to share common grievances and empathise with other women? The WAF initiative explores the possibility of building a multi-ethnic polity defined by women's politics and women's ways of doing things.

Background to Disaffection

To understand the sources of the MQM conflict, we need to look at the political mix of the population in Karachi—the multiplicity of ethnicities, religions, sects and political groupings. Karachi is in effect a mini Pakistan. Moreover, state policies have aimed at consolidating central power and have refused devolution of power thus aggravating regional tensions. Populations have been further fragmented through policies exacerbating ethnic and sectarian divisions.

In Pakistan, all governments—whether they comprised political parties, and hence were democratic or army dictatorships—have employed the politics of convenience. Their focus has been on the narrow interest of getting to power. For this, they have appeased some groups at the cost of others, compromising the national interest.

The MQM is a political party mainly confined to the Urdu-speaking immigrant population from India with its power base in urban Sindh. It came into existence in 1978 and caught on as a party by 1980. Its main focus has been the social, political and economic rights of the immigrant community. This brought the MQM in direct confrontation with Sindhi nationalists, who were agitating for the rights of the Sindhi-speaking population. They refused to accept Mohajirs[1] as their partners in sharing power and jobs.

After the partition of the Indian subcontinent in 1947, the Mohajirs had settled down in the urban centres of Sindh. The two-nation theory propounded by the Muslim League (a party for Muslims led by Mohammed Ali Jinnah) had divided the Muslims and the Hindus in the subcontinent. The Muslim League demanded a separate homeland for the Muslims comprising the Muslim majority areas. This resulted in the creation of Pakistan on the partition of the subcontinent amidst a huge carnage in which a million people lost their lives. Several million migrated. A large number of Muslims from the Hindu majority areas came to Pakistan in search of safety and better economic options.

The bulk of the population came to Karachi, the only port city. They were awarded evacuee properties left behind by the Hindus. 'Soon Sindh became a multi-ethnic province with the majority of jobs held by Mohajirs and agricultural land was appropriated by the Punjabis (awarded to armed forces personnel).'[2] Later on a large number of Pathans migrated to Karachi as construction and factory workers. They took over the transport system in the coming years and became a powerful community during Ayub Khan's military regime (1958–69).

The ruling party, the Muslim League, comprised mainly the ruling and land-owning elite of Punjab and suppressed the impulses towards provincial self-assertion of the movement for greater Baluchistan, the Sarhad Pashtoon movement and Sindhi nationalism. The Muslim League government created its own allies in each of these provinces to suppress these movements and choke the voices of dissent. The Mohajirs who had left their homes for a unified Pakistan became the natural allies of the ruling Punjabi-dominated army-bureaucracy oligarchy.

In the first general elections based on adult franchise in 1970, Karachi was polarised between the socialist Pakistan People's Party (PPP) and the religious parties upholding the banner of Islam, Quran and Kashmir. The latter's opposition to socialism suited the business and middle classes. Also, the Mohajirs disliked Bhutto and the rise of PPP, though a sizeable Urdu-speaking population did back the PPP in the 1970 elections.

After the emergence of Bangladesh in 1971, the two-nation theory which provided the basis for Pakistan was no longer intact. Nationalist movements were emerging in Baluchistan and Sindh, while the Pakhtuns had always held on to their separate political identity. But this fragmentation did not permeate the public consciousness of the forces in control at the centre, which regardless were centralising power. For the first time, the Mohajirs felt alienated from mainstream politics which so far they had participated in along with the ruling army and bureaucracy. In time, as they were no longer needed by the ruling Punjabi elite, the Mohajirs began to lose their substantial hold on the bureaucracy. As for the army, it remained dominated by Punjab.

This coincided with the rise of Sindhi nationalism and PPP rule was seen as its manifestation. Tension arose between the *vaderas* (landowners) holding power in Sindh and the educated Sindhi middle class seeking new jobs and opportunities. The first ethnic riots between the Urdu- and Sindhi-speaking population took place in 1972 when Sindhi was introduced as an official language in Sindh.

Mohajirs tried to align and re-align themselves with Pathans and Punjabis to further their perception of a united Pakistan. In the next martial law under Zia-ul-Haq, the Mohajirs supported Zia-ul-Haq when he stripped Bhutto of his power and hanged him. The cleavage between Sindhis and Mohajirs sharpened. The 1985 elections on a non-party basis gave impetus to ethnic and sectarian considerations. The ethnic riots between Mohajirs and Pathans started in the same year and reached their peak in December with the Aligarh Colony massacre.[3]

Later, when the MQM was faced with a backlash, the MQM supremo, Altaf Hussain claimed that it was not an ethnic party, that it represented lower- and middle-class people including Punjabis and Pakhtuns who had settled in Sindh for over 25 years. This claim however lacked conviction. What was widely accepted was that MQM managed to rally people on economic issues rather than religious or sectarian slogans.

Nature of Conflict

The MQM has its origins in the All Pakistan Mohajir Students Organisation (APMSO) which was formed in 1978. The MQM announced its entry into the political arena on 7 August 1986 in a rally at Nishter Park to the accompaniment of celebratory gunfire. Since its inception and amazing success at the local body polls in 1987 (claiming the mayorship of Karachi and Hyderabad), the organisation has been involved in confrontations with almost all the ethnic and political forces in urban Sindh. First they wiped out the religious parties which had held sway for years. Then came the political parties, Punjabi-Paktoon Ittehad and the Sindhis. Later, bloody battles were fought in the congested streets of Karachi and other cities.

The 1988 election saw a brief period of respite when the PPP and MQM formed a coalition government in Sindh. But soon disagreements arose and MQM withdrew support and collaborated with Nawaz Sharif, the leader of the Punjab Muslim League. Things took an ugly turn in 1992 when Nawaz Sharif's government ordered a military operation against MQM militants, alleging that Karachi was being run as a 'state within a state'. It is difficult to assign the major responsibility for the mass killings in Sindh. It is alleged that in-fighting between the two factions of MQM (Altaf and Haqiqi) resulted in targeted killings.[4] But the law enforcing agencies are known to have played an incriminating role. The MQM responded by disbanding its organisational network; its leaders and activists went into hiding. Altaf Hussain took refuge in London and still operates from there.

Karachi, a city of 12 million people, came in the grip of unprecedented violence. Hyderabad and other cities were also affected. Before the military operations, abductions for ransom and the killing of opponents had become routine. Afterwards there was pitched confrontation between the MQM and government agencies. A faction of MQM dissidents was propped up and supported by the law-enforcing agencies. The jails and police lock-ups were bursting at the seams. In 1993 Benazir returned to power. The military operations continued. The two factions of MQM targeted each other's activists and unabated murders and atrocities were committed. It was dubbed a 'mini-insurgency' and law-enforcing agencies were given unlimited powers to deal with the situation. The year 1995 was the worst. It claimed 2,095 lives in Karachi alone.

Karachi division has five districts, the most affected were districts central and east. The composition of Karachi's population by age group reveals that the under-30 years group accounts for approximately one-fourth of the city's population. The highest percentage of the population, that is 26 per cent resides in district central, and 24 per cent of the households live in district east. The district central also has the highest literacy rate in the city, which is 76 per cent (66 per cent being the average literacy rate of the city) and over 25 per cent are graduates and degree holders. The concentration of the Urdu-speaking population is 74 per cent in district central and 61 per cent in district east. It makes Karachi a city of migrants from India, and two million (illegal) immigrants from Bangladesh and Burma and job seekers from all over Pakistan. What affects Karachi must affect all Pakistan.[5]

The demographic data shows very clearly that MQM has the support of the middle class, and the young, educated urban population. They are the ones who are unemployed and believe they are disadvantaged due to their ethnic background. The small shop owners, artisans, skilled and unskilled workers were drawn into the rank and file of the MQM. A large number of women also joined the MQM along with their men, due to the same reasons. They recreated a Mohajir identity by calling all Urdu-speaking women their 'sisters' and wearing bangles and *dupattas* (scarves) in the MQM flag colours and taking an oath of allegiance to the Mohajir cause.

Women in MQM

The situation of the MQM women like other women of Pakistan, had deteriorated as a result of the so-called Islamisation process. On top of it they were dragged into the ethnic conflict and became targets of violence, both by the state machinery and the warring factions. A large number of women were affected by displacement, loss of male family members, death of close relatives and continued harassment by the police. Many ended up as sole caretakers of the family. One could see them in newspaper photographs crying over dead bodies, queuing up outside *thanas*, jails and courts. Women were also being arrested, killed and tortured. Though the direct victims were not many, numerically speaking, every second household in the conflict zone was affected. It became a 'no-go' area for the rest of the city. Women from other urban centres were also facing the consequences of violence. But Karachi was the city where the battle for control was being fought.

The MQM mobilised a large number of women. Since 1947, there has not been such a major political mobilisation of women. In February 1989, 7,500 women workers enlisted in the MQM in a single day, and broke the barriers which hitherto had confined women in their homes. It was the first time in the history of the country that so many female political workers were mobilised in a single city. It was said to have brought women at par with men in shouldering responsibilities. An advertisement in a newspaper celebrated their coming out—'Women are saluted for their exemplary struggle to make the *Haq Parast Movement* [Urdu name for MQM] a success'. 'The Mohajir women were exhilarated and adorned themselves with dopattas and glass bangles in the white, red and green colours of the MQM flag.'[6]

The reason that this was possible was because the MQM was an urban middle-class phenomenon and women were under less social pressure than their counterparts in the rural areas. Even those who wore *burqas* (veil) had no restrictions on their mobility. In all MQM meetings and processions women were very visible. But very few were in top positions. Virtually not a single woman was put up as a national assembly candidate in the general election, in spite of thousands of active workers. Somehow the MQM leadership always thought that the time was not ripe for fielding women candidates. Despite the mass presence of women in the MQM, they were not involved in decision-making. In fact, the militant and fascistic nature of the MQM left very little room for political manoeuvre. Their opinion was not sought, their voices never heard, they were just there to implement.

The 'Mohajir identity' was recreated in women by the menfolk. Undoubtedly the state's violent response to reassert its exclusive centralising identity increased regional identity politics. In such situations, not only will women's identity get subsumed, but they will be expected to embrace the community identity being redefined by fathers and husbands and their symbolic extension in the person of the MQM patriarchal leader, Altaf Hussain. As Nighat Saeed Khan describes in her introduction to 'State and Ideology',

> Identities will be forged by men whether Sindhi, Baluchi, Christian, Mohajirs, working class or peasants. Women will be expected to choose the identity imposed by the husbands and fathers. An appeal to their family loyalty, motherhood and wifehood will override their identities as individuals with the right to choose their own course of life. Economic and other emotional factors will also be a form of pressure on them to choose with the family.[7]

A number of women expressed the need for 'Mohajir identity' in terms of better jobs for their sons or husbands. Some spoke of emotional blackmail as well as threats from their men. Interviews conducted with activists, affectees and sympathisers of the MQM reveal that women's participation and commitment to the MQM movement comes from more than just economic reasons. Women see the MQM as embodying a struggle against injustice, and hence their commitment is both at an emotional as well as cerebral level. They justify MQM's stand quoting several examples of nepotism by Pathans, Punjabis and Sindhis. As such there is no deep-rooted hatred against Sindhis, but they are definitely considered rivals in competing for jobs.

All communal and ethnic movements create their own icons and symbols to be used for political ends. The leadership seeks legitimacy by popularising these symbols among the masses. Masses of women were mobilised for a show of strength by the MQM. For example, all over the city huge iron gates were installed in the name of providing protection to 'Mohajir mothers and sisters'. Women went door-to-door to collect funds for erecting iron gates. The imaginary threat was supposed to be from Sindhis who threatened to attack and rape them. In fact these gates were meant to protect their own militant men, but it was carried out in the name of women and family honour.

Out of their own inherent sense of insecurity, women accepted the perceived threat of rape and molestation. 'We did not question the use of arms and ammunition within the movement. We were convinced that it was for the safety of our sons and daughters,' remarked a diehard activist, but she refused to be involved in any arms transaction herself. 'I knew my husband used to carry guns and he said it was for his protection.' He was the most sought-after person (by the security forces) due to his involvement with the movement. 'The police was after us all the time and we were fighting for the Mohajir cause. We were being pushed against the wall by the establishment.'

There were all sorts of stories of women being involved as couriers, protecting militants, running torture cells, transferring arms and hiding guns for their men in demonstrations. How far this was true and to what extent they were involved, whether it was voluntary or coercive, remains an enigma.

As far as the activist women were concerned they just obeyed the party's commands. The women rallied around the leadership for the Mohajir cause and generally played a subservient role. They were motivated to have faith in the leadership, accept their decisions unconditionally and strictly abide by them. Some of the leading women workers publicly expressed their commitment and total faith in the leadership of Altaf Hussain. They also took an oath of allegiance and unconditional support. It was not for the cause but to their leader. The type of slogans that became popular were: 'death for all who betray leadership', 'we need our leader and not the destination'. A few women workers confided, 'There was a remarkable difference of treatment between those who took an oath of allegiance and those who didn't. We were just supporters and not allowed to attend indoor meetings, only religious ceremonies and demonstrations which were used as a show of strength.'

A variant of how sexist ideology gets used in conflict was demonstrated in the manner in which betrayal was constructed. In 1993 in

Lahore the party central command was obliged to take an oath to remain faithful to the leadership. Those who violated it 'would be mother and sister fuckers'. Neither the MQM women nor women of any other political party objected to the use of sexist language. The Women's Action Forum was the only organisation to lodge a strong protest through a press release.

MQM in Crisis: Women Take Responsibility

The MQM was in the throes of a crisis as the establishment had propped up a 'dissident group' (MQM Haqiqi) against Altaf Hussain. It was the militant faction of the MQM which had developed serious differences with the leadership. The party went through a process of purging and eliminating doubtful persons. The dissident group with full backing of the establishment went on a rampage in June 1992, taking over party offices, tearing Altaf Hussain's life-size posters and eliminating the diehards. Altaf Hussain fled to London and has hot returned yet. This was a major blow to MQM's myth of invincibility.

Women workers were not targeted but with their men being eliminated or going underground, their roles changed. They were called upon to take over responsibilities in the headquarters. They were asked to give day and night duties, receive phone calls and organise religious ceremonies (Quran reading, etc.). It was said to be a cover for passing on important messages and instructions.

Things took a further ugly turn when Nawaz Sharif's government fell and Benazir Bhutto took over in 1993. The army operation continued but it was twisted into a Sindhi-Mohajir conflict. Benazir Bhutto was seen as the oppressor and the focus shifted from Punjab to the Sindh leadership. In Hyderabad the situation was already tense since the massacre of Mohajirs on 30 September for which a Sindhi nationalist party was held responsible. Sindhis fortified themselves in separate localities and lines were drawn between Sindhi and Mohajir localities.

In the clashes between the MQM and the security forces, women were not spared. They were used by their men and attacked by the others. During one notorious army raid on Pucca Qila, an MQM stronghold, women came out to resist. They were holding the Quran and Zia-ul-Haq's pictures in their hands and raised slogans against Benazir. The men were following behind. It was alleged that women were carrying guns in their *burqas* which they passed on to the men. Some militants fled clad in *burqas*. The women were kept in the forefront by the organisers to provide a cover. In the violent clash several women were injured and manhandled. Sources in the MQM claimed that horse-riding personnel were let loose on them. There was no evidence to support this claim. The women themselves narrated their woes to the Human Rights Commission's investigating team. There were allegations of rape but the investigation team could not find any proof. On their part, Sindhi nationalists also alleged the rape of women by Mohajir terrorists but no victim came forward. It could not be ascertained if there was any rape on either side.

Even in the most violent phase of MQM it was not established that women were playing an active militant role. They were fully aware that their men used guns but they were not involved in any planning. At that time, no woman even admitted to being used to transfer arms. The allegations of torture cells being run under their patronage was vehemently denied by women publicly and privately. Though as we shall examine later, we did come across some hearsay evidence, but the woman in question did not admit to it. However, there is no denying that MQM women approved and justified the actions of their party. They did not question the use of violence and fully supported the 'mission of their sons, husbands and brothers'. They themselves were convinced that the fight for Mohajir rights was vital for their survival.

One could attribute these attitudes to their lack of proper education and exposure, common in the women workers of all political parties but actually the seeds of subservience lie in our patriarchal culture. Even educated women leaders did not challenge or find anything wrong with their subservient role. The MQM's only woman senator Nasrin Jalil[8] expressed similar views in an informal meeting, when she was interviewed while under house arrest. 'Women of our party perform all office chores. They clean, sweep, make tea, make calls, receive messages and attend public meetings when they are asked to. They are not involved in decision making because politics is not their field. Most of them are not educated and do not understand the complexities of the situation.' Replying to a question about a women's agenda, she said, 'there is no specific agenda but we believe in equality . . . whatever it means. Our leader always makes it a point to address women especially and praise their role in the struggle.'

Another woman leader praising the leadership said, he (Altaf Hussain) always addresses them as mothers and sisters. Often he shows his concern by asking boys to marry girls who have lost their brothers in the struggle. She quoted the example of several such marriages. 'In better times our public service committee organised marriage ceremonies and provided *jahez* [dowry] for poor girls.'

Even in an urban-based, middle-class party, the role envisaged for women, from top to bottom, was no different. It was the same gender-based stereotyping. Women were used as a reserve force whenever required, otherwise they would perform their household duties. The party leaders, when confronted by women's groups, always took the plea that they were working in a crisis situation and could expose their women to the hazards of elected politics. But that did not stop the MQM men from sending women to violent demonstrations, to *gherao* (encircle) police *thanas* and to collect bodies of militants when it was too dangerous for the men to come out. Women have even carried bodies to graveyards. In Muslim culture women never go to bury their dead. But cultural norms and social practices are put aside when women are needed in a struggle. Even their privacy and sanctity is violated.

In 1996, when an MQM activist's sister was allegedly gang-raped by terrorists of the dissident faction, the girl and her mother were dragged to a press conference, escorted by the party leaders. The proceedings of the conference were relayed to London on telephone. Addressing the media, Altaf Hussain expressed concern for the victim and appealed to his 'good boys' to come forward and marry her. There was complete lack of sensitivity about how traumatic all this could be for the victim and her family. There was no understanding that if the boys started queuing up to ask for her hand in marriage, it would add to her misery. The family quietly left their house and nobody heard about them later on. Women's groups were denied access to the victim. However, they did make a hue and cry about the politics of rape and women being used as tools.

Women's groups in Pakistan, especially the WAF, resent the patronising attitude towards a rape victim. On the one hand there is an attempt to minimise the crime against society. Also, the person who has been violated has the right to decide whether she wants to reveal her identity or get married. The trauma of rape continues for a long time and each person resolves it in a different way. Nobody has the right to impose marriage as a solution. Moreover, the notion of 'honour' linked with rape is further feminised and used with negative connotations. Women suffer not only as a biological entity but as collective social beings also. In case of a rape, the honour of the family becomes the dominant discourse rather than the violation of a woman's body. The immediate concern is with marriage, which is supposed to restore her honour. In all patriarchal societies, the ideology of the state determines the dominant discourse. The women's movement has to define an alternative discourse, keeping in mind the feminist perspectives.

Regarding the status and role of women in MQM, we can arrive at a few tentative generalisations:

(i)   A large number of women were involved, but they played a passive role.

(ii) Their passive role changed in a crisis situation when they took over responsibilities which men had been performing.

(iii) The women undertook unprecedented tasks like protecting militants, burying their dead, encircling *thanas* and transferring arms. But there is no evidence of their involvement as militants.

(iv) They were subjected to violence and torture by warring factions and law-enforcing agencies, e.g., arrests, harassment and taken as hostages to induce male relatives to confess.

(v)   Masses of women were mobilised for a show of strength but were not given any share in power and decision making.

(vi)   There was no specific agenda for women in the MQM.
(vii) With a few exceptions, MQM women were from the lower middle class.

The WAF Initiative

The Women's Action Forum is a radical organisation which has taken a political stand on various issues from a broad feminist perspective. In the wake of violence and state repression in the urban centres of Sindh, WAF, like others committed to peace, felt helpless and shocked. Political parties blamed each other for the violence. The newspapers were thriving on the number of bodies being found everyday. Torture and killing were assuming new forms and intensity. After all what could a small group of women do in the midst of an armed conflict? Who would listen to us? How should we respond to the situation?

Twice in the past, WAF's attempt to contact MQM women had failed. First, in 1988 WAF had tried to contact them as part of a peace-making process in Karachi, but the high command disallowed it. On the other hand the Sindhiani Tehrik (women's wing of the nationalist Sindhi party Awami Tehrik), a counterpart of WAF, declined to have any dialogue with MQM women. Sindhiani did not agree with WAF's position of bringing such diverse groups on the same table.

Again in 1989, on the issue of gang rape, WAF contacted women from all political parties for a demonstration but met with a refusal from the MQM. Since neither the girl raped nor the rapist was a Mohajir, it was not an issue for them. This amply illustrates the fragmentation in Sindh. Women who did not accept this view, dared not protest.

Making Contact

In Karachi, the situation in 1995 was very tense and many areas were inaccessible. We had heard how the women of MQM men were isolated and under tremendous pressure. (The author is a member of the Women's Action Forum.) We realised that it was not possible to go to them directly, as the women were not ready to talk to strangers. We spent a lot of time finding some common contacts. We tried to discover a common link through friends of victims' families. But their families were scared and even relatives had stopped visiting them. We asked them to explore the possibility of speaking to us. Some of them responded, others totally refused. But it gave us the breakthrough we needed. Two teams, comprising two members of WAF went into the affected areas like Nazimabad, Golimar, Jehangir Road and Korangi. We managed to contact eight families. Our focus was on those affected by violence, irrespective of their political and ethnic affiliation. We even contacted the families of the law-enforcing personnel. The idea was to bring these women together on one platform and listen to their suffering and to break their isolation. As a women's group we wanted to ascertain the reality and share the grief.

We had lengthy discussions over what our purpose was and what we wanted to achieve. Some of us thought we might be able to bring women together for a peace initiative like the Mothers Front in Sri Lanka. Others thought this goal was too ambitious. But there was consensus on one point—women are suffering and we need to hear them. Hence it was necessary to reach out to other violence affected families and not only the MQM.

Witness to Violence

We wrote letters on behalf of the Women's Action Forum, War Against Rape and Karachi Peace Committee (Human Rights Commission of Pakistan [HRCP] joined later) asking women to come to a meeting to listen to the tales of suffering of other women. 'As they talk, we shall only listen; and in this act of listening, we will be witness to the violence inflicted on them. How the listening affects us cannot be predicted. However, we hope that we would experience a solidarity that would strengthen our determination to work for peace'.[9]

It was further emphasised in the invitation that,

> In organising this collective act of listening, we have been non-partisan. We believe that all violence must be condemned and empathy established with those women who have suffered, irrespective of their class, creed, religion, sect and ethnicity. We believe that peace is an imperative for human development, and can be claimed if all those who believe in peace and non-violence come together.

It was decided that nothing was to be disclosed to the media. We invited selected journalists, writers, human rights activists, and representatives of lawyers and psychiatrists. The response was almost 100 per cent.

On 23 March 1996, more than 50 women turned up and out of the five families who had committed themselves, three women showed up. The other two women were not permitted by their menfolk. Of those who came, one was the wife of a police official, who had been allegedly killed by terrorists. The other was a teacher whose young daughter was killed by Pakistan Rangers (paramilitary). The third was an MQM activist's wife, who was shot in an alleged encounter.

We called the meeting 'witness to violence'. At first there was nothing but apprehension on both sides. But once the ice was broken and empathy established, the women spoke of their grief for the first time. It was a painful process.

Mrs Qamar, a middle-class teacher, had lost a 21-year-old daughter. 'It was dark. We had gone to drop a relative who had come to visit us,' she said. 'While coming back we were stopped by rangers. My son got nervous and didn't apply the brakes fast enough. They fired and we drove for our lives. We were very near our house. It was only when she didn't come out of the car that we realised she was hit in the chest. It was an instant death.' The mother choked. The women were sobbing.

Next was a police inspector's wife, who was widowed with five children. Accused of killing many activists, he was allegedly killed by MQM terrorists. Several eyebrows were raised at her presence.

But when she narrated how she was alone when her husband was shot in the car and she fell unconscious, women could feel her pain. 'When I came to my senses, he was in a pool of blood and breathing his last. I ran from pillar to post but no one came to help. Somehow my family came to know and rushed to the scene. Since then our house is not the same. I don't know what he did outside but he was a caring father and a good husband. Now I am left alone. The government hasn't paid any compensation.'

The government had announced compensation which was given to some of the police personnel. The successor government, under an agreement, awarded a large sum of money for the victims of violence, which was distributed by the MQM to the faithful. Some women refused to take the compensation and stuck to their demand for a judicial inquiry and punishment for the killers. One woman, Aziza, refused compensation for her two sons.

I have lost two sons. There was no FIR registered against them in any *thana* of Karachi. One was killed by an unknown assailant and the other was gunned down in a fake police encounter. I swear by God, my son never brought any arms into the house. He was in charge of the students' wing. Our family is very close and my sons shared everything with me. They were active workers but not involved in any crime. I challenge the government to prove that he was a criminal and I will accept it, but nobody has an answer. He was caught unawares because of his friends. He was just being used. He did not know their true identity. How can there be any compensation for my flesh and blood? I will not accept anything for two precious lives. Who made them criminals, if they were involved in any crimes?

Some of the survivors did take the money but the women, especially younger ones, had no control over it. Nazia was an 18-year-old girl with an infant on her lap. She was witness to a fake police encounter in which her husband and three others were killed. She was two months pregnant and taken into police custody as she was the sole witness. She was taken to Islamabad but was released after she gave birth to a daughter.

She was pale and nervous as she spoke.

My husband was not staying home because of the army raids. We had been married for only a few months. He would visit every night and we had to keep changing places. I didn't like it all. I used to tell him, I want to lead a normal life. That night he came with three other friends. I told him that I was pregnant. He was thrilled and decided to spend the night. His friends did not like the idea but he forced them. He promised me that very soon we would get out of the country and live peacefully with our child. At 3 a.m. the law-enforcing agencies raided the house. They took everyone away, including my father and brothers. I was put in the same car as my husband. Early in the morning, all four of them were put in the car with their hands chained and shot. The sight of so much blood made me dizzy and I collapsed.

The next thing I remember was being put on a plane. I asked about my husband. They laughed and used filthy language. I spent seven months in solitary confinement. My father and brothers were kept separately. They used to tell me that they have killed them. No male member is spared and if I give birth to a boy, he will be killed. They used to kick me in the stomach. God knows how I survived. [She broke down.] My mother was an activist but I was not involved in anything. My husband was living . . . most probably hiding in our house and he had asked for my hand. My family agreed and that is how I got married. I knew he was a hardcore worker and had many cases on him. But I loved him and he treated me very nicely. The police wanted him dead or alive and had announced a huge reward. I was convinced that he was fighting for a great cause but never believed that he could be a terrorist. He was kind-hearted and couldn't kill an ant. I did see a gun on him but it was for his own protection. He wanted to leave everything and go away. Like every girl I used to dream of a peaceful home with my husband and children. He was sick and tired of running and living in terror. It all came to an end.

We interviewed Nazia again, three years later. She said,

Before, I was living but dead. I got a new life when I started going to WAF meetings. Everywhere else, I had to hide my identity but there I was myself . . . felt wanted and cared for. I loved to work with the group but the higher-ups stopped us. We started going to Nine Zero [MQM Hq]. For a while they bothered about me and wanted me to get into active politics. Then I realised it is not easy for a young widow to be in politics. Every other day somebody would make a pass and there would be a scandal. Once again I succumbed to family pressure and married my husband's younger brother. He is nice, not so actively involved but still when things go bad, the police hound him. Recently, he was arrested and I sold my gold bangles to get his bail. The party does not do anything for us anymore. We got nothing . . . not even the compensation for the killing of my husband. My in-laws got that money. Now I have another son. We are in a crisis again. I am fed up of living in constant fear.

These narratives portray the situation of women caught in the conflict. There were mothers, wives and daughters of MQM activists, militants, law-enforcing personnel and innocent citizens. Their suffering as women was a common factor. They could empathise and share their grief. For WAF it was a unique experience which emotionally drained us. For these women, who were suffering in isolation it was energising. They felt lighter and strengthened. These women had lost sons, husbands and brothers. They were running from pillar to post for the release of male family members who were in jail.

As the information spread about our fortnightly meetings, the number of distressed women started swelling. Just listening to them was not enough any more. They needed legal help, medical help and financial support. The WAF, being a non-funded pressure group, was not equipped to handle it alone. Realising that most of the women were suffering from trauma, we inducted the help of the Pakistan Mental Health Association (PMHA). They sent a team of two psychiatrists weekly. The WAF members started going to jails, *thanas* and courts. We organised meetings with lawyers and police officials. Our stand was very clear. The due process of law should be followed. If the courts find them guilty they must be punished but their families should not be harassed. They should be given access to relatives in jails.

The WAF took on a political campaign when on 13 April 1996, it organised a public meeting asking for the repeal of terrorist courts. Lawyers, journalists and police officials were invited. The women who had initially been reluctant to speak to us, were now ready to speak on a public platform. They had gained tremendous confidence and trust in us. That night one of the speakers was arrested. She had lost a son who was killed in a fake police encounter, and had spoken about it with details. She was an important witness. The police got alarmed and picked her up. We managed to get her released. This incident boosted their morale and cemented the process of trust building. 'We know that you women care for us . . . it provides us a lot of support at a time when even our own relatives have left us,' one of them remarked.

We had about 50 women and their children coming to the WAF meetings regularly. In six months these women had changed immensely. They were vocal, happy and confident. It was an amazing experience. The feedback was overwhelming as we see in this polyphony of voices:

'You have changed our lives. We were dying and your support has given us new strength.'

'When we were abandoned by our own party and relations, you provided enormous strength.'

'We owe this life to you. We will do whatever you people are doing.'

'We are hated as the mothers and wives of terrorists. Everybody criticised us. Here we got a new identity of being a woman, a human being.'

'We were very apprehensive, because you all came from a different class, but we felt no class difference. We all sat on the floor together. You cried and laughed with us. You gave us tea first and had it yourself later. We were never treated like this before.'

'I have lost two sons but it has been compensated by so many friends. I now feel for the cause of humanity.'

The young girls were particularly inspired. There was a new dimension in their lives. A struggle for women's rights had become meaningful. The issues of domestic violence, discriminatory laws and injustice to women were discussed. Sometimes films were shown and discussions were held. Their thinking, perspective and politics were changing gradually. They would now open up and talk about the violence in their lives and how they hated it.

'You cannot resolve anything with violence. You have to learn to co-exist with all ethnic groups.'

'We wait for the whole week to come here. It makes us feel good.'

By this time we thought they were ready to form a group of their own. The formation of the Muzloom Aurat Ki Awaz (MAKA) was formally announced on 27 November at a press meet with the mothers whose sons had been killed. In the same gathering were present the victims of feudal violence from Tando Bahawal with a view to bring Sindhi and Mohajir women on the platform. It gave them a broader view of widespread violence and poverty in Sindh. In Tando Bahawal, nine men of the same family were killed by the landowners with the connivance of an army officer. The poor family could not get any justice and out of frustration two young women had publicly burnt themselves. It was an eye-opener for those who saw Sindhis as oppressors only.

MQM Protests and Women's Resistance

The announcement of MAKA sparked off a negative reaction within MQM. It was seen as a threat to their integrity. The WAF was too small a pressure group to challenge a powerful party like MQM. Besides, our focus was not only MQM women but all those who were affected by violence. In our meetings women came from different ethnic and political groups. But since in Karachi the operation was against MQM, their number surpassed all other groups. Sindhi women were either too scared to come onto a public platform, or were stopped by their male relatives, or the family had left the city. So the group of affected women were overwhelmingly Mohajir and some Punjabi-speaking women from MQM. Though there were always a few Sindhi women among the audience.

The turning point was the formation of MAKA which coincided with a change in government. Benazir Bhutto stepped down and a new schedule for elections was announced. Again women were needed by MQM for their election campaign. Though a very small number, about 50 to 60, were coming regularly to our meetings, they were now stopped from doing so. On Saturdays, parallel meetings were organised at Nine Zero and everyone was asked to attend. Absentees were questioned and reprimanded. Most of the women still kept coming to our meetings. Only a few gave in to the pressure. Gradually they stopped coming but still kept in touch. In December 1996, none other than Altaf Hussain addressed a specially called meeting of women and asked then not to mix with us. Mrs Zaid, who had lost two sons and thus enjoyed much respect, got up and challenged those who were questioning our integrity.

'WAF women cared for us when you people didn't bother. They do their own work and are honest. They don't hate anybody. We have given enough sacrifices for you. You cannot run our lives any more.' Her speech created a stir in the crowd. Never before had anyone dared to confront the leadership. It was handled tactfully. But later on pressure was increased. Somehow we managed to retain 32 women with their children, who were also being looked after.

The women had confided to us about the strange behaviour of their children who had seen a lot of violence in life. Two members of WAF, with the help of a psychiatrist, were handling them in a separate group. They had managed to get some funding for their rehabilitation from 'Save the Children Fund'. Al-Falah Trust, a social welfare organisation, also started some income-generation activities. It made quite a few women financially independent. There were success stories and failures. But women learnt different concepts, which changed their perspective about politics.

Our intervention was on a small scale but it had far-reaching effects. Other NGOs who had been scared to make contact with MQM, considering it highly politicised, changed their attitude. There was a constant flow of invitations to MQM women to attend meetings and seminars on women's issues. The Aurat Foundation (AF) was one such NGO. Shirkatgah was also involved through WAF. Now besides WAF, there were other organisations constantly clamouring for women's agenda. Gradually women were allowed to participate in the activities with the permission of the MQM higher-ups.

The WAF's concern was women and we decided to operate independently, which was not taken as a friendly act by the MQM. Consequently, whereas in 1996–97, 8 March, International Women's Day was celebrated as a joint venture with other NGOs and MQM women were there as participants, in 1998, when WAF organised the first function for women in an MQM stronghold, the MQM opposed it. The WAF had announced a separate programme on 6 March, for the greater participation of area women. The MQM headquarter responded by announcing a 'Women's Day Celebration' on the same day and at the same time. As a result, our turnout was very poor and they had much better response. Though some women decided not to go anywhere, or to show up at both places to avoid any conflict.

MQM Co-opts Women's Agenda

For the first time, the MQM supremo Altaf Hussain addressed women workers on the occasion of International Women's Day and co-opted most of our demands. He supported the struggle for women's rights, criticised discriminatory practices and stressed the need for political participation of women. Senator Nasrin Jalil, the only woman in the MQM coordination committee invited a senior member of the Aurat Foundation to the MQM meeting to celebrate

International Women's Day and asked Altaf Hussain to demand 33 per cent reserved seats for women, which he did. The Aurat Foundation advocacy group, in its report on the event stated, 'Senator Nasrin Jalil fully endorsed the recommendations of the Report of Inquiry Commission of Women' (a very radical report in many ways).

Mehnaz Réhman,[10] a senior member of the AF advocacy group has been in touch with the MQM leadership. Describing how the Aurat Foundation has been able to establish a link, she explained,

> Well WAF took the initiative and we took it further. But still they are not that open. Nasrin Jalil, a senator and the only woman in the co-ordination committee, is throughout very helpful. She consults four on five other women also. Due to their support and the advocacy of AF, on 16 March 1999, the Sindh Assembly unanimously passed a resolution to restore and increase the reserved seats for women, as recommended by the Inquiry Commission Report.[11]

Mehnaz thinks the response of MQM changes according to the political situation.

> If it is easy then they will withdraw or not respond well. Under political pressure they are more open—but definitely from a no-agenda for women to the present day there is a significant change. When Nawaz Sharif announced the introduction of the Shariat Bill, MQM opposed it tooth and nail, saying it was detrimental to women's rights. Even when the NGO bill was in the offing MQM expressed a strong reservation.

About the role of women in the MQM, Nasrin Jalil, said,

> We take into consideration how much time a female activist can give and then she is involved accordingly. MQM women who contested elections were harassed by the administration that is why we did not give them tickets in 1997 elections. However whenever MQM passes through an emergency period, the women take over all the responsibilities. We also want to activate more women to participate in elections at all levels.

Nasrin Jalil strongly recommends that the Inquiry Commission Report should be implemented and the political parties act should be changed to make it compulsory to induct women in the party hierarchy.

According to Dr Farooq Sattar, an ex-minister and leader of the MQM in the Sindh Assembly, the MQM women's wing has 300 active female members in Karachi. These are activists who can be gathered on one phone call. In interior Sindh, there are 200 such female activists. Policy-wise MQM does not discriminate against women, but women have to face a lot of restrictions from their families and they cannot cross the limits prescribed by their families, he explained.

In the coordination committee of the MQM there is only one woman, i.e., Nasrin Jalil. While making important decisions, four or five ladies of the women's wing are always invited for consultation. Mrs Mumtaz is in charge of the women's wing. In the employment cell of MQM, there are always four to five girls out of 10 members. The election cell is mostly dominated by men but there are one or two women. In the legal aid committee, there are four to five female lawyers but they are not bold enough to attend press conferences held by MQM. The fact-finding committee is dominated by women; actually the membership is 100 per cent women. In the media committee the membership is mixed.

Dr Sattar said, 'We intend to involve more women at every level but at the proper time'. That proper time has not come yet. When the MQM was in power, women were only involved in celebrations. Most of them went back to their household chores, even the diehard 300 activists. Only when the MQM is under pressure are the women activists called upon to take over responsibility.

Given the women's lack of education and awareness, it has been easy to manipulate them. But 'violence and arms' is still considered a male domain and as we see in the testimonies below, women do not feel comfortable at all. There is a marked ambivalence about their husband's or son's involvement in violent activities and a total denial of their own complicity, if any, in violence. Also, there is a growing realisation that the 'politics of arms' has not paid any dividends. Most of the mothers regret that they have lost their sons in the process. Some still believe that they have given their lives for a great cause. But very few still vow to fulfil the mission of their loved ones, i.e., the achievement of economic, political rights and justice for Mohajirs. That does not mean that they do not believe that there is injustice and prejudice against Mohajirs in every field. As Qaiser Bengali observed, 'Their sense of injustice remains strong and can be summed up as unemployment, lack of control over local resources, and virtually complete absence of effective participation in provincial and political decision making'.[12] But they have come to realise that violence, arms and hatred are no solution to their problems.

Nafisa Shah in a collection of testimonies of affected women in 'Women in the Crossfire',[13] observed,

'Most women would eulogise their sons. Those who were convinced of the *Cause* would revel in their elevated status as a *shaheed's* mother. MQM people would call them *shaheedon ki mayen*—mothers of martyrs—as in the case of Aziza and Kauser. This in a strange way would comfort them and then they would say that they had to "fulfil the missions of our sons".'

Aziza (55) is quoted as saying,

I had never been to Nine Zero, but I vowed on my son's bleeding body that I will fulfil his mission. I felt revived when I met a group of nice women. They did not have the courage to stop me from going to WAF meetings. I was furious when they made baseless allegations against WAF. They respect me for being a '*shaheed's* mother'. It feels good when people respect you but it is not enough. I will not be in peace until I establish that my son was killed wrongly. Every mother says that they think their sons are innocent. But my point is different. If they prove him guilty I will accept it, otherwise they [police] should announce publicly that he was innocent. It is my only desire now.

Most women, Shah recalls, stayed away from articulating a determination to seek justice or revenge. They would simply settle for remembering their husbands or children with fond memories.

Saida is quoted as saying, 'My son was innocent. He never yelled, never shouted. He was so responsible that he wanted to take over all the burdens.' Shah adds that although she never asked they would on their own say, 'My son was not in anything.' If he was an active party worker, the mother would forcefully say, 'My son was just an active party worker but nothing else.' Most women believed their husbands or children were innocent. This perception was reinforced because of the state's use of extrajudicial killings to tackle a political problem.

Impact of Violence

Many women who had been widowed were more concerned about the future of their children. A lot of them said, 'What will happen to the children if something happens to us?' Several widows had become victims of recurring cycles of violence, that is, victims twice or even thrice over. Widows had lost husbands in the ethnic violence in the 1980s and were now losing sons. Widows did not seem to have settled down even years after their husbands had died. Kauser had lost her husband in ethnic riots in Hyderabad and now in the 1990s had recently lost her son. Her son had never seen his father. She was in a state of depression and was anxious about her children. 'We alone know how we are faring. Every day I die and every day I live.'

Husain and Yusuf—two Kutchi sons—died one after the other. 'If a person who is the life-source of a family falls ill, a hundred dependents fall ill. And now it seems that it is not just one Husain who had died, all of us have died,' Husain's mother said, echoing the sentiments of the many women whose cohesive families have broken down. Women had to bear not only the emotional brunt of living in conflict but also the deteriorating monetary implications of the loss of earning members.

Khursheed's (63) narrative evokes the utter devastation that conflict has caused to her and her family's existence. A resident of Orangi town, Khursheed's five sons and three daughters were living comfortably.

My sons were earning enough to keep their families well fed. We had our own house. Daughters were married and two of them lived in their own house. One of them was living with me. One of my sons N who had a good earning joined MQM. Two brothers followed suit. One night the police came looking for N and picked up the two others. N disappeared. The police would beat up everyone and threaten us with dire consequences. One day our house was attacked by the rival group. They broke windows, doors and made us leave the house. We had to take refuge with a relative but they asked us to leave. Since the police had announced a reward for my son N, nobody wanted to have anything to do with us. Meanwhile my daughter who used to live with me died, leaving behind four children.

Later we were to learn that her daughter was killed by N, allegedly for being an informer. But Khursheed denied it. She insisted it was an accident.

We are like gypsies, always on the run. My two sons were released but now all three of them are in jail. First they were arrested in 1995 and released in 1998. Again the two were picked up when they went to the court. Finally N was apprehended and is being tried for a number of criminal charges. The police took all of us to the police station and beat us women up. If my sons are bad why should they punish us?

The family lives in the suburbs of Karachi. The mother and two daughters were hardly on talking terms. They blamed each other for working for rival groups of MQM. Bare survival was difficult as they had fallen below the poverty line. Most of the time the men were in jail and the daughters-in-law were in bad shape with six to eight children each. So were the daughters. Two boys of one of the daughters were in jail—one of them was hardly 14 years old. Another daughter N had six girls. One of them committed suicide when her fiancé was killed by the police. It was a strange household, quarrelling with each other and facing all kinds of miseries.

But Khursheed was not just a passive victim of the conflict. There were reports that she had helped her son N run a torture cell in their home. Khursheed broke down, vehemently denied any knowledge of a torture cell, swearing upon God. She kept crying. But unlike other mothers, Khursheed did not eulogise or defend her son's role. She would say,

Why don't you ask them what they have done? I am an unfortunate mother who is being dragged into the street at this age. Don't you see our miserable condition? If any of my sons had made money, we would have something to eat. What I know is that we were better off before, living peacefully in our home. God knows what kind of a party this is. It has destroyed us. Men are languishing in jails or are on the run all the time. Women are left to bear the brunt. There is no end to our suffering. I wish we all die.

The families of Khursheed and Aziza were all active in the MQM. But there were others like Jahanara (35), whose misfortune was that they were living in the conflict zones and were too poor to move out. 'I am not an activist and there is none in our family, but we live in a stronghold of MQM militants,' she said.

The young boys carry arms and the whole area supports them. We have seen a lot of bloodshed and violence in our lanes and the streets. Whenever the situation is bad, the neighbourhood is besieged by rangers and the police who are looking for militants. There are a lot of hiding places. When it gets really bad, the men leave the area, and women and children stay behind. The militants make us cook their food, wash their clothes and ask the children to get cigarettes. They are good to us but because of them we are besieged by law enforcement agencies. They warn us not to give any information and to warn them if we see any new person in the area. Once the whole neighbourhood moved out because it was so dangerous. But I had to stay with my five girls and ailing husband. We had no place to go. All the time we heard gun shots. The police invaded our house and turned everything upside down. They asked all kinds of probing questions but did not take us with them. We were poor and resourceless; they could see it for themselves.

Jahanara recalled how on one occasion she heard that a girl was shot. It was a time of a lot of disturbances in October 1998. She was the daughter of a Punjabi family living there. Shama was the eldest daughter and was working somewhere. One evening she got a telephone call and left the house in haste. In the early morning the police intercepted a van and opened fire. One person was shot dead and the other fled. This girl was caught trying to escape. The next day the family got a call to come and identify her. They refused to go. Some neighbourhood people went and said she was hardly in any state to be recognised. The police claimed that she was involved in arms transfers. 'Her family moved away to Punjab. No one heard about them afterwards. Perhaps she was buried by *Edhi* [charitable] Trust.'

Increasing police atrocities mobilised the women to organise a few protest demonstrations against the police.

After that they were not so bad with women. Nowadays, we are relieved. All the militants are gone. Either they have been arrested, killed or have fled. They never bothered women but they brought guns and violence to the area. Drugs and other crimes also increased. We were scared all the time. Some people helped them out of fear.

The interviewer had visited the area in October 1998, soon after the girl was killed. The situation was very scary and sensitive. Though a resident had accompanied her, she was told to clear out by armed men. 'You are an outsider and we suspect every stranger to be an informer.' She was talking to a group of women about the girl who was killed. Some kept quiet, others just nodded. They were afraid of the armed men who did not want them to talk to new people. They seemed to be under their control and remained tight-lipped. 'Talk to us, they don't know anything,' claimed one armed man.

In the politics of arms, women feel helpless and their choices are not taken into consideration at all. In Karachi, with the violence pitting brother against brother in internecine rivalry, mothers like Bilquis (40), were caught in the middle, helpless. Bilqis had three sons.

> One of them who used to live with me was in the Haqiqi (rival group). I had asked him repeatedly to leave it. This kind of politics is risky but he wouldn't listen to me. A year ago the police took him away. He was released after some months. They raided our house and also took away my younger son for questioning. He was beaten up very badly. My elder son M who lived with me, was gunned down by the other group on 27 July 1996. His two friends were with him. They also died on the spot. Some people had seen the boys who killed them. But they [police] did not register an FIR. Now we live alone. My husband has been a heart patient. I miss my son a lot. He loved us very much. As a woman I feel very helpless and sad all the time.

Younger women like Farida (24) were left destitute with young children to bring up. Farida's response to her husband's refusal to give up MQM politics shows how women's daily experience of conflict pushes them to get involved, to take control of their own lives and politicises them: 'How could I keep out of it [his politics] when my household was affected?' she said.

> My husband was in MQM. I would beg him not to get involved in politics but he said, 'You don't know. You are a woman. Keep out of it.' How could I keep out of it when my household was being affected? He would never work regularly. He used to drive a rickshaw or taxi. Sometimes he would bring money and sometimes not. He would often bring his party friends home—they would stay with us. When the trouble started they all ran away. We had no money to go anywhere. I always had to work since his income was not regular. We kept shifting from one place to another to avoid the police. Once we went to Hyderabad, but the police came to know and raided our house. So we came back to Karachi. Once on his way to Sohrab Goth, he was arrested. Since then I am very lonely and alone in coping with hardship.

Farida has four children. The eldest is 7 but none of them goes to school. She has no money for their education. Sometimes her mother and brother help but it is not enough. Farida's family survives on the Rs 40 she earns wrapping 2,000 *paans* (betel leaves) working into the night with her two elder children. 'Each time I go to see my husband in jail I spend Rs 500. What has he got out of this politics?'

While hardly any of the women spoke about the transference of political violence in the public arena to the home, the linkage between political violence and domestic violence has been recognised in many conflicts. One of the women told us that her husband who used to be very submissive before had started threatening her with a gun at home.

One more factor which became visible during the course of our interaction with affected women was that it was not easy for them to find a match for their young girls. Either they got married to so-called terrorists or stayed home. Sadia (30) is still single. Her elder brother was in the MQM. She remembers going into his room with some food for his friends and finding them cleaning guns. One night during a police raid, they found a gun. Her mother and she were hauled off to the police station, made to sit on the floor and abused. Next morning her brother surrendered. They were released. His friends too were caught. It was rumoured that Sadia's brother had become an informer. He was killed within weeks of his release. 'We were poor but we have become poorer now. No one wants to marry me,' she said.

Widows and wives of jailed MQM militants have had to take children, especially daughters, out of school and face the prospect of daughters remaining unmarried. Drops in income levels have resulted in girls being kept at home to save the expense of an education and also in the interest of security. For example, all of Ruqaya's six children used to go to school before—now only the sons go. 'My daughters are from 18 to 12 years old and are helping me in sewing clothes. Otherwise how will we survive? When my sons, who are 6 and 8, grow up we will have some hope. My biggest worry is how am I going to marry off my daughters?'

Many mothers insisted that their sons were 'not involved', their friends were. Khushi was adamant her young son was no 'dacoit'.

Her testimony about her son's killing in a so-called police encounter alarmed the police. She was arrested but WAF's intervention got her released. Khushi is destitute with eight mouths to feed. Only one son and daughter work while she works as a 'maasi' (cleaning woman). She received no compensation on her son's killing. 'They (MQM) don't accept him.'

The ethnic strife of Karachi has become an old story but women are still suffering as a result of conflict. Either they have become widows or lost a son and have to raise their children and run their households. More than 80 per cent of the women interviewed were from the Urdu-speaking community. In terms of killing and violence, the Mohajir localities were the most affected. The crisis was not only losing the male members of the family but the constant relocation due to police harassment. The age group of the women interviewed varied from 20 to 60 years. We found that it was easier for the young girls to recover from their trauma if they had the support of their mothers. The older group was more desperate and depressed.

Most of the families were from lower income groups. As a result of the conflict, the income of affected families fell considerably, and in half of the cases they had absolutely no means of income. The drop in incomes changed the pattern of households drastically. Most women who had never worked outside their homes became the main bread earners. They had no skills or training for jobs. Attempts to make them financially independent by the Al-Falah Trust met with little success. Out of 50 women, about 10 started earning, depending on the conditions of their area. A few of them survived on the help of relatives and charity. Considering that we had a small group of 50 women, our experience of the impact of the conflict was limited.

Conclusions

The WAF's initiative, though on a very small scale, had its significance in many ways. It was an experiment in the first step towards conflict resolution by a small group of women. Our experience

shows that it is possible to bring women from differing sides together on a neutral platform, where they can share their common
grievances and empathise with each other.

One may argue that the scale of the study is limited and so is the
intervention by WAF. But the nature of problems and their preva-
lence was quite generalised. More or less the impact of the conflict
was common given the class background. Thus it is possible to state
that in the endemic violence of Karachi and urban areas of Sindh we
can identify some basic characteristics regarding the impact of political violence on women there:

  (i)   Women are the sufferers in the long run,
  (ii)   Women are not directly involved in armed conflict,
  (iii) Women are sometimes direct victims, but mostly second-
         ary victims, and
  (iv)   Women do not take up arms of their own volition unless
         forced by circumstances.

Here I would argue that women by nature resist participating
actively in arms politics. It is considered a male domain and when
women are dragged into it they do not feel comfortable. There may
be a few hardcore women militants in armed struggles but their
number is small.

We learnt from our experience that women empathise with each
other, irrespective of their ethnic or political affiliation. This awareness is further borne out by several stories of the partition in 1947
which describe how Hindu, Muslim and Sikh women saved women
and children of other communities. The realisation that all women
suffer in an armed conflict brings them together. The story of
women's vulnerability and subjugation is a common thread among
women of warring communities. It makes them a natural ally for
peace.

Unfortunately the power structure of MQM is totally male-
dominated like other political parties. The 'Mohajir identity' as mentioned earlier, was recreated in women by the menfolk and accepted
by the women in the overall environment of a community which
was targeted with massive repression. A number of women expressed

the need for 'Mohajir identity' in terms of better jobs for their sons or husbands. Some spoke of emotional blackmail as well as threats from their men.

This is where the WAF intervention came in. Given the rampant violence which affected every house, it has become necessary for women to negotiate their sense of self among and with each other. It is a painful journey and an uphill task. In the midst of multiple identities and overwhelming pressure, each woman will have to decide where she wants to go. It is vital for the women's movement to provide a common platform for women from diverse communities to come together. By sharing each other's experiences, concerns, sufferings and joys they can break the isolation of domestic spheres. It will bring about a collective consciousness in this fragmented world.

The realisation that the 'personal is political' inculcates a sense of togetherness. That is how one woman's story becomes every woman's story. Those who are involved with the women's movement need to address the issue of conflicting identities. They need to have clarity to make a right political choice. To quote an example, it was the women's movement in Pakistan which condemned the atrocities of its own state's army in 1971, and apologised to Bengali women[14] for the violence committed against them. Women need to break the barriers of ethnicity, politics, class and religion to make this world a place where people can live together even though they may be different. That is where the hope for peace lies.

APPENDIX A

To the Women of Bangladesh on 3rd March 1996

Dear sisters:

As Bangladesh celebrates its 25 years of independence, the state and the people of Pakistan must reflect on the role played by the state and the Pakistan military in the unprecedented and exceptionally violent suppression of the political aspirations of the people of Bangladesh in 1971. Continued silence on our part makes a mockery not only of the principles of democracy, human rights, and self-determination which we lay claim to, but also makes a mockery of our own history.

The community of nations had (*sic*) now not only recognised that even in cases of war, and various forms of conflict, there are certain parameters beyond which violence cannot and must not be condoned, and further that those perpetrating and/or responsible for such violence should be held responsible even in retrospect. In view of this and in the larger interests of our own humanity as a nation, we must condemn the repression by the state of its own citizens in 1971. As Pakistanis who stood silently by, we must also judge ourselves as history has already judged us.

Women's Action Forum would like to use this opportunity to build public awareness on the issue of state violence and the role of the military in 1971. At the same time there is a need to focus on the systematic violence against women, particularly the mass rapes. While we try to focus the nation's attention towards a period in our history for which we stand ashamed, Women's Action Forum, on its own behalf, would like to apologise to the women of Bangladesh that they became the symbols and targets in the process of dishonouring and humiliating a people.

In common struggle and sisterhood.

Women's Action Forum
Pakistan

Notes

1. The term 'Mohajir' was used for Urdu-speaking refugees who had settled in the province of Sindh. While in Punjab, the bulk of the immigrant population was Punjabi-speaking and did not create any ethnic or linguistic problems. They amalgamated and adapted the lifestyles of the local population. On the contrary, the Urdu-speaking immigrants maintained their separate culture and identity and regarded themselves superior to the locals.
2. Haroon Ahmed, 'Conflict Resolution in South Asia: A Case Study of MQM', *Liberal Times*, Vol. 4, No. 1, 1996, pp. 27–29.
3. It was the third ethnic riot and worst of its kind. The Aligarh Colony massacre claimed more than 100 lives in a day.
4. It was in the Karachi streets that the turf war for the control of the Mohajir leadership was fought between the rival claimants, the Muttahida Quami Movement (Altaf Hussain faction) and the splinter group MQM (Afaq Haqiqi faction) with the state allegedly collaborating with the Haqiqis to undermine the dominant Hussain faction.

5. Kamal Azfar, 'Karachi: Past, Present and Future', Monograph, Karachi, 1993.
6. Sheen Farrukh, 'Women and Ethnic Identity: Case of MQM', in Nighat Saeed Khan, Rubina Saigol and Afiya Shahbano Zia, eds, *Locating the Self: Perspectives on Women and Multiple Identities*, ASR Publications, Lahore, 1994, p. 207.
7. Khan et al., *Locating the Self*, n. 6, p. 18.
8. She is an educated upper middle-class woman. Her husband is an ex-minister of MQM.
9. Invitation letter from WAF, WAR and Women's Committee for Peace, commemorating International Women's Day (1996) by focusing on the women of Karachi who have suffered in the violence.
10. Coordinator of Aurat Foundation, a middle-class, Urdu-speaking activist from the left.
11. The Inquiry Commission was set up to improve the status of women in 1994. It comprised women's rights activists and lawyers. A senior judge was the head. The commission gave a very radical report in 1998, recommending 33 per cent seats for women and a number of changes in family laws. The report recognised domestic violence and marital rape as crime against women. In spite of pressure from women's groups it has not been implemented so far. But still it is a valuable document in the history of women's movement in Pakistan.
12. Qaiser Bengali, 'Defining Mohajir Grievances', *Daily Dawn*, 13 February 1996.
13. Nafisa Shah, *Women in the Crossfire*, Human Rights Commission of Pakistan, Karachi/Lahore, 1997.
14. See appendix A for text of apology to the women of Bangladesh.

Where There Are No Men: Women in the Maoist Insurgency in Nepal

6

SHOBHA GAUTAM, AMRITA BANSKOTA AND RITA MANCHANDA

Introduction

In whole villages in the western hill districts of Nepal, there are no men. This is the epicentre of the Maoist insurgency. From three districts in February 1996, the Peoples War has swept across two-thirds of the Himalayan kingdom of Nepal. Remote, backward hill districts have been transformed into guerrilla zones and 'base areas', provoking massive police repression on predominantly poor, peasant, minority ethnic groups of Nepal. To escape being picked up by the police or targeted by the Maoists, the men have become *farari* (absconders), who have fled into the surrounding jungles or melted into the cities of Nepal and across the open border into India. Left behind are the women, the stable element, who keep alive family and community in the midst of conflict. Traditionally, women form the backbone of the semi-feudal subsistence agrarian economy and even under normal conditions, a 45 per cent rate of underemployment drives the men to seasonally migrate in search of jobs to cities in Nepal and India. This time, the men have not come back.

In these villages without men, the women have been left to work with conflict, to negotiate with the police and the Maoists, the survival and security of their families. It is women who feed and shelter the Maoists who come at night. It is women who have become the heads of households, the providers for the children and the aged. It is women who have had to break tradition and take on the 'male' job of ploughing the land. It is women who in the space vacated by men, are challenging gender relations in both the private and public spheres with structural implications, difficult to reverse post-conflict.

Women are also getting directly involved in the Peoples War as propagandists and guerrillas. In the Maoist strongholds every third guerilla is a woman. As in its inspirational revolutionary model, Peru's Shining Path, the presence of women in the propaganda, logistic and fighting ranks is critical for the success of the Peoples War. Women, especially poor, peasant, illiterate and *jan jati* (tribal) women have achieved a political visibility never before imaginable in Nepal's politics. The majority of the women in the Maoist movement come from Nepal's disadvantaged Tibeto-Burman ethnic groups. Relatively speaking, they are culturally less oppressed than Hindu upper-caste Aryan women. Their identity is not constructed around a religious ideology. However, as in any community, women have the least rights and suffer on top of class, ethnic and regional oppression, gender oppression.

The ideological thrust of the Maoist movement is oriented towards expanding the rights base of the poor and the marginal, including women. In a predominantly rural society, the New Democratic Revolution is essentially an agrarian revolution, where land reform is at the centre, both for women and for men. The movement has a strong appeal for women as its 40-point charter supports property rights for women.

This chapter focuses on the experience of poor peasant women as protagonists in the swirl of war, i.e., women negotiating survival and women joining the ranks of the guerrillas. Empirically, it is based on field interviews with peasant and rural women in two contrasting situations—(*i*) illiterate poor women in underdeveloped Rolpa and Rukum districts in the mid-western hills, and (*ii*) literate women in the more developed and prosperous Gorkha district in the central hills. Gorkha district stands out for the large number of girl students who have been drawn to the Peoples War.

Also interviewed were 'guerrillas' in prison, and top ranking woman leader, Hisila Yami. The interviews are oriented towards revealing through their life histories and memories of events, women negotiating conflict and their notion of violence and justice. The questions which arise, emerge from the lived experience of the women.

How do we understand women's transformative experience from relative invisibility to visible protagonism? What does the shift in the roles of these women mean for the religiously sanctified socio-cultural structures of feudal-patriarchal communities? The 'exclusions' which all Nepalese women face span right from the household level to the state level, i.e., political, economic and cultural domains. What does it mean for women socialised in conservative patri-archal cultures to become armed guerrillas or area commanders?

Is this one armed class struggle in which the women are not being told that the women's question has to wait till after the revolution? Evidently, the Peoples War ideology has created space for women to claim rights but the women joining the movement have also helped shaped that ideology. How have women defined the movement and how has the movement structured women's roles?

Leftist armed resistance movements tend to argue that the spe-cial conditions of revolutionary struggle make gender differences unimportant. That the liberation of the peasant/proletariat will in the process emancipate women from gender oppression. Is the Maoist movement in Nepal the exception? An analysis of the role of women in the Shining Path, the acknowledged model for Nepal's Peoples War, suggests that despite the fact that women achieved an import-ant presence at all levels within the movement, Sendero was not capable of programmatically incorporating their gender interests. 'Shining Path established an instrumental relationship with its fe-male members that re-produced patriarchal relations to benefit the party.'[1] Is the situation of the women in the Maoist movement in Nepal different?

In Nepal's Maoist movement, initially, among the top leader-ship, were women with accomplished political qualifications like

Pampa Bushal, co-leader of the United Peoples Front, the political platform of the Maoists. Hisila Yami, as head of the Women's Front was also in the circle of the top leadership. But as the struggle has got more militarised and more hierarchically structured, the participation of women in the top policy making councils seems to have diminished. Women have become area commanders, party committee secretaries, but are the women in policy-making positions in the central leadership?

This chapter also dwells on the failure of Nepal's democratic political agenda to deal with the central issues of poverty, development and ethnic, caste and gender oppression. Its corollary is the weakness of the democratic forces in Nepal to forge solidarities on the humanitarian front of the war story and strengthen social capital needed to build a just peace.

Historical Prologue

Nepal's dominant historical narrative is structured around the reunification of the petty principalities of the territory of Nepal nearly two-and-a-half centuries ago by the Shah dynasty which established a Hindu kingdom from the fiefdom of Gorkha. Nepal's palace history is presided over by the Shahs as conquerors, titular heads during the hereditary Rana prime ministers, as absolute rulers and as constitutional monarchs in a multi-party democracy. Power, however, remains monopolised by a minority governing elite of a few upper-caste Brahmins and Chettri families with the co-optation of some Buddhist Newar merchants and Sanskritised ethnic Magars. The system is feudal in nature and land remains the primary resource.

According to a Food and Agriculture Organisation (FAO) study, the rich peasants make up 10 per cent of the population and own 65 per cent of the land, poor peasants make up 65 per cent of the population and own 10 per cent of the land and 8 per cent of the peasants are landless.[2] The landholding structure in Nepal has not changed much. Nepal remains a semi-feudal, subsistence agriculture economy with low productivity and high underemployment. Seventy per cent of the population lives below the poverty line and the number of the absolute poor has doubled in two decades.[3]

Nepal's three distinct ecological regions, mountains, hills and plains accentuate inequalities and diversities. According to Nepal's Human Development Index the central hills which include Kathmandu and the Gorkha districts score the highest. The lowest scoring region is the mid-western hill area. The most backward and the most underdeveloped regions are also where the indigenous and ethnic groups are in a majority, so that there is a confluence of regional, cultural, linguistic and religious discrimination and regional deprivation. There are 60 ethnic groups and 60 living languages. The physical ruggedness of the region and the feudal structure of land relations have resulted in an enduring resilience of localised cultures and community life. The Maoists have tapped into this cultural tradition of tribal cooperation and the historical sense of deprivation and injustice. Rolpa, Rukum and Jajarkot, the flashpoints of the Maoist insurgency, are in the backward mid-western hills. Gorkha is in the central hills.

The restoration of democracy in 1990, the setting up of a constitutional monarchy and multi-party elections in 1991, found the ultra left parties joining parliamentary politics. Nepal has a long tradition of left activism and left factionalism. The historical roots of the Communists are entwined with those of the centrist Nepali Congress in the final days of the anti-Rana struggle in 1949. But many of the radical left groups owe their origins to the 1971 Jhapa rebellion, which paralleled the uprising across the border in Bihar and Naxalbari.

In the first multi-party elections, the Nepali Congress secured a comfortable majority with the Communist Party of Nepal-Unified Marxist Leninist (CPN-UML) establishing sway over a third of the seats. Its main electoral rival on the left was the United Peoples Front or UPF (Samyukta Jan Morcha), an umbrella organisation of avowedly Maoist parties who came together under the chairmanship of Dr Baburam Bhattrai. The UPF won nine seats. By the 1994 mid-term elections, the UPF was disenchanted. It split and the majority unit under Bhattrai pulled out of parliamentary politics along with the Communist Party of Nepal (Maoist) under Pushpa Kamal

Dahal, alias Prachanda. Preparations began in earnest for a protracted armed struggle modelled on Peru's Shining Path.

In February 1996, barely six years after the restoration of democracy, the Communist Party of Nepal (CPN) (Maoist) launched the Peoples War to overthrow Nepal's constitutional monarchy and effect a socio-economic revolution—a New Democratic Revolution. Parliamentary politics had failed to make any difference to the people's grinding poverty and disempowerment. Nepal's tryst with multi-party democracy had produced in 10 years, eight governments comprising right and left coalitions of cynical convenience.

In the political vacuum, the Maoists have emerged as the voice of Nepal's poor and marginalised, the indigenous ethnic peoples, the lower castes, peasants, workers, students and women. Through their mass propaganda mobilisation, development activities and pro-people guerrilla actions against the symbols of rural oppression like the Agricultural Development Bank and local tyrants, the Peoples War has spread from three districts in 1996 to 45 of Nepal's 75 districts.

The district of Rolpa, the stronghold of the Maoists was in a sense a rehearsal of things to come. Two years before the launch of armed struggle, the UPF concentrated on political, cultural and developmental activities to strengthen the potential for class struggle. The state hit back with savage repression.[4] The UPF's supporters were targeted, false cases framed against them and more than 1,000 people arrested. The Maoists also hit back at political and class enemies. As the clashes between the two flared up, the government launched Operation Romeo in November 1995, a draconian police operation which drove 10,000 out of 200,000 able-bodied men into the jungle to escape police atrocities.

Three months later the Peoples War was launched with guerilla action, sabotage and propaganda. On 13 February 1996, there were lightning strikes on police outposts, state-owned Agricultural Development Bank offices and local feudal bosses in the districts of Gorkha in the central hills, Rolpa and Rukum in the mid-western and Sindhuli in the eastern hills. In the police repression which followed, thousands were arbitrarily arrested on charges of dacoity, arson and murder. Human rights organisations have documented the extrajudicial executions, rape and arbitrary arrests by the police and the killings, extortion and destruction of property by the Maoists.[5]

According to the home minister of Nepal, Purna Bahadur Khadka, in the last four years of the Peoples War, 1,128 people have been killed, 836 are Maoists, 115 police personnel and 177 are 'common men'.[6] The level of violence has been determinedly kept low. The weapons used by the Maoists are, largely, 303 rifles, *khukris* and farm implements. This is remarkable given that Nepal sits at the crest of South Asia, a region awash with AK-47s. Nepal has not deemed it necessary to call out the army. Moreover, its big neighbour, India appears to be not worried. The territory of Nepal abuts onto India's volatile state of Bihar and it is highly unlikely that India will tolerate a successful social revolution in Nepal before one in India.

So far the Peoples War has not appreciably impacted upon life in the capital, Kathmandu or in the plains of Terai bordering India. Except for a few high profile executions of political leaders in the western hill districts during elections, the Peoples War is regarded as a sideshow in Kathmandu. The upper-caste Hindu Brahmin-Chettri power elite of Kathmandu treat it as essentially a law and order problem in the remote hills where largely, ethnic groups like Magars are killing other Magars. The Magars, the third largest ethnic group in Nepal, comprise 7 per cent of the population (Table 6.1).

TABLE 6.1
Castes and Ethnic Groups in Nepal[7]

Parbatiyas 40%	Newars 5.6%	Ethnic Groups (hill tribes) 20%	Madhesias (plains) 32%
Brahmin 12.9%	Brahman 0.1% Shrestha 1.0%	Magars 7.2%, Tamangs 5.5%	Castes 16.1% Ethnic Groups 9%
Chettri 16%	Bajracharya/ -Shakhya 0.8%		
Gurungs 2.5%	Maharajan 3%		

Source: David N. Gellner, Joanna Pfaff-Czarnecka and John Whelpton, eds, *Nationalism and Ethnicity in a Hindu Kingdom*, Harwood Academic Publishers, Amsterdam, 1997, p. 53.

In its fourth year, the Peoples War has spread far beyond the Magar areas to two-thirds of Nepal's districts. The 40-point demand of the political front of the Peoples War, the UPF, calls for a new peoples' democracy based on a new constitution, seizure of mon-archial privilege and protection of the rights of women, the oppressed nationalities, the downtrodden and the regionally disadvantaged. It calls for radical land reform, property rights for women, debt relief and guaranteed employment. Taking an anti-India stance, it calls for the repealing of unequal treaties with India and the regulation of the open border with India.

Women in Nepal: From Invisibility to Protagonism

The majority of the women directly involved in the conflict zone, either as negotiating survival or as party cadres and guerrillas are drawn from non-Aryan groups, especially the Kham Magars. However, many of the leading women in the Peoples War are upper-caste women like Pampa Bushal, or from the Buddhist merchant Newari community like Hisila Yami. In focusing on women's experience of the Peoples War, through their life stories, inevitably, there is a misleading tendency to emphasise women's 'visibility' and 'protagonism' in the conflict situation and assume dormancy and invisibility before the crisis of the Peoples War. As we shall explore below, there were also important continuities in the experience of the women. Notwithstanding this caveat, we argue that the conflict situation is producing a certain threshold of change or shift in gender relations for women directly involved in the conflict with implications for the disadvantaged status of women in Nepal, in general.

Gender discrimination in Nepal has actually increased, despite the kingdom's accession to the Convention on the Elimination of (all forms of) Discrimination Against Women (CEDAW) and other international instruments.[8] Women suffer from 23 discriminatory laws in Nepal. Nepal tops South Asia's gender inequality ratio at 1:6, a notch above India at 1:5 and way above Sri Lanka at 2:3. In Nepal, women's lifespan is shorter by two-and-a-half years. Women make up 49 per cent of the population. Nepal's maternity deaths are the highest in South Asia. Abortion is illegal. Work burden for women is four times that of the adult male. Literacy index is 54.3 per cent for males and 21.3 per cent for females. Gender disparity is similar for rural and urban areas. However, disaggregation across regions and social collectivities shows swings in the Human Development Index (HDI) and widening gender disparities in the mountainous regions. Gorkha stands out with 24.5 per cent adult literacy for women as against Rolpa with 8.7 per cent. The enrollment patterns for children aged 6 and above for the mid-western hills, the Maoist epicentre, is, for boys—46.9 per cent, for girls—17.6 per cent, i.e., an average of 31.8 per cent. The Nepal average is 40 per cent.

In Nepal's *mulki ain* (civil code), the daughter has no claim to parental property unless she remains unmarried till 35 years of age and then can claim her share, if it is still intact but forfeits it, if she marries. Women form the backbone of the subsistence economy, accounting for the bulk of agricultural work and animal husbandry, but have no legal rights over property. Currently, a bill on property rights for women is hanging fire in parliament, but the militant opposition to it demonstrates the difficulty of passing legislation guaranteeing property rights to women under the present system. Its opponents argue that property rights for women will destroy the very basis of the Hindu family. Officially, 98 per cent of the population of Nepal is Hindu. Given the geographic and economic isolation of the hill districts, acculturation to dominant Hindu beliefs and customs among communities like the Kham Magar, is limited but growing. Women's groups in Nepal blame women's lack of rights, especially property rights, for a social structure of exploitative practices, such as polygamy, *jari* (a man who takes away another's wife pays him compensation for the loss of his goods), wife beating and mass trafficking of girls to the brothels of India and the Gulf. Every year 5,000–7,000 Nepali women are trafficked across the border. The majority of them belong to the minority ethnic groups.

Religiously sanctified, 'exclusions' which Hindu women face span right from the household level to the state level and cover political, economic, and cultural domains. Citizenship is through the male line. Socio-cultural practices detailed in ancient Hindu codes like Manusmriti, have enshrined oppressive patriarchal structures, subjugating the Aryan upper-caste Hindu women, in particular. Women from the Tibeto-Burman communities like the Magars, Gurungs and Rais, have fewer religio-cultural restrictions. Widow remarriage is possible and divorce does not entail a loss of ritual status. The identity of the Magar women is articulated in a secular idiom.

As a result, the Kham Magar woman has access to a variety of economic options which gives her socio-economic independence. She is responsible for many important decisions concerning selection of seed, cropping, and disposal and sale of agriculture and household products. Informal entrepreneurial activity like the sale of *raski* (country liquor) is centred on women. Augusta Molnar in an anthropological study of the Kham Magar women of Thabang, before the Peoples War, demonstrated that although the women are denied legal right to land and family property, in the economic sphere they are accorded a position of complementary authority. It is a status they retain on divorce or widowhood. Women have primary responsibility for agriculture and animal husbandry. Ploughing is done by men but seed selection by women. Traditionally, men's work burden has been much lower than that of women.

Given that one in two households is involved in seasonal migration, women are obliged to take decisions in the absence of men. However, decisions on sale and purchase of land are rarely taken without consultation with a male but women determine how much of grain is to be consumed and how much set aside to make *raski*. Through the informal institutions of women's work groups women manage a wageless labour exchange and small entrepreneurial activity. The household responsibilities of women channelled through the work groups provide women, more than men, with access to information and informal political power. Indeed the traditional esteem enjoyed by the Magar women in society has made socially acceptable for young educated Magar women to compete with males for posts as village officials.[9] However, after the Peoples War, it is illiterate peasant women who are emerging as protagonists.

Poor peasant women, and women from the oppressed nationalities have been the most active in joining the Peoples War. Nearly
70 per cent of the women in the Peoples War are from the Tibeto-
Burman and non-Aryan communities, e.g., Magars, Tamangs, Kamis
and Gurungs. The harsh conditions of life have made Tibeto-Burman
and non-Aryan women tough. In a socio-economic power structure dominated by upper-caste Brahmin Chettri elite, the ethnic
groups suffer from social, linguistic, cultural, economic and political discrimination. Their oppression is further reinforced by the
backwardness of the regions where they are a majority. And, as in
every community, the women are the most oppressed and the most
marginalised.

In Nepal there is a tradition of armed political activism and struggle by women of ethnic and indigenous groups. Nepali history
records the fight women and children gave the British at the battle
of Nalapani in Dehradun in 1815. More recently, in the movement
for democracy, the women of Lalitpur from the Brahmin, Chettri
castes as well as the ethnic groups, were particularly active in their
support, but behind the frontline.

Living between the Maoists and the Police

Mirule, a village in Rolpa district is a village without men.[10] It is a
Kham Magar village of 265 houses without men. In the first year of
the insurgency, Mirule held the record for the largest number of
killings in Rolpa district. This village is a case study in the 'making
of Maoists'. Mirule's remoteness and inaccessibility reflects its abject neglect and backwardness. It is an arduous eight-hour walk from
the district headquarters in Libang. The presence of the Nepali state
is visible in the police post set up during Operation Romeo in 1995.
The police stay on the other side of the river, watchful but do not
cross over. When our all-women journalists' team went to Mirule,
there seemed to be an apparent lull both in Maoist and police activity. But the women do not dare light a lamp, as dusk falls. The
police have proscribed it. Outsiders are regarded with suspicion.
'This one or that one might be the man who puts on a mask and

comes to kill at night or the informer who brings in the police', a student said.

Sympathisers of the UPF, teachers, farmers and in the end, all the able-bodied men, had fled in the wake of arbitrary arrests and killings. It started with the killing of Mulman Budha, the 'smart' farmer of the village who was organising the community's drinking water project. Mane Karne, the son of the local village *mukhiya* (chief) now allied to the Nepali Congress used the police to settle political and personal scores, targeting Mulman Budha. Just two days before, he had begun adult literacy classes. Maoists retaliated and killed the 'informer' Man Bahadur Rokka. The police hit back charging 42 people with his murder including in the charge-sheet the names of all those associated with the UPF and others whom Mane Karne wanted to get even with—women and men. Police justice was dramatically demonstrated when four men were picked up one night. Kumari Budha (23), the daughter of one of the men went with food and clothes for her father. She too was detained at the police post. Kumari Budha was raped and killed. The five half-burnt bodies were found smouldering the next day. It is a memory which even the children obsessively recall.

Those implicated in the omnibus charge-sheet, did not wait around. They became *farari* (absconders). Raji Maya, who had been with her children in the fields staying in a *got*, a cowshed, when Rokka was killed, was also charged. She was arrested and imprisoned till she produced her land title deed as security for bail. Young men routinely harvesting potatoes in the upper slopes were picked up by the police and arbitrarily executed on the say so of village informers. Hundreds were arrested. For two years, Buji Maya (16), a Kham Magar girl, has been behind bars in Libang jail. She still does not know why she was arrested. She is charged with dacoity and murder. She was picked up on suspicion of feeding and sheltering the Maoists. It is not an unfounded suspicion, for who are the Maoists, but brothers, fathers, uncles and aunts in a tightly knit tribal village community. 'When they come for food, who can say no. Then, come the police,' said Asapura Gurung, a village ward member.

The men slipped away into the surrounding jungles, some to join the Maoists, others to melt into the crowds of the cities. The women were left alone, to deal with the police. Girls grazing live-stock in lonely slopes were open prey. Anyone carrying food was suspected and imprisoned. Female relatives of *fararis* were threat-ened and physically abused. After her father and brother became *fararis*, Pura Budha (17) too fled, unable to take the nightly harass-ment and threats of the police. Her younger sister and she lived in the forests for six months, hiding from the police. All the members of their four interrelated families fled. 'After six months the situ-ation cooled down and I decided to come back. It is difficult to spend all your life hiding in the forest. I have lost all the people I loved. Let them kill me even if I am not involved in any Maoist activity,' she said. Pura Budha was busy repairing the roof of the farm house. She is now the head of the household, responsible for her younger sibling, her elderly grandparents, the land and the livestock.

Traditionally, women are not allowed to plough the land and risk social ostracism and punitive action. But in Mirule as in many other villages in the affected 'guerrilla zones', there are no able-bodied men. The handful of men still left in the village, largely state employees, defensively explain that if they help *farari* families, the police come after them. In some cases, where the Maoists hold sway, they have collectively ploughed the land garnering much goodwill. Significantly, the women who have been ploughing the land, do not rationalise it as necessitated by the absence of men. They explain it as a practical demonstration of 'there's nothing women can't do, if we have to do it'. It is an assertion of capability.

The absence of men has also meant opportunities opening up for women to step into public life. Moreover, the sharing of communal labour and responsibility has facilitated women's access to debate and decision making in the public sphere. When elections took place for the wards of the Mirule Village District Council (VDC), there were no men to contest. Women came forward and all six elected members of the ward are women including the chairperson. A peasant illiterate woman like Asapura Gurung, who had been active in informal politics, became the nominated ward member. Not sur-prisingly, she too has been charge-sheeted by the police. In the ab-sence of men, the women have been left to negotiate not only with the police but also with those remnants of the state who have not fled Mirule, e.g., the drunken schoolteacher who opens the school at noon and his co-conspirator, the VDC secretary. The women are outspoken in their criticism of the cost of being in a 'guerrilla zone'. It has meant a critical break in the immunisation programme, bad or no schooling, fall in land productivity and a halt in non-government organisation (NGO)/international non-government organisation (INGO) development activity.

Despite the very obvious humanitarian plight of the women and children in the Maoist affected areas, there has been no forging of solidarities between national level women's groups in Nepal and local women. Some Nepali human rights organisations have been active in documenting excesses by the police and the Maoists, but Nepal's many women's groups have been indifferent to the violation of the basic rights of women and children in the Maoist affected areas. Investigative press reports by a team of women journalists on the experience of women and children in Rolpa Rukum and Gorkha were denounced and labelled Maoist propaganda. Nepali women journalists who dared to urge a political and humanitarian intervention, met with hostility and threats, even from women's groups. Although property rights for women are central to the Maoist revolutionary agenda, mainstream women's groups lobbying for property rights for women have not considered it desirable to enter into a dialogue with the All Nepal Women's (Revolutionary) Association (ANW[R]A) which is politically affiliated to the Maoist movement.

Evidently, this demonstrates how much gender is intersected by class, caste and ethnicity. For women's groups in Kathmandu, the Maoists armed struggle against class oppression has eclipsed their fight against gender oppression and left no room for even an engaged analysis, let alone a dialogue.[11] Moreover, there seems to be a determination on the part of the state to discourage and prevent any forging of solidarities on a humanitarian front or on women's issues. This is reflected in the police's brutal attack on a public meeting of the ANW(R)A in Thapathali campus in Kathmandu in November 1998. Some 168 women were arrested including radical left political leaders, teachers, students and women and children.

Maoist Justice vs Police Justice — Making Choices

In the Maoist influenced areas, the dominant chorus we heard was, expectedly, one of people trapped between the police and the Maoists. 'The police come and ask about the Maoists and the missing children and the Maoists come and ask why the police came?' But listen to the silences of the people in most affected districts of Rolpa, Rukum and Gorkha. In the attitude of the 'ordinary' people towards the terror of the Maoists and the police, a difference is discernible.

On the one hand, the people have to face massive police excesses against 'innocent' women and men. The brutality and arbitrariness of the police operation Kilo Sera–2 in 1998 drove many people towards the Maoists. On top of that is a defunct local administration, rampant injustice and abject poverty and neglect. In Musikot, Rukum district, after multi-party democracy won against the Pancha (royalist) system dominated by the old feudal elite, the people filed a case against the local tyrant, thinking their day had come. Meanwhile, the former Pancha, had switched parties and joined the ruling Nepali Congress. He filed a counter case naming the 65 people who had accused him. The police took his part.

On the other side there is Maoist terror, but also Maoist justice and community support activities like collective farming and redistribution of grain 'looted', the people say, from the labour of the people by the local petty feudals. The Maoists through their attacks on the symbols of rural debt, the offices of the Agricultural Development Bank and the local usurers, the burning of debt bonds and misappropriated title deeds and the punishing of rapists and wife beaters, have garnered much popular support, especially among the women. Moreover, in their stronghold areas, the Maoists have been dispensing pro-people justice through *Jan Adalats* or People's Courts.

In Libang, the district headquarters of Rolpa, the Administration and Land Revenue Office have seen no new cases for months. The people are going to the parallel administration offices opened by the Maoists in many Village Development Councils. Out of the 52 VDCs in the district, some 26 VDCs are said to be in the control of the Maoists.[12] As a demonstration of their hold over the people, in 1997 the Maoists did not allow local elections to be held in 87 VDCs. In August 1999, in a bid to strengthen their parallel administration, the Maoists conducted their own local VDC elections in Rukum district.[13]

In addition, the Maoists, through their political and cultural propaganda activities have been mobilising villagers. Pro-Maoist publications have projected images of heroic Maoists and their pro-people activities. The anecdotal grapevine, in constructing the myths of the popular history of the Peoples War, has picked on how in one of the first attacks on a police post, Maoist insurgents tied up the police and left covering the men with quilts. It was bitterly cold that night.[14] In Kavre district, a group of Maoists knocked at the home of an old peasant woman late at night and demanded food and shelter. She had nothing but a small bag of seed. They made her cook that and left her in despair. A week later a sack full of grain was left outside her home and Rs 10,000.

In Surkhet district the people tell of a Maoist Peoples' Court. An all-women guerrilla unit with the area commander came to a village at 10 p.m. to hold court. On trial was a husband who was habitually drunk and mercilessly beat his wife. He was warned. Everyone was told to bring out their bottles of *raski*, locally made and purchased. The bottles bought were to be returned to the shop. The Maoists would warn the shopkeeper. The home brewed alcohol was destroyed after keeping some aside for medicinal and ritualistic purposes. A homily was delivered on the ill effects of alcohol, and the linkage between alcohol, immiserisation, wife beating and illiteracy explained. After holding an adult literacy class, they left.

In the preparatory phase, the Maoists had concentrated on students and teachers as a priority sector. Maoist ideology has seeped into the schools, adult literacy classes and in women's work groups and village women's collectives for income generation and forestry management. It had even seeped into the prisons. They have become workshops for Maoist indoctrination. In the prison in Libang, on the walls are life-size portraits of Marx, Engels, Lenin, Stalin and Mao. All the 57 'political prisoners', men and women, may not

have been Maoists when they went in, but they would go out as
Maoists when they were released.[15]

In Maoist strongholds like Rolpa, it is commonplace for children
to say: 'The police are our enemies. They will be cut down to size
by the absconders. It will go on like this for two years more at the
most. Then we'll have our government and you'll see.' Indeed, one
of the professed objectives of the Maoist strategy is to draw in children into the guerrilla war. The party organ, *The Worker* celebrat-
ing the participation of women in the guerrilla war, adds that through
the women, 'another bonanza is the drawing in of children into the
process of war and politicisation.'

Reports of Maoists putting up gates and establishing liberated
zones, may be exaggerated but what is evident is that in their strongholds, the Maoists seem to inspire self-confidence and empowerment while the police are seen as brutal, corrupt and on the defensive.
As a young girl student from Rukum district said, 'Before the police used to kill "innocent" people because of their beliefs. Now the
junglees [absconders] will kill the police even if they hide under water.
Because of fear of the *junglees*, the police have stopped filing false
cases.'[16]

A caveat needs to be added that in the districts where Maoist
influence is dominant, it is not surprising that the voices opposed to
them are quiet. It is only when an incident provokes public outrage, that these voices are emboldened to speak out. The killing of
Yadu Gautam, the UML parliamentary candidate for Rukum district, did provoke public outrage. But was the popular vote in favour
of his widow Tirtha Gautam, a vote against Maoist politics or in
honour of the white she wore, a symbol of widowhood? In Nepal's
fourth parliament sit two widows of Maoist terror but party political divisions, UML and NC, seem to be more significant than their
common grief and anger against the Maoists. The two have rarely
even spoken to each other. Moreover, their loss, essentially, is cast
in personal and not political terms.

Tirtha Gautam denies that her husband was a Central Intelligence Department (CID) agent, as alleged by the Maoists who executed him. She insists he was a sympathiser of the Maoists. Given
the reality of the Maoist domination of her area, Rukum district,

she was careful to echo support for the causes the Maoists stood for. Even while deploring the killing of her husband, she added, 'There were so many other people, class enemies, why didn't they kill them? Why her husband?' Tirtha was insistent that there was less sympathy for the Maoists than terror. People were pulled out and forcibly taken away for indoctrination through cultural events and money was extorted, she said. But there is also the reality of local development workers, who speak in support of the pro-people activism of the Maoists. This is despite the fact that many of these development activists have seen their INGO supported activities closed down by the Maoists.

However, the strident propaganda about growing and enduring sympathy for the Maoists rings a little hollow when there is a public outcry against an unpopular Maoist action as in the case of the killing of Shyam Sunder Shrestha of Gorkha district.[17] Shyam Sunder was a leader of the Nepali Congress Students Union of Gorkha campus. In December 1998, he was killed with a *khukri* because of rivalry for political control of the Gorkha campus. Evidently, Shyam Sunder was a popular teacher who far from informing against the Maoists, used to stand witness for Maoist supporters framed in false cases. Even Maoist sympathisers among the teachers in Gorkha campus criticised his killing as unjustified. The police reprisal which followed, further alienated the village people.

Hundreds were arrested. Eighteen people were killed, including six women. Nepal students union supporters went on a rampage and the Maoists hit back with ambushing activists going to address Nepal students union gatherings. People were terrified that the Maoists would come to their homes to hide and the police would come after them and loot their homes. People were heard speaking out against some of the local Maoists. 'For some, insurgency has become a business.' The mother of one Maoist was quite pleased her son was a Maoist, because he regularly brought home money to rebuild the house and money to marry off his sister. Was it an example of the revolutionary struggle getting corrupted?

The police's dramatic raids on Maoist hideouts in Gorkha district, indicated their success in infiltrating the movement. The government-sponsored press in 1998 also played up reports of a lengthening list of Maoists, men and women, who were surrendering. Much publicity was given to reports of surrender by women combatants. Hisila Yami,[18] the former head of the Women's Front, was doubtful whether for women, return could really be an option. 'Sons will be welcomed back with open arms, but for the daughters, can there be a return? When they become guerrillas, the women set themselves free from patriarchal bonds. How can they go back? That is why, the women are more committed,' she explained.

Police Victims and Maoist Victims—Challenging Victimhood or Surrendering

The difference in the attitude of 'ordinary' people towards Maoist justice and police justice, is poignantly exposed by juxtaposing the manner in which the women survivors of the victims of the police and Maoists construct the 'injustice' or the 'justness' of the killing of their family members. In the former there is a determination to take revenge, to empower themselves by joining the Maoists; in the latter, there is resignation and dependency on the state.

Sita Kumari Pun was 11 years old when her 23-year-old brother was killed by the police while he was on the upper slopes harvesting potatoes. A passer-by brought the news that a man and a woman had been gunned down by the police and buried. She never saw the body. Afterwards, the police came and beat up the family. Her father suffered a paralytic stroke. Sita had to leave school and at 13 manages the house and the fields while her 14-year-old brother tends to the livestock. Sita blames Mane Karne, the former village chief's son for setting the police on her brother. He had nothing to do with the Maoists, she insists. Sita vows to revenge the killing of her brother, a 'simple, ordinary man'. 'It doesn't matter whether we have to use a *khukri* or a gun, we will avenge ourselves against our enemies, and the police, in league with them.' Two years after her brother was killed, Sita, choking back her sobs, ended her story on a note of defiance resonating with Maoist rhetoric. 'Yes, my brother has been killed. But we have another 1,000 brothers of the same kind. We will all come together and take revenge. We will not spare those responsible for our grief,' she said.

From a 13-year-old girl to a 70-year-old mother, the language of revenge against injustice shrilly echoes in the hills of Rolpa and Rukum. Lali Roka was called to a police post, raped, killed and her body burnt in a cowshed. Doja Rokka, her mother, is adamant that Lali Roka was only a dedicated health worker. The villagers insist she was not involved in any political party. The police claim she was a Maoist and killed in an encounter. The Maoists, too, post facto a killing, have adopted the practice of claiming the victims of police terror as Maoists, although many may not have been linked to the movement, except by their killing.

In the case of Sabita Gatri, her husband was killed along with five others while they were digging potatoes. She believes he was not political. But Sabita recognises the advantages of being a martyr's widow. 'Who would have cared if my husband had died falling off a cliff or a tree? But because the police killed him, the society honours him as a martyr. They help me too. From now onwards, I'll be a party worker too.' Sabita had no hesitation in acknowledging her sympathy for the Maoists.

Sabita's badge of resistance is the *sindoor* (vermilion) vivid on her forehead and her *pothay* (red beaded necklace), symbols of a married women, which she wears in defiance of her widowhood. When the dead bodies were brought down to the village, the police forbade her to mourn her dead husband by ritualistically discarding the public symbols of a married woman. Now, Sabita wears them as a show of resistance. It is a language of support and resistance, which is rooted in the cultural space of women and revolves around widowhood or motherhood.

In an effort to mobilise women's support for the Maoist movement, widows of martyrs are helped and their 'sacrifice' for the revolution is publicly lauded. Publications close to the Maoists like the *Yojana* weekly project Nanda Kumar Shrestha, the wife of a revolutionary, as a role model. When her husband was killed by the police she refused to mourn. *Yojana* quotes her as saying, 'He said, I was not to cry, if he was killed by the enemy. That I should not go into ritual mourning, for a revolutionary never dies.' Nanda, in true Maoist style asserts, 'I am ready to lift a gun to follow my husband's beliefs. I will make his dream come true.'

Whether it is the public avowal of Sabita's support for the Maoists or Sita's vociferous vow to avenge her brother's death by joining the Maoists, there is in their assertiveness, a sense of defiance and even empowerment. It is in sharp contrast to the tone of resignation and defeat which has overcome the women relatives of the victims of the Maoists. Some like Sita Oli (27) have left their village and moved to the district headquarters with the help of the compensation paid by the government. Sita's husband was a pharmacist and a Nepali Congress party activist. Sita is aware that her husband was a police informer against rival political activists. He was not a 'good' man and addicted to gambling, she said. Sita has no intention of pursuing her husband's killers. One has been killed by the police, as for the others, 'the police will arrest them and then free them for a bribe,' she says cynically.

Another widow of Maoist violence is Puranmaya Rokka who says she fled Maoist terror to live in the shadow of the police post in Libang. When Mul Bahadur Rokka was killed in Thabang by the Maoists on the charge of being a police informer, the Maoists threatened to kill her and looted NRs 700,000 from their shop, she claimed. However, in Thabang, the villagers had a different version. She was under no threat and could have stayed on. As for losing NRs 700,000: 'Who would have thought that a shop in a poor village would be worth so much money?' The point is not that Puranmaya exaggerated her plight, but that the 'ordinary' villagers, in what is undoubtedly a Maoist stronghold, defend Maoist justice as just.

Many families of the victims of the Maoists and the police live cheek by jowl in the villages. While the relatives of the victims of Maoist violence appear to live on in the village without much fear, the families of the 'Maoist' victims of police violence, seem to live in terror of the police. Routinely, women relatives are sexually harassed and raped. There are reports of police contracting multiple marriages and abandoning pregnant women. What makes women even more tragically vulnerable is that in Nepal, abortion is punished as infanticide. The Maoists do not seem to have taken a public stand on this issue. On issues of sexuality and reproduction, the Maoists have been careful to project a conservative code of conduct.

Morality, Sexuality and the Peoples War

The issue of sexuality is a particularly explosive one in a conservative society like Nepal. Although, among the non-Aryan ethnic groups 'virginity' is not considered as sacrosanct. The sexuality of the widow is not seen as ritually dangerous and widow remarriage is possible. However, with young people becoming *farari* and living together in the jungle, there has been a great deal of adverse publicity about licentious behaviour encouraged by the Maoists. In the popular press, it is reported that every unit has a woman to sexually serve the men.[19] Sources close to the Maoists give a very different spin on the presence of two or three women in every *daffa* or guerrilla units. It is to ensure discipline and restraint during any action. And there are few reports accusing Maoists of sexual violence against women.

A major propaganda plank of the anti-Maoist drive of the government is to slur the image of the Maoists by reports in the media about condoms found in the pockets of young guerrilla fighters. Moreover, sackfuls of condoms have been found in their hideouts and in the pockets of dead guerrillas. Sources close to the Maoists explain three quite novel uses of condoms freely distributed by INGOs, (*i*) for antiseptic purposes on a cut, (*ii*) for carrying water, and (*iii*) as a protective cover for a musket-rifle.

Far from encouraging sexual licence, Hisila Yami insists that the Maoists impose strict discipline against sexual misconduct. 'A code of conduct is formulated for women and men, particularly for the combatants, so that sexuality leads to marriage, if both partners are not married,' she said. 'If one or both are married, they are warned and punished,' she said. Does this effort of the leader–patriarch to control the private life of the members indicate a reproduction of traditional gender relations? In the case of the women in Shining Path, especially the women who surrounded Abimael Guzman, Cordero argues, 'it is clear that they were also responsible for the care and attention of the personal and survival needs of the patriarch'.[20] In the Peoples War in Nepal, while there are ambiguous reports of the growth of a cult around the supremo, Prachanda, there is little, as yet to suggest any instrumental (sexual) relationship with the women in the movement.

How seriously the issue of the 'morality' of the brothers and sisters of the revolution[21] is regarded in the Peoples War, was demonstrated with exemplarity when a top leader of the UPF, Pampa Bushal was punished for sexual misconduct with a married comrade, 'Badal'. Pampa was suspended and sent to an obscure village post, for re-education. Badal was dropped from the central leadership, though he has, since, climbed back.[22] There has been no come back for Pampa Bushal. Her exemplary punishment demonstrates the politics of gender at play in the 'morality' of the sisters of the revolution.

Why are Women Becoming Maoists?

'The women have more to gain than the men from the Peoples War. That is why the women, especially the Tibeto-Burman and non-Aryan women constitute such an important part of the movement.'

—Hisila Yami

Women are visible at all levels of the Peoples War. Four years since the Peoples War was launched, women are visible in mass actions, cultural and propaganda organisations and the guerrilla units. In the mass torchlight processions women are seen massed at the head. At all-women rallies and the Women's Front district level meetings, 3,000 to 5,000 women pour in. Whether it is collective farming or a mass action to raid the granary of a local usurer, the women are the first to mobilise. The tribal socialisation of women from the oppressed ethnic groups, especially their experience of communal sharing in women work groups, makes them particularly responsive to collective action.

In the Peoples War, women are involved, directly and indirectly as cultural activists, members of village defender groups, couriers, guides, nurses, visitors to jail and to the families of the martyred and those in custody. Women are also combatants and spies.

According to Hisila Yami, in the Maoist strongholds, every third guerrilla is a woman. In the new districts where the Maoists are becoming more active, every tenth combatant is a woman. Women have become area commanders.[23] Some of the most violent actions against local 'tyrants' are associated with all-women guerilla squads armed with *khukris* and sawed-off muskets.

What does it mean for a Hindu woman in Nepal to take up arms? In a religiously sanctified culture where women are structurally excluded from political, economic and cultural domains, what does it mean for Nepali women who are becoming Maoist guerrillas? Are the women flooding into the movement because of their desire and expectation of new liberatory spaces for participation opening up for women or is it because of a Maoist sensibility that incorporates gender interests in the Peoples War's revolutionary project? As we shall see, it is a mix of both. Moreover, as we saw in the analysis of the situation of women, particularly the women of the oppressed nationalities and disadvantaged regions, there is a tradition of prot-agonism in public space, at least at an informal level.

Also, for women, especially poor peasant women of the oppressed nationalities, violence and death are very familiar. Violence is struc-turally all around them, domestic violence, social violence and the violence of the state apparatus. Women watch one out of eight chil-dren under five die in infancy. In Nepal, the maternal death rate is the highest in South Asia. It breeds a fatalism which the socio-religious culture reinforces. 'You've got to die sometime so why not die for a new order', is commonly heard in the Maoist strong-hold areas. Fatalism acquires a quixotically empowering nuance in the talk of a 'meaningful death'.[24] There is unconscious irony in Hisila's statement that 'the Peoples War gives all of them [women] a meaningful life and a meaningful death; it allows them to prove their worth is equal to the men'.

The majority of the women in the Maoist movement are from the Tibeto-Burman and non-Aryan ethnic groups, but women from upper-caste Brahmin-Chettri and Newar-Buddhist communities have also been attracted to the Maoist movement. For upper-caste women, joining the Peoples War holds out the liberating possibility of escaping an oppressive socio-cultural milieu sanctified by religion.

Going to the forest is for these women a possibility for empowerment.

At the outset of the Peoples War, few women were directly
involved. The death toll of women killed in the first two years of
the insurgency was six, three by the police and three by the Maoists.[25]
In 1998, the number of women killed by the police rose to 44, indi-
cating a much higher participation of women and the serious targeting of women in police action.

The party organ, *The Worker* in its special issue on women titled
'Fury of Women Unleashed'[26] celebrates the participation of women
at all levels, ranging 'from party committee secretaries, guerrilla
squad commanders to local volunteers and propagandists'. Inevitably, parallels will be drawn with the women in the Shining Path
who had achieved a very significant presence in the revolutionary
struggle in Peru. However, as analysts like Cordero show, even
though the women surrounding Guzman, at the time of his capture, held high party posts, they 'were there as a result of loyalty,
reliability, dedication and operational efficiency'.[27] Cordero empha-
sises the difference between their intellectual, ideological and political qualifications and those of the few women who were in the
previous central committee of the Shining Path. How different is it
in the case of the relatively young Peoples War in Nepal? Hisila
Yami maintains that there is no discrimination against women at
the political level, but there is no woman in the central committee.
Pampa Bushal who was once co-chairperson of the UPF has been
marginalised.

Mobilising Women

The Maoist strategy is consciously oriented to drawing women into
the Peoples War. In a woman-run subsistence economy, where one
in every two men is involved in seasonal migration, women form
the majority of the rural community. You cannot have an agrarian
revolution without mobilising women and putting them in guerrilla fatigues. *The Worker*, in its 'Reports from the Battlefield',
acknowledges that the 'fury of the women' has given a qualitative

leap to the development of the Peoples War in the whole country.[28] In Maoist propaganda women guerrilla commanders have been projected as formidable fighters, more committed, disciplined, reliable and militant. It also exemplifies the limits of the space reserved for women in the movement.

The Maoists have championed the cause of autonomous governments for the oppressed nationalities; they have opposed discrimination against the downtrodden and the practice of untouchability. As for women, they are 'subjected to class, gender, national and regional oppression simultaneously', says *The Worker*. The participation of women is promoted through an active propaganda network. Anecdotes eulogise the exploits of women guerrilla leaders who are cast in a heroic, self-sacrificing and self-effacing mode like Shanti Shrestha or Kamla Bhatta. To instill grit, determination and revolutionary fervour among raw recruits, much play is given to the heroic defiances of comrades like Devi Khadka. Even after she was gang-raped by the police, her spirit was not broken. She vowed to fight on and take revenge.

Young girls from schools and colleges in Gorkha district are shown joining the long list of volunteers eager to enrol with the Maoists. Stories are spread of students becoming heroic guerrilla fighters. A schoolgirl had been arrested by the police. Her 'feudal' father bailed her out but she gave him the slip and went off to join the Maoists. In a reversal of the saga of widows of martyrs vowing to carry on their husband's work, *Janadesh*, a Maoist influenced paper spotlighted a report from Bardia district of widowers of martyred women vowing to join the movement.

How central the woman guerrilla is in the public construct of the Maoist movement is evidenced by the prominence given to women in the Peoples war in the propaganda windows of the Maoists. Their website carries the image of young women marching in battle fatigues carrying guns. Prachanda, the Commander of the Peoples War, in a recent interview with the organ of the Revolutionary Communist Party (RCP), USA, the *Revolutionary Worker*, celebrated the militant activism of the women in the movement.[29] Prachanda's comments also reveal the limits of the space reserved for women in the movement. He commented how initially it was

difficult to find illiterate peasant women who could assume leadership positions but since then women are visible at all levels. In the
politico-military leadership of the district committees there are 40
to 50 women. But has the presence of women at the level of area
commanders and party secretaries influenced the programmatic
content of the movement?

Programmatically Incorporating the Women's Question

Traditionally, socialist ideology has recognised gender oppression,
but most left revolutionary struggles have dealt with it as a social
problem to be resolved with the overthrow of capitalism. The
women's question remains marginal, indeed, postponed till after
the struggle is over. Within the revolutionary struggle the issue of
gender discrimination is treated as something that dissolves when
primary questions of feudal exploitation and class oppression are
resolved. In short, gender oppression will melt away as more radical commitments are made by women and men.

In the Peoples War women make up a third of the movement.
What impact has the massive presence of women in the Maoist
movement had on redefining the women's question in the Peoples
War ideology? Prachanda, the General Secretary of the Communist
Party of Nepal (Maoist) admits that before the launch of the Peoples
War, they had not taken the women's question 'seriously' but afterwards with the dramatic importance of women's activism in the
Peoples War, the women's question has been ideologically and programmatically incorporated. In programmatic content, the Maoist
struggle at the ground level has given space to an anti-alcohol campaign, issues of sexual violence and women's exploitation. But on
the issue of abortion, which is illegal in Nepal, Prachanda steers
clear of the legal/illegal issue but engages with it at a gender-practical
level, i.e., in the context of the Maoist women cadre who become
pregnant and may be obliged to quit the movement. There is no
inflection of a gendered discourse of women's rights.

With a third of the Maoist guerrillas being women in the areas
where the Maoists are most active, practical considerations have

obliged the party to put on the agenda the issue of maternity and child care of the women in the fighting ranks. Prachanda, in a wide ranging interview to *Revolutionary Worker*,[30] mentions the practical difficulties of women guerrillas becoming pregnant and the provision of foster care structures for children. Gender neutral discourses of revolutionary struggles often flounder on issues of sexual morality and when women guerrillas become pregnant. It is noticeable that in social-political revolutions, it is mothers who are expected to leave their children behind, not fathers. In Nepal's 'Peoples War', is there serious questioning of the feminisation of parenting or for that matter cooking?

At the ideological level, just before the launch of the Peoples War, the UPF had released a memorandum of 40 demands. Taking on board the women's question, No. 19 demanded: 'Patriarchal exploitation and discrimination against women should be stopped. The daughter should be allowed access to property.' The key phrase is the daughter's 'access to property'. In an agrarian revolution, women's 'access to property' means women's right to land.

The 'roots of women's oppression must be sought not only within the sphere of production but also reproduction, i.e., not only in the economic structure but also in the social and cultural structure,' asserts Hisila. The CPN (Maoist) ideologically reaches out to women to join the Peoples War and smash the state, because the state treats them as 'second class citizens . . . [victim to] rape, trafficking and the process of commodification through advertisments'. Implicit is the recognition of a continuum in the structure of oppression for women which stretches from the family, society, the labour market and to the state in all its manifestations.

However, it is surprising, given the flood of women getting involved in the Peoples War, that the ideological patron of the Maoist movement, Dr Baburam Bhattrai does not engage with the women's question in his political writing on the New Democratic Revolution (NDR). Clearly, the importance of the presence of women in the movement is recognised, but Bhattrai, in a detailed analysis of the logic and structure of NDR and its core, land reform, finds no space to incorporate a gender analysis. In his article 'Politico-Economic Rationale of People's War in Nepal', gender oppression is subsumed in the overall struggle against feudal and imperialist oppression. With the shedding of the fetters of feudalism and imperialism, patriarchal oppression, automatically, will be cast off. The writings of the movement's ideologue, Bhattrai rarely make any serious mention of the women's question, in contrast to the focus on the question of oppressed nationalities.[31]

Hisila denies that the Peoples War subsumes gender oppression in class oppression. She maintains, that 'since the NDR is antifeudalism, it will at once remove feudal Brahminical Hindu rule which sees women in relationship to men. The anti-imperialist nature of NDR will discourage unequal trade relations with imperialist and expansionist forces, thus saving women from sweat shops where they are exploited sexually and economically. It will prepare the ground for removing prostitution, consumerisation and commoditisation of women in Nepal.' It is a rhetoric which echoes the dominant narrative of other revolutionary struggles, that gender oppression will dissolve when 'feudal exploitation and class oppression' is defeated.

But there is also the counter reality of how women in the movement have reshaped the ideology of the movement and ensured that at the ground level the women's question is not postponed. In the Maoist stronghold areas, most of the mass actions are related to getting women justice, punishing rapists, wresting back the usurped land of single women, punishing men for polygamy and mass action against liquor dealers. 'The women have more to gain than the men from the Peoples War', says Hisila Yami. 'That is why the women, especially the Tibeto-Burman and non-Aryan women constitute such an important part of the movement.'

In an incident narrated earlier, in Surkhet district, an all-women guerrilla squad punishes a wife beater, promotes anti-alcohol and adult literacy and creates political consciousness at the ground level of a structure in which oppression, poverty, wife beating, alcoholism and illiteracy, all coalesce. It is anecdotal, but reflects what is popularly spoken about as happening in thousands of villages where the Maoist women are active.

But this is essentially at the grassroots level. Have women been able to reshape the programmatic agenda at the ideological and policy determination level? Hisila maintains that women are given due representation in the political power being exercised in the 'embryonic new democratic state'. Women are party committee secretaries. Does it imply gaining policy responsibility? The experience of women in high party posts in the Shining Path counsels a cautious assessment of how empowering is the women's access to area commander or party committee secretary positions in Nepal's Maoist movement. However, it should be mentioned that there are armed struggles like Zapatista movement in Mexico, where women are once again highly visible as protagonists and commanders. Here the revolutionary project seems to have as its goal not only the transformation of relations with the state but also gender relations.[32]

As for the Peoples War in Nepal, four years after it was launched, women co-leaders of the movement like Pampa Bushal, are no longer prominent. Presumably she is one of the 'bourgeois intellectual women' denounced by Prachanda. There are no women at the regional or central committee level. The majority of the women in the movement are illiterate or neo-literate. The exception are the students and teachers of Gorkha district who are joining the movement.

Gorkha: Classroom to Jungle

The epicentres of the Maoist insurgency are the remote underdeveloped mid-western hill districts of Rolpa, Rukum and Jajarkot. The mass of the people who have fled to the forests to take up arms are poor and illiterate peasants. Next only to these Maoist flashpoints is the Gorkha district. The fact that the Maoists should establish their influence in the relatively prosperous Gorkha district in the well-connected central hills, has to do with a history of radical left activity in this area. In Gorkha district, it is literate women and men who are joining the struggle. Ironically, it is the success of the adult literacy campaign which has paved the way for women to become active in the public life of the community, for girls to go to schools and for girls politicised in school to be drawn into the armed struggle.

Gorkha district has a tradition of radical left politics. The top politico-military leadership of the Peoples War hails from Gorkha, including Dr Baburam Bhattrai, Pushpa Kamal Dahal alias Prachanda. Some of the better known women guerrillas like Kamala Bhatta and Shanti Sreshtha were from Gorkha, one from the Brahmin community, the other a Newar Buddhist.

Pampa Bushal, the former co-chairperson of the UPF is a Brahmin. Hisila Yami, the head of the Women's Front, comes from a Newar Buddhist family of the Kathmandu valley. She is associated with Gorkha by marriage to Dr Baburam Bhattrai. Hisila Yami, coming from a Newari Buddhist family of six daughters and an only son, had been weaned on gender sensitivity. Political consciousness, too, came early. Hisila's parents were involved in the anti-Rana struggle. In Delhi to study architecture, she met and married Bhattrai who introduced her to Marxism and a pro-people activism.

In Gorkha, women militants come from both Aryan Hindu castes and the *jan jati* or ethnic groups. Young women have been politicised in schools, the adult literacy classes and NGO-sponsored income generation women collectives. During the preparatory phase of the Peoples War, students, teachers and schools were priority areas for Maoist ideological indoctrination. Gorkha district schools too came under the sway of Maoist influence, with not only young men but also young women getting radicalised. The Gorkha district stands out for the significantly higher number of girls in schools. The experience of the Gorkha district is reminiscent of the Nicaraguan phenomenon of 'girls in the literacy class when 13 and in the militias when 14'. Literacy campaigns supported by INGOs designed to promote the empowerment of women, inadvertently encouraged many conscientised young women to choose subsequent empowerment through armed struggle.

In Gorkha district female adult literacy level is above the national average and nearly three times as much as that in Rolpa and Rukum (Table 6.2).

In the villages of Gorkha district, adult education campaigns for women, initiated by international NGOs like Save the Children (USA) helped women appreciate the value of education for empowerment and support education for both girls and boys. Surveys done

TABLE 6.2

	Life Expectancy		Adult Literacy %		Mean Years of Schooling		Gender Development Index (GDI)
	F	M	F	M	F	M	
Nepal	52.4	55	21.3	54.3	1.1	2.5	0.27
Gorkha	51.8	54	24.5	47.8	1.5	2.8	0.27
Rukum	49.1	51	9.8	50.2	0.5	2.4	0.19
Rolpa	50.1	52	8.7	50.7	0.5	2.4	0.19

Source: *Nepal Human Development Report 1998*, Nepal South Asia Centre, Kathmandu, 1998.

in villages like Takukot in Gorkha where Save the Children had been active for 15 years revealed that of the women who participated in the programme, 90 per cent of their schoolgoing children are actually in school.[33]

What is striking is the dramatic increase in the number of girls studying in village schools where earlier, barely any girls were seen. Sancharika, a Nepali women's organisation claims that 50 per cent of all students are girls in Gorkha district village schools. One reason may be that parents are sending their sons outside the insurgency-affected Gorkha district to study in Kathmandu. They fear their sons will get politicised in schools and campuses which are under the sway of Maoists. Also boys will be the first to be picked up in an environment where all students are suspects. Left behind are the girls at school, many of whom have come under the influence of the Maoists.

Indoctrination in the Gorkha district begins young. Ask a 10-year-old girl about the Maoists and promptly comes the reply— 'Maoists grab the property of the rich and give to the poor. The Maoists are fighting for justice for the poor. The Maoists are tortured and killed by the police because they are working for the poor.' Ask about the victims of the Maoists, and there is not a trace of remorse. 'He was killed because he was a fool, or worse, an informer.' Younger people exposed to the radical political thinking of teachers and older students are particularly susceptible. With the police targeting relatives of Maoists and student-cultural activists, many girls and boys have been pushed underground.

For many Gorkha women in the movement, the road underground to the forest, armed struggle and capture or death, often begins with the overground student-based cultural activities of the Peoples Front as in the case of Niru Pokhrel. She was arrested as she was walking to a neighbouring village to do a cultural programme. In the case of Shiva Kumari Biswakarma, a college student in Kathmandu, she was arrested by the police when she went with her room-mate to visit a brother in jail. The minute they said they were from Gorkha, they were arrested. She was a cultural activist in a sister organisation of the Communist Party of Nepal-Maoist and not a party member, she said.

Young family members of known Maoists are harassed and it is almost a foregone conclusion that they will be forced to go underground. When Gupta Bahadur Nagrachi was killed in an 'encounter', his sister, was closely watched at the mourning ceremony. 'It was only a question of time', the villagers said, 'when she, too, would go underground.'

Maoist women like Sarla Srestha, an efficient organiser and an area military commander, are spoken of as role models. She was a charismatic student leader, who mesmerised her audience. Sarla was in Class X when her hide and seek with the police began till she was killed a couple of years later. Local villagers tell tales of her courage under fire. She was in the student committee when the Peoples Front directed local cadre to organise torch processions on the eve of the Peoples War in February 1996. Students in Gorkha grow up on the revolutionary heroics of women guerrilla martyrs.

Police Targeting Women and Children

In protracted, internal conflicts, with the women left to negotiate the public sites of confrontation, the communal tap, the marketplace, the health centres, the schools and the administrative offices, it is inevitable that they will be at risk. Indeed, in guerrilla conflicts, police terror or counter-terror is directed at making the 'conflict' itself the primary problem, eclipsing the structural injustice at the heart of the conflict. In this strategy of terror and counter-terror, women living with conflict, i.e., the stable element of the community, become obvious targets.

More directly, women are becoming victims of police violence because of the importance of the presence of women at all levels in the Maoist movement. The increase in the number of women 'rebels' killed in the Peoples War, reflects their growing numbers as guerrillas. Also, women's open defiance of traditional roles and empowering themselves by taking up arms in the jungle, may have provoked a double punishment for what is seen as a double challenge to the social–political order. In this context, the rape and killing of women 'Maoists', is not an aberration but a systematic instrument of terror and repression. Rape is routine and the 12 women interviewed in Lalitpur jail from Gorkha district, spoke of rape and torture when in police custody.

How seriously the coercive state apparatus regards the challenge of the women's revolt may be indicated by the excessive zeal shown by the police in firing on women and children at a cultural programme in Kavre district in 1999. Incidents such as the arrest of hundreds of women in Kathmandu who were attending a public meeting of the legal All Nepal Women's (Revolutionary) Association, further strengthens this view. In November 1998, at a programme organised by the ANW(R)A to discuss 'Future Strategy for Nepali Women's Liberation Movement' in Thapathali campus in the heart of Kathmandu, 168 persons, women and children, were arrested on suspicion of being Maoist sympathisers. Following a court order 36 were held back in custody and others were released after being detained for two to 15 days.

As for children, the Peoples War strategy of integrating them in the guerrilla struggle, has legitimised the targeting of children by the police. According to the INSEC *Human Rights Yearbook 1999*, on the charge of supporting the Maoists, in 1998, 11 girls and one boy (under 15) were killed by the police. Some of the captured guerrillas locked up in jail are child soldiers.

The Peoples War propaganda lauds the fact that with the women come children, who in the process get indoctrinated. On these potential revolutionaries will rest the future of the Peoples War. But what about their future and the future of societies where children are in militias? At a time when they should be in school they are fighting in the jungle for a new dawn when their government, their education system will be in place. Children, as the wars in Africa have shown, who grow up with the gun, are likely to look for opportunities to pick it up again as adults.

The Maoists insist that in Nepal, politics is in control of violence, but there are too many scarred battlefields where violence has become an end in itself. For many young people in schools, girls and boys, the road to empowerment has become the barrel of a gun or in this case a *khukri*. Poverty breeds extremism and the failure of existing parliamentary politics to promise even the hope of change, radicalises politics. The failure of the democratic agenda to make any difference in the people's grinding poverty and neglect, has driven the young into the Peoples War. And the government's policy of militarily responding to what is at the core a political protest against structural injustice, can only intensify the conflict.

NOTES

1. For a detailed analysis of the Women in the Shining Path, see Isabel Coral Cordero, 'Women in War: Impact and Responses', in Steve Stern, ed., *Shining and Other Paths: War and Society in Peru 1980-1995*, Duke University Press, Durham, 1998, pp. 345–74. The book as well as the cited article tends to emphasise people's resistance to the Shining Path.
2. See Dr Baburam Bhattrai's article 'Politico-Economic Rationale of Peoples War in Nepal' (1998) available on the website *http:/www.maoism.org/misc/nepal*, Maoist Documentation Project. The landholding pattern of Thabang village, one of the 'liberated zone' villages in Rolpa district gives an insight into the relative deprivation of the peasants. Landholding of a third of the households was more than subsistence, a third was barely subsistence and a third was less than subsistence, with one member in active service and 10 per cent who drew pensions from the Nepal, Indian or British armies. See Augusta Molnar, *The Kham Magar Women of Thabang. Status of Women in Nepal*, Vol. 2, Pt 2, CEDA, Tribhuvan University, Kathmandu, 1981.
3. According to official statistics 45 per cent of the population is below the poverty belt. However, *Nepal Human Development Report 1998*, Nepal South Asia Centre, Kathmandu, 1998, p. 295 (Study submitted to UNDP, Nepal), estimates it to be more likely 70 per cent. See also Dr Baburam

Bhattrai, *Nepal: A Marxist View*, Jhilko Publication Pvt Ltd, Kathmandu, 1990.

4. *Nepal Human Rights Yearbook 1996: The Maoist Peoples War and Human Rights*, Informal Sector Service Centre (INSEC), Kathmandu, 1996, and South Asia Human Rights Documentation Centre, 'Midnight Killings in Rolpa', Human Rights Killing in the Maoist War, 1996.

5. *Nepal Human Rights Yearbook 1997: Criminalization of Politics*, INSEC, Kathmandu, 1997, and 'Red Salute to the Immortal Martyrs of the People's War,' *The Worker*, June 1996.

6. *The Kathmandu Post*, 28 January 2000.

7. David N. Gellner, Joanna Pfaff-Czarnecka and John Whelpton (eds), *Nationalism and Ethnicity in a Hindu Kingdom: The Politics of Culture in Contemporary Nepal*, Harwood Academic Publishers, Amsterdam, 1997, p. 53.

8. *Nepal Human Development Report 1998*, n. 3. 'Beyond Beijing Mid Decade Meet in South Asia: Nepal Monitoring Platform, Pledge and Performance', report presented by Beyond Beijing Committee, Lalitpur, Kathmandu, August 1999.

9. See Shree Khadka, 'Decision Making Role of Magar Women in Bukeni Village of Baglung District'. Ph.D. thesis, Tribhuvan University, Kathmandu, 1997.

10. Empirically based on the field investigation of an all-women team of Nepali and Indian journalists who toured Rolpa and Rukum in May 1998.

11. See the section on 'Human Security and Social Protection in Nepal', report to the Beyond Beijing review, n. 8.

12. *The Kathmandu Post*, 14 May 1998.

13. *The Kathmandu Post*, 1 & 8 August 1999.

14. 'Red Salute to the Immortal Martyrs of the Peoples War', n. 5 and February 1998. See Maoist website *http://www.maoism.org/misc/nepal/nepal.htm*.

15. Rita Manchanda, 'Maoist Insurgency in Nepal', *Frontline*, 12–25 September 1998.

16. Gyanu Pande, 'Situation in Rolpa and Rukum', *Himalaya Times*, 4 June 1998.

17. Empirically based on interviews done by Banskota and Gautam in April 1999.

18. Hisila Yami was interviewed after she went underground in 1997. Hisila Yami is the wife of Dr Baburam Bhattrai.

19. Tirtha Gautam, Member of Parliament from Rukum, was full of reports about the sexual excesses of the Maoists. The Nepali press is full of allegations and lurid reports of the sexual licentiousness of the guerrillas.

20. Cordero, 'Women in War', n. 1.

21. Diana Mulinari writing about sexuality and sisters of the revolution during the Sandinista war in Nicaragua, says, 'The morality of the sisters of

the revolution is central to understanding the politics of gender within the political leadership. A link existed between women's credibility and their sexual activities. To be taken seriously women must act as morally correct—in the words of Andrea, "they have to respect you as a campanera. You cannot go to bed with any of them. If you do so . . . they don't respect you afterwards".' 'Broken Dreams in Nicaragua', in Lois A. Lorentzen and Jennifer Turpin, eds, *The Women and War Reader*, New York University Press, New York, 1998, p. 160.

22. The fact that three other senior male comrades who were found guilty of sexual misconduct, were left unscathed, lends suspicion to the conspiracy theory of a power struggle to sideline the popular Badal with Pampa playing an instrumental role.

23. Parallel to women guerrillas in the Peoples War, Nepali women have been joining the police and the army. There are 234 women including 29 officers but in non-combatant roles. Nepali women legislators have been demanding that women be recruited for combat duties. *The Kathmandu Post*, 15 August 1999.

24. Nancy Scheper-Hughes, 'Maternal Thinking and the Politics of War', in Lorentzen and Turpin, eds, *The Women and War Reader*, n. 21, pp. 227–33.

25. *Nepal Human Rights Yearbook 1999: Political Corruption in Nepal*, INSEC, Kathmandu, 1999. Peoples War sources claim that seven women were martyred in 1996 and two more in 1997.

26. Maoist website; *The Worker*, February 1999.

27. Cordero, 'Women in War', n. 1, p. 353.

28. *The Worker*, February 1999.

29. 'Red Flag on the Roof of the World', interview with Comrade Prachanda, general secretary of Communist Party of Nepal (Maoist), *Revolutionary Worker*, 20 February 2000; website *http://www.mcs.net/rwor. org*.

30. 'Red Flag on the Roof of the World', interview with Comrade Prachanda, n. 29.

31. Cordero claims that no official documents of the 1980s Shining Path nor Guzman's 'interview of the century' of 1988, contain any reference to the problem of gender. In a private Shining Path event, Guzman is quoted as saying 'We must see that we sidestepped the popular feminine movement, women being the half that holds up the sky: to fight the enemy that is transitorily strong with one arm tied behind one's back is foolish. The struggle for the emancipation of women is part of the liberation of the proletariat—this is the Communist way of understanding the problem—from which derives equality before law and equality in life.' Cordero, 'Women in War', n. 1, pp. 351–52.

32. Mariana Mora, 'Zapatismo: Gender, Power and Social Transformation', in Lorentzen and Turpin, *The Women and War Reader*, n. 1, pp. 164–74.

33. Save the Children has now wound up its work in Gorkha. One of the most dramatic early Maoist actions was the attack on the SCF office in Gorkha. The Maoists in their memorandum of demands had accused INGOs and NGOs of being tools of imperialism. Ironically, it was the adult educational campaigns of SCF and the Lutheran World Service which encouraged women to go to school, lead and participate in women's groups, take part in community meetings and work as community health workers which politicised them.

7

Women's Narratives from the Chittagong Hill Tracts*

MEGHNA GUHATHAKURTA

Introduction

It is interesting to note that most of the research works on the Chittagong Hill Tracts (CHT) in Bangladesh have been conducted from the point of view of strategic studies and/or from consider-ations of domestic and regional security. Conversely some materials have been written from the angle of human rights concern in the region. Very few works in recent years tell us about social change in the Hill Tracts or recent living patterns and lifestyles there. The available works on anthropology or sociology deal with unchang-ing timeless concepts of 'tribal' life and livelihood, which hardly touch questions of a political nature. The reasons for this are not hard to fathom. From the time that the Parbattyo Chattogram Jana Samhiti Samiti (PCJSS or JSS), the central organisation for the strug-gle for autonomy of the Hill Tracts was formed in the Chittagong

*Acknowledgements: I am deeply grateful to my research assistant Shomari Chakma. I also thank Shuvro Jyoti Chakma and Hasina Ahmed for their help with this research. I am especially indebted to all the women who trusted me enough to share with me their experiences and understanding.

Hill Tracts, the area became a national security zone. Consequently, news and reports about the area were almost totally blacked out in the media. Information, apart from that screened by the military command, could only be made available through the international press or organisations like Amnesty International and the Chittagong Hill Tracts Commission. Some of the more serious treatises on the CHT have dealt with the politics of nationalities, identities, and the inadequacy of a modern nation-state or unitary constitution in accommodating such identities as well as looking at the problem in the light of a post-nationalist discourse.

Just as this state of affairs led to Bengali civil society being ignorant about social and political life in the CHT, it also led to the construction of the dominant notion of the CHT as a security zone, in which the logic of insurgency and counter-insurgency prevailed and civilians had little to do or say. This left a wide gap in the literature on the CHT. Just as the hill peoples' perception of the conflict was left unsaid except when it became a human rights issue, women's perceptions of the conflict and their role in the conflict beyond that of victims were left unrepresented. It is the intention of this chapter to explore whether there is a women's version of the struggle. What are their different ways of coping with conflict and when are they considered as agents? Is there space for exploring the woman question within a struggle of identity politics? How do women reformulate questions of peace? Are they marginalised in the peace process and if so why?

Although the current research project has set out to answer the above questions, answers have been difficult to gather in the context of the CHT. This is due to the absence of a systematic study of social and political change in the CHT, since virtually nothing has been written about women's changing position in the societies of the Hill Tracts. Therefore, in researching the question of women in conflict situations, I have had to base most of my assumptions on the basis of primary data gathered. My conclusions therefore are specific to the time and space I have conducted my interviews[1] in and must not be generalised for all the people of the Hill Tracts.

In my analysis I will attempt to locate the position of women in the context of the emerging civil society activism in the Hill Tracts.

It was the civil society groups which spearheaded the political resistance and raised their demands in a more democratic framework
within the polity of Bangladesh. I will assess the general political
awareness of women, especially with regard to state, ethnicity and
nationalism. Then I shall see how women negotiate conflict in both
public and private domains and finally look at women's active agency
as an organised form of protest.

Changing Nature of the Conflict

The main events and features of the conflict in the CHT are not an
entirely untold story.[2] It has been told time and again from the
perspective of a dominant security concern as well as from a human
rights concern in the literature on the CHT. The CHT occupies a
physical area of 5,093 sq. miles or 13,295 sq. kilometres constituting
10 per cent of the total land area of Bangladesh. It shares borders
with India and Myanmar. Out of the total land area of the CHT,
only about 3.1 per cent is suitable for agricultural cultivation, 18.7
per cent is under horticulture and the rest 72 per cent is used for
forestry.

The CHT is inhabited by about 13 (according to some estimates,
10) ethnic groups among whom the Chakmas, Marmas and Tripuras
constitute the majority. Non-indigenous hill people, i.e., Bengalis
who are predominantly Muslims, also at present live in the CHT.
According to the 1991 Census, the total population is 974,465 out
of which 501,145 (i.e., 51 per cent) are from groups of different
ethnic origins. About 49 per cent are Bengalis. It is to be noted that
about 70,000 refugees who were in the Indian state of Tripura from
1986 to 1998, are not included in this census report.

It has also been reported that fertility rates are not as high among
the hill people because of the instability in society. The average
family size for Rangamati, Khagrachari and Bandarban districts in
CHT is 5.4, 4.9, 5.2 respectively compared to 5.6 for Bangladesh as
a whole. Hill people also apprehend that the state's family planning
programme is another device to keep the population low, so that
Bengalis can become the majority ethnic group in the CHT. Census

reports revealing a demographic shift in favour of Bengalis tend to confirm these apprehensions.[3]

The CHT conflict involves issues like the land question, the transfer of population from plains districts to the hills, the control of administration by non-inhabitants of the CHT and the discrimination, deprivation and exploitation of the hill peoples in social, cultural, economic and political fields and the programme of assimilation of the indigenous hill people into the majority Bengali population. These concerns have attracted attention, national and international.

However, when we focus our attention on women in conflict situations, a slightly different scenario of events and perceptions proves to be more relevant and important. This relates to the evolution of organised resistance movements in the area, the incorporation of women and their perspectives into the movement as well as how and in what way the hill people perceived and remembered the changing nature of conflict in the region. This is what I will try to outline in this section and will simultaneously try to depict its consequences for women in particular and how women perceived or engaged themselves in the evolutionary characterisation of the conflict.

The people of the hills also perceived different markers, which distinguished one period from another, and they were not always related to the change of government in Dhaka but had to do with the different policies followed by successive regimes. From the perspective of the hill people, the conflict in the Hill Tracts may be categorised into the following phases: (*i*) early mobilisation phase, (*ii*) the demand for autonomy and the growth of armed struggle, (*iii*) army raids and operation, (*iv*) the settlers issue and clustered villages as counter-insurgency measures, (*v*) ceasefires and the growth of civil society movements of the hill people, and (*vi*) the accord and post-accord situation.

Early Mobilisation Phase

Much of the written history of the Chittagong Hill Tracts has been sketched in accordance with what happened in the dominant political system and the changes brought about by dominant politics, for example, the partition of British India, the independence of Bangladesh, the assassination of Sheikh Mujib, or President Ziaur Rahman; or in the developmental sphere, for example, in the construction of the Kaptai hydro-electricity project; the forced settlement of Bengalis from the plains, the creation of the Hill District Councils and other administrative measures. All these left their impact on the lives and livelihood of the Jumma people. But they were not silent spectators to these events. They responded and intervened both individually and organisationally.

The first step to organise resistance was against the construction of the Kaptai hydro-electricity dam (1957–62) which made thousands of people homeless.[4] Manobendra Narayan Larma, a headmaster, spearheaded the movement to make the hill people aware of their rights and it became popularly known as the 'headmaster's movement'. A political colour was added to the movement when some leaders started organising it as the Rangamati Communist Party. In post-independence Bangladesh, it was under the leadership of M. N. Larma that the Parbattyo Chattogram Jana Samhiti Samiti was formed on 7 March 1972.

A students' front, the Pahari Chattra Samiti already existed with a strong base in Rangamati College. This Samiti also had women members. We found one such woman in the course of our research. Mithila Chakma, now in her 40s and married with two children, had been the vice-president of the Pahari Chattra Samiti, Rangamati College in 1973. She remembers how the demand for autonomy gained ground among the people of Rangamati. She was present at the meeting where Sheikh Mujibur Rahman, the prime minister of Bangladesh gave a speech where he declared that all hill people were 'Bangalees'. She remembers people feeling irritated and gradually dispersing soon after he uttered the word. As the demand for autonomy gained ground, she was active in awareness raising programmes comprising rallies, leafletting and poster pasting.

Mithila described how she perceived her role in the organisation in those early years. She was a dancer and had won an All Pakistan Dance Award in 1968. She therefore emphasised the cultural aspect in the students' front. She felt that if Paharis were to have a different identity from Bengalis, then they must demonstrate it in their

culture. So she started to learn the dances of all the indigenous people and taught these dances to a group of hill women. In this way a
cultural troupe of the students' wing was formed by the name of
'Giri Shur' (music of the hills). They performed their first show
called *Ek Mutho Alo* (A Fistful of Light) in 1972. Later they were
asked to perform at the victory day celebrations in Dhaka. Mithila
claimed that because of her endeavour, the government of Bangladesh was forced to recognise cultural differences and later appropriated it into state practice by setting up a tribal cultural centre in
Rangamati.

The Demand for Autonomy and the Growth of Armed Struggle

After the assassination of Sheikh Mujibur Rahman and the promul-
gation of martial law, things became worse. As the campaign for
autonomy gathered momentum, the Bangladesh government, after
1975, unleashed a reign of terror against it. The JSS responded by
organising an armed resistance group called the 'Shanti Bahini'. From
then on, the situation rapidly turned into that of counter-insurgency
operations under the administration of President Ziaur Rahman.
M.N. Larma fled to India.

The history of the CHT was to become a series of killings, violation of human rights and displacements of people from their homes
and land. The people of the Hill Tracts realised that the struggle for
autonomy had brought them into direct armed confrontation with
the Bangladesh government and the army. Mobilisation continued
among the people in many forms. One of the ways in which the
people were encouraged to join the Shanti Bahini was through patriotic songs. According to reports heard, one particular song proved
to be so emotionally arousing that it was banned from being played.
The lyricist Ranjit Dewan was reportedly hunted by the army and
forced to flee to India. The first few lines of the song were:

Jimit Jimit Juni Joley	The fireflies spark
Muru Desat Deao Toley	Among the hills, under the skies
Iaan Aama Dech	This is my country

| *Iaan Toma Dech* | It is yours |
| *Iaan Bego Dech* | It belongs to us all |

The meaning of the song may appear mundane but if listened to carefully the words are strangely evocative to the Bengali ear as it is reminiscent of a famous anti-British Bengali nationalist song '*Dhono Dhanya Pusphey Bhora, Amaderi Boshundhara*' (This Bountiful World of Ours) used profusely during the Bangladesh liberation war and then inducted as the slow marching tune of the Bengali nation! The tune is a hill tune and the words appropriate the symbols of Bengali nationalism in a reverse manner quite effectively. For example, *Sonar Desh* is used as opposed to *Sonar Bangla*. The symbol of the mother and brother as patriotic symbols is the same as that used in *Dhono Dhanya Pushpey Bhora*. So is the act of valorising the land of birth over the rest of the world. The last phrase is in contrast to some of the images used in Chakma folk songs where a common theme is the lament of a Pahari yearning to go outside the hills to see and explore the world.

Army Raids and Operation

In the early 1970s, the whole of the CHT was brought under military control and the local civil administration undermined. Counter-insurgency operations in the CHT produced fresh waves of refugees into India during 1979–86.[5] Whole villages were uprooted for security and developmental reasons, displacing thousands. Between 1980 and 1993, the Bangladesh army and Bengali settlers were implicated in 11 massacres and the plunder and destruction of villages in the CHT. During the confrontation between the JSS and the army, military raids on villages were common. People lived in perpetual fear of the army. A young girl, currently a university student, reminisces about her childhood in this way:

> I don't like writing about my childhood. Why? The answer for me is too painful. The atmosphere in which I grew up was more filled with fear than pleasure. Whenever we used to go out and

play or go for a swim in the river, fear used to accompany us. We had to be on constant alert, ready to run home and warn our father, 'Hide, the army is coming' or tell our uncle, 'Quick, run'! Or the neighbour's son, 'Please hide!' The girls would all go inside until the army left the village. Only old people would come out. Sometimes even they were not spared. And the goats, the chicken, the fruits that we grew. . . all had to be surrendered to them at their command, free of cost. Or else we would be taken to the Camp. And Camp was a terrifying place!

Curfews were routine and passes were necessary to go to the market. Rationing of goods was common. Every Pahari was looked upon with suspicion as a potential Shanti Bahini. During this time there was hardly any scope of resistance from the civilians. After a ceasefire was agreed upon between the JSS and the Bangladesh government, people could relax a little because the raids were not that frequent, except when the Shanti Bahini violated the ceasefire or the military felt they had something to defend.

The Settlers Issue and Clustered Villages as Counter-insurgency Measures

Another watershed in the inter-communal relations between Paharis and Bengalis in the hills was the planned settlement of Bengalis from the plains. They were settled in clustered villages with military camps surrounding them for protection. Chakma, Marma and Tripura villages in the vicinity suffered as a result. Many hill people claimed that as a result of this, inter-communal tension increased. Also, the advent of plains settlers caused a deterioration in law and order. One of my interviewers described the situation as follows: 'Before people left their doors open because there was no fear of theft. But then they started locking doors. Beggars also grew in number. Intermingling with each other was not the done thing.' The hatred between the old and new settlers was strong and reflected in the derogatory terms they used for each other. Chakmas often called them *bhangti poisha* (old change), or *shoronarthi* (refugees). They in turn called the hill people *chakkus* and *moghs*. Even the resistance movement drew a difference between old Bengali settlers and those forcefully settled by the military.

Ceasefires and the Growth of Civil Society Movements of the Hill People

On 21 October 1985, the first formal dialogue between the JSS and President H.M. Ershad's government was held and the CHT problem was identified as a political one. The JSS tabled its five-point demand, including demands for provincial autonomy with legislature, withdrawal of all Bengali Muslim settlers who entered the CHT after 17 August 1947 and restoration of traditional land rights and power for land administration. The government rejected them. In February 1989, the government passed three Hill District Local Council Acts and constituted the Rangamati, Khagrachari and Bandarban Hill District Councils in June 1989. In the last nine years, of the 22 subjects the Councils were empowered to address, only 12 subjects were transferred with nominal powers.[6] In 1991, the Bangladesh Nationalist Party headed by Prime Minister Begum Khaleda Zia assumed power. The JSS unilaterally declared ceasefire from 10 August to 10 November 1992. Subsequently, till March 1996 six rounds of meetings were held but no agreement was reached.

During this period of prolonged ceasefire, the beginning of talks between the Ershad regime and the JSS, as well as the setting up of the District Councils, the hill people felt there was more political space than before to register their protest against army atrocities. Although the JSS asked the Jumma people to reject the District Councils, the political space which was opened up led to the formation of the political wings of the JSS, the Pahari Gono Parishad (PGP), the Pahari Chattra Parishad (PCP) and later in the 1990s, the Hill Women's Federation (HWF). The HWF became active on the issue of rape as an instrument of counter-insurgency. Among the many crimes committed against the people of the Hill Tracts, sexual violence such as rape, molestation and harassment was particularly prevalent. These civil society groups spearheaded the resistance and raised the autonomy demand in a more democratic framework within the polity of Bangladesh.

The Accord and Post-accord Situation

The Bangladesh Awami League headed by Prime Minister Sheikh Hasina took over power in June 1996. From 21 to 24 December 1997, a 12-member National Committee on CHT Affairs comprising the Bangladesh government and the JSS held seven rounds of peace talks. The JSS placed its modified Five-Point Charter of Demands, which included demands for regional autonomy, withdrawal of Muslim settlers, constitutional recognition of the ethnic entity of the indigenous hill people, restoration of traditional land rights and administration, and withdrawal of armed forces.

The peace talks held between the government and the JSS from 1985 to 1997 had been arranged through a liaison committee named CHT Co-ordination Committee. But the Chittagong Hill Tracts Peace Agreement was signed between the Government of Bangladesh and the PCJSS on 2 December 1997. This accord with the subsequent surrender of arms on 10 February 1998 was hailed by the Bangladesh government and foreign governments as a positive step towards maintaining peace in the region. However, nationally the agreement has created much controversy and polarised political as well as civil society. The government and its supporters regard the treaty as the best possible settlement of the CHT issue; while the mainstream opposition party, the Bangladesh National Party (BNP) in alliance with Jamaat-e Islam, term it as unconstitutional, a sell-out to the 'terrorists' and above all a violation of state sovereignty. This is due to India's involvement in the conflict as provider of refuge to fleeing civilians and arms to 'insurgents'. In this highly polarised debate, a faction of the Hill Peoples Organisations, which used to operate within the political boundaries of Bangladesh as the civilian wings of the armed PCJSS, expressed their dissatisfaction over the terms of the agreement claiming that their demands were compromised by their leaders.

It was expected that with the arms surrender of the JSS, armed confrontation would come to an end. But no word was mentioned within the treaty or even in the peace process on the question of demilitarisation. Three cantonments exist in the area and three brigade headquarters in each district capital. According to one

estimate the ratio of military personnel to hill people is said to be
1:6. The mainstream opposition has resisted the withdrawal of armed
forces from the area and the ruling party has been defensive about
it. The reality in the Hill Tracts is that two decades of virtual military rule in these areas has undermined the civil administration and
civil society. There is no sign of this changing overnight.

When the JSS surrendered and signed the treaty with Sheikh
Hasina's government, there was a split in the civilian wings of the
organisation. Public opinion was substantially with the 'accordists'
but disillusionment with the government's failure to implement the
accord in any meaningful way has drawn many into the anti-accordist
camp. Lately, the PGP, PCP and the HWF members who were
critics of the accord have joined to form a new political party, the
United Peoples Democratic Front (UPDF). They have pledged
to continue the movement for full autonomy within the polity of
Bangladesh.

Women Caught in Conflict: Victimisation and Coping

It cannot be denied that in a militarised situation, Jumma women
constitute the most vulnerable section of the population. Among
the many crimes committed against the people of the Hill Tracts,
sexual violence such as rape, molestation and harassment was especially prevalent. In 1990 information from one refugee camp in India
indicated that one in every 10 of the total female population had
been a victim of rape in the CHT. According to a survey, over 94
per cent of the alleged cases of rape of Jumma women between 1991
and 1993 in the CHT were by security forces.[7] Of these rape allegations, over 40 per cent of the victims were women under 18.[8]

However, aside from these outward manifestations of violence,
women were affected in a number of ways during military rule, not
least in their daily activities of household chores, procuring food
and looking after children, all in an environment that became hostile to their very existence. Their stories are most powerfully told
in their own words through the following histories.

Voices—Chakma and Bengali Women

Kabita Chakma is now a leader of the women's resistance move-ment and president of the Hill Women's Federation. She comes from a large family of six. Her father was a primary school teacher. She remembers the terror of the army raids, when she was in class I and II in school. They had to learn how to defend themselves quite early in life. All the grown boys and men used to run away. Her mother used to take a sickle in her hand and pretend to work in the field clearing the jungles with the little ones by her side.

Women also went to the market instead of boys, since boys were often suspected and caught. Women were harassed on the streets as well, but even that seemed a lesser price to pay than if the boys were caught or murdered. The army used to come and steal or demand chickens. Her father was a *karbari*, a village headman. He was re-sponsible for counting heads and reporting to the army any missing persons or guests. If there was anyone missing, then they would beat up those who happened to be present.

Memories of witnessing violence and torture were quite com-mon among both the old and younger generations of women. When Kabita was in class VIII, the army gathered all the villagers to inter-rogate them about the Shanti Bahinis. She saw them threatening to kill people unless they told the truth. She saw one boy being beaten up as he was a suspect. An army camp stood by the side of their village. Hence their raids were frequent. Neighbouring Bengalis would attack them sometimes. During the raids, everyone took shel-ter in the hills. One night they had to flee while they were eating their evening meal. Because her father was the *karbari* he had to return to the village. This time he was the target. The army noticed her father and chased him into the jungles. He managed to escape but was badly scratched and bruised by thorny bushes.

Kabita's father was not so lucky another time. He was caught one day as he went to report the guests in the village and imprison-ed for several months. He was tortured, needles were pierced through his fingers and his arms smashed by bricks. The army then declared all the houses in the village should be dismantled and cleared. Forced eviction of whole villages was not uncommon. People were to tear down their own houses and go elsewhere within one month. Most people left for India. Kabita's family left for their aunt's place. They saw their neighbours tearing their houses and storehouses and granaries with their own hands. They did the same.

This was the turning point of her mother's life. From a simple housewife she had to take up the task of sole bread earner and responsibility for the welfare of the family. This included pleading with the security personnel to free her husband. Her mother who had been a simple housewife took up a job as a schoolteacher. She used to run after the officials to get her husband released. Kabita once remembered going to see her father. He was almost mad. He kept asking for money from other prisoners. After nine–10 months he was released. She remembers a *daroga* (a police inspector) who used to visit their house regularly. Her mother used to plead with him to release her father. The *daroga* took a liking to Kabita and tried to talk to her. Kabita found it repulsive and demeaning but knew that her mother would scold her if she was not nice to him. She therefore used to run away when she sensed him coming.

Women not only faced violence when there were raids or army operations, their daily lives and aspirations were transformed by the overall conflict situation. Such was the case of Sheila Chakma, now married with a daughter. She came from a farming family in a *mouza* (revenue unit) of Rangamati district. Although she claimed that she had never lived through an army raid in her village, she said that people always lived in fear of one. For that reason they always had a bag packed in case they had to flee at short notice. Once, like many others in their village they had to sell off their cattle and land because of the uncertain situation. They sold them dirt-cheap and often were not able to buy them back again. Sheila did mention that the Bengali settlers in their village sometimes helped them. Sometimes, villagers who fled would leave their lands and cattle in the care of Bengali neighbours. Many had their land and cattle returned to them on return. But when things became really bad, they would be careful about their Bengali neighbours. For example, they would exchange fruits and vegetables with each other, but would only go to their houses during the day and avoid them at night.

The family income declined and often the price would be the education of the girl child. Sheila being the youngest could not study beyond secondary school level. Like many other young persons residing in the Hill Tracts, Sheila used to go to a school some distance away. Both girls and boys would gather at one spot in the village and go all together to school. It was a way of defending themselves from possible harassment by the army. They took a path through the rice fields to keep away from the main road used by the military trucks. A captain of the division, posted in the vicinity of the village, used to frequently visit the school with some of his friends. His orders were that two or three girls of Class VIII and IX should parade in front of him each day so he could pick one out. He took a liking to a girl called Shikha and began to visit her home and put pressure on her family and neighbours to make Shikha marry him. When the wedding took place, the army had a big feast and deliberately cooked two different types of menu: *biryani* and beef for the Muslims and pork for the Chakmas. They forced the villagers to attend the wedding. The captain used to make Shikha wear traditional Chakma attire thus showing everybody that he was respectful of her cultural tradition.

Bengali women settlers in the area had a different view of the conflict, i.e., for them the enemy were the Shanti Bahinis and not the military. But the violence all around affected them as well. Ismat (35 years) said that when the war with the Shanti Bahini was raging, they suffered a lot. They were virtually imprisoned in the clustered villages. They could not go anywhere and practically had no work. Those who had businesses could not tend to them.

We lived in dread of the Shanti Bahini. We feel happy about the accord. We can have peaceful relations with our Chakma neighbours. We live in constant interaction with them. We often take their advice. A Chakma teacher resides with us. The Shanti Bahini has been rehabilitated, but what about our rehabilitation. We too are poor; we have to marry our daughters. The Shanti Bahini has been empowered [*shokhom hoechhey*] but the Bengalis have not been empowered.

Hanufa (60 years) complained that during the struggle, women (she did not specify Bengali or Chakma) could not move around freely. They lived in fear and often had to flee to India. But according to Hanufa it was the Shanti Bahinis who created the reign of terror. They used to come and set fire to their villages and kill people. Amidst all this, Hanufa had to protect her household, cook and feed them and keep watch constantly. Her exact words were, '*policer moton guard diye beraichi*'.

Had to keep watch like a policeman. Many a night have I spent like this. Once, during the Ramzan month [in 1975] when we women were sitting down to break our fast at the end of the day, we suddenly heard screams of fire all around us. We ran in all directions. There was firing too. Bullets missed our heads by inches. The Paharis who are our neighbours are good. They too live in danger. They say we too are targets. Sometimes they give us shelter from Shanti Bahini. When we run, they run, too. We protect each other. Problems are caused by outsiders.

The conflictual situation caused many women, men and children to flee to India and a large number to be displaced internally. Elora Dewan, an activist, claimed that to this day she is afraid of headlights in the dark, because that was the most feared thing when whole villages of people were silently fleeing their homes in the cover of the night. Children grew up in an atmosphere of uncertainty. Moitri, a young activist, recalled her childhood nightmare-like experience of hiding.

We had to flee to the jungles for a week. That was the worst nightmare in my life. On the one hand, I feared ghosts! On the other hand, I was frightened of tigers, bears and the army! The days used to go by somehow. But at nightfall, my fear was intolerable. There was no sleep in my eyes, only tears. Whenever I think of those days it fills me with dread. As children, if we cried, our parents used to threaten us by saying 'Hush, the army is coming, or the Bangali *shoronarthi* [refugees] are coming'. Our tears dried up, instantly. You didn't need toys or dolls to keep you quiet. So much did we dread the army and the refugees.

Families were fragmented as a result of forced evictions and dwindling resources. In the case of families who had members fighting in the Shanti Bahini, the pressure from collaborators and spies often produced internal migration. Those who were in schools and colleges had to stay at a relative's home in order to continue their studies or drop out for a year or two. Village schools were especially affected as the army used them as camps or torture centres. Almost all women interviewed related stories of how they remembered scenes of torture being conducted in the school grounds. Men or boys were beaten black and blue and often hung head downwards from a tree. Women and men were usually separated and lined up with their faces toward the sun. Men who were under suspicion were often taken inside the school building and tortured. Women were not allowed to cry out or scream when they heard sons, brothers and husbands screaming in pain, only weep in silence.

Dynamics of Civil Society and Women's Resistance

It is clear from the above that given the nature of militarisation in the Hill Tracts, the growth of civil society was not an easy or smooth process. There were nevertheless historical factors, which contributed to its growth. Also, as mentioned earlier, the 1960s witnessed a drive for education and awareness of the rights of the hill people known as the headmaster's movement. This was instrumental in raising the literacy rate of the hill people, especially in Rangamati, above the general literacy rate for Bangladesh.

The lower rate of literacy for women especially in the Khagrachari and Bandarban districts, demonstrates that not only was the headmaster's movement more effective in Rangamati district but also more among men than women. Women in the outlying districts especially, were disadvantaged. This has direct bearing on the potential for civil society organisations in this region. However, no matter how high the literacy rate, the militarisation of a society

TABLE 7.1
Literacy Rate of Population over 7 Years and Above

Districts	Total %	Male	Female
Khagrachari	26.3	34.6	16.9
Rangamati	36.5	45.8	24.7
Bandarban	23.8	32.2	13.5
Bangladesh	32.4	38.9	25.5

Source: Bangladesh Bureau of Statistics, *Bangladesh Population Census, 1991*, Government of Bangladesh, Dhaka, 1993.

gradually erodes civil society. Basic infrastructure like schools and colleges cannot grow. I remember a trip to the CHT in 1977 when I was asked to participate in a United Nations International Children's Emergency Fund (UNICEF) project for teaching science at primary schools. We saw many schools totally neglected by government authorities. In many cases the school inspector who came from the plains did not visit these schools. Furthermore, army operations often meant that schools were closed for long periods. Temporary displacements meant dropout rates were high. According to one newspaper report, there were no first class results recorded from Rangamati College. This is not unusual considering the conditions in which the hill people are required to study.

Another aspect of militarisation which blocked the effective formation of civil society was the divide and rule policy of the military whereby one community was pitched against the other. This was aggravated by the recruitment of indigenous groups of people as collaborators and spies for the army.

Despite all this an embryonic civil society was in the making in the Hill Tracts and the incentive for this came from the struggle which the people were waging against state repression and the suppression of their fundamental rights. The Pahari Gono Parishad, Pahari Chattra Parishad and the Hill Women's Federation were crystallised expressions of such civil society organisations. The PGP emerged as the civilian wing of the PCJSS and the PCP as the consolidated version of the students' wing. It may be recalled that the precursor to the PCP was the Pahari Chattro Samiti, which in certain localities was accompanied by women's organisations called the Nari Samiti. Hence, the PCP was born out of a strong legacy of students' activism which had characterised politics in the hills. Both these organisations emerged during the late 1980s in the space created by the cessation of armed hostilities and in keeping with the spirit of the anti-autocracy movement, which was rocking the country during the last years of General Ershad's rule.

The Hill Women's Federation formed around 1989 by Pahari women students at Chittagong University actually came into its own only around 1991. This organisation drew its support from a young generation of educated women some of whom had past activist experience either in the Nari Samiti or as women members of Pahari Chattro Parishad. Given such a history, it was quite natural to expect a certain amount of overlapping among the members of these organisations. Both the PGP and PCP allow men and women to become members. The HWF is a women-only organisation. It was formed to address issues of sexual harassment and violence against Pahari women by the armed forces and Bengalis. The detailed activities of this organisation will be discussed in a later section. However, the point to be made here is that although structurally and technically separate, all three organisations are closely knit together and it is not uncommon that decisions in one proliferate to the other. Since the power structure in both PGP and PCP is male dominated, it has particular implications for the working of the Hill Women's Federation. This is an issue which will be taken up in the section on women's resistance.

Because many of the leaders of the students front were studying in Dhaka and Chittagong, it was easy for them to strike up alliances with the Bengali intelligentsia, human rights and political workers who sympathised with their cause. This however did not mean that such support in any way reflected the mainstream of Bengali intelligentsia. However, these organisations were particularly successful in rallying together opinion against some of the worst massacres and genocide committed by the security forces, especially the Logang massacre in 1992 and the Naniarchar massacre in 1993. The joint movement, which demanded justice for the abduction of Kalpana Chakma, the organising secretary of HWF has been dealt with in a later section.

Civil society groups like the PGP, PCP and the HWF claimed their orientation to be secular and in the interest of the Jumma people, a category that was invented in the context of the struggle for autonomy of all the ethnic groups residing in the hills. This categorisation often ran contrary to some of the more religious-oriented or community-based organisations which already existed, e.g., the Tripura Samiti or Marma Samiti which were often headed by religious leaders. People of the older generation too were sceptical about the term. Those in the resistance movement in turn rejected their objections since Samiti members were compromised because of their collaboration with the establishment, for example, with the District Councils. In this way a bone of contention was embedded in the civil society of the Hill Tracts, a phenomenon which the military always took into account in their counter-insurgency plans.

In my interviews, I also discovered that the concept of a Jumma identity was not simply a political construct but had practical and daily usage in the Chakma language. In most literature it is mentioned that the word is derived form *jhum*, the slash and burn cultivation technique traditionally practised by the hill people. However, as the word is currently used in the Chakma language it refers to a collectivity. For example, one may say, '*ek jhak jummo etton*' (a group of *jhum* people is coming). At other times it is used with humour or affection when someone makes a mistake, e.g., '*mui hoyong jummo, ki gortung*' (so, I am a jummo, what can I do?). There is another Marma word that is used similarly, but whether other communities accept these categories could not be ascertained in this research. However, in Chakma community and among those exposed to the word, it has become a symbol of a new collective identity which transcends the specific community (Chakma, Marma, Tripura and Bom), lineage (*goza* or clan) and religion.

Transposed on this by the state is the identity of the *upajati* (literally translated as sub-nation) which has been reasserted in the peace accord with JSS and the Bangladesh government. Chakma and other intellectuals and politicians have vehemently refuted this nomenclature, but the state has continued to use it in its official parleys. It may be noted that the Bangladesh state has continuously rejected the notion of giving indigenous status to the hill people since according to international law that would mean conceding them certain land rights. Thus we see that the formation of identity politics in the hills has been and still is a complex and difficult one.

Position of Women in the Hill Tracts

Few secondary sources are available about the current status of women in Chakma, Marma and Tripura societies in terms of their changing relationships. Most anthropological literature deals with such society as static and unchanging. One particular article in Bengali however talks about women in the Chakma community, which is the largest of the indigenous groups in the Hill Tracts.[9] It states clearly that Chakma society is a patriarchal one, where men are more valued than women, because they inherit the wealth of the family. However, more and more educated families are making wills in favour of their daughters. It is often the practice that mothers reserve ornaments for their daughters and sons' wives during their lifetime. Legally however, *stridhan* cannot be given away without the permission of the husband. Widows cannot inherit wealth if they remarry unless they have sons. According to one of my interviewees however, the concept of ownership is not as strong in Chakma society as it is in Bengali families.

Divorce is allowed but maintenance is available only if the husband suffers from a terminal disease, has oppressed the woman or got married a second time without permission. (Polygamy is not forbidden among the Chakmas though it is not common.) On the other hand, a wife may be denied maintenance if she has a bad character or has taken up another religion or name. Needless to say, character assassination of the wife has become one way of evading maintenance. A legally divorced woman does not enjoy custodial rights over children, although this system has been modified in practice. Since sons are considered the guardians of the household, they alone have the responsibility of performing the last rites of their parents. In the absence of sons, any other male member of the clan may perform such functions.

In the public domain, Chakma women enjoy relatively more freedom than their Bengali sisters do, but here too their freedom is more curtailed than their male counterparts. They are given education but depending on the family income. Where income is restricted, the boy gets preference over the girl. Although women put in equal labour to men in the production process, their labour is not as fully recognised as that of the men is. According to one of my interviewees, 'A Pahari woman's oppression lies in the fact that she has a double burden of work. She works in the fields as well as in the home. Sometimes her husband gets drunk and the burden falls on her.' However, things are changing and during normal times, hill women definitely enjoy more mobility than Bengali women. Many women said that their parents would allow them to go out with boys if the family knew them. Both men and women claimed that women were never teased on the streets or market-place until the army came. Sexual harassment of women in public spaces was something they related directly to the establishment of military rule.

Women in the Hill Tracts have been highly politicised through their struggle against state oppression, especially with regard to ethnic and national identity. Earlier it was explained how the term Jumma, a source of collective identity has been used as a marker to give the hill people a new sense of being. Women too have internalised this in many ways. This is evident in the protest songs and poetry written during this period and sung by activists. Kabita Chakma, a young activist poet's famous poem is called *Joli No Udhim Kittei* (Why Shall I not Resist).

Why shall I not resist!
Can they do as they please—
Turn settlements into barren land
Dense forests to deserts
Mornings into evening
Fruition to barrenness.

Why shall I not resist?
Can they do as they please—
Estrange us from the land of our birth

Enslave our women
Blind our vision
Put an end to creation.

Neglect and humiliation causes anger
The blood surges through my veins
Breaking barriers at every stroke
The fury of youth pierces the sea of consciousness.

I become my own whole self
Why shall I not resist!
(Translated by the author from Chakma, 1992.)

Kabita's poems echo the more articulate educated voices of Chakma women. Women in their own way have admitted that despite differences in culture and language among the different communities, the hill people have been drawn together by the common bond of resistance against the repressive forces of the Bangladesh state. Many women claimed that they needed to participate in the resistance movement because it was the only way to safeguard their dignity and protect their existence, both physical and cultural. Even if they did not directly participate in the movement they gave economic or moral support.

Women of the CHT have been negotiating conflict both in the public as well as private spheres. We have seen how women caught in the conflict have been engaged in the struggle for survival, i.e., going about their daily chores, looking for food and going to the market, and in the process how some of them have had to adapt and rework traditionally gendered roles. We saw how housewives whose husbands were away or arrested had to cope not only with daily household chores but manage public relations with officials and the army to procure the release of a husband or appease the army during raids.

Parenthood also took on a new meaning during the struggle. Parents of many young girls and boys were at first hesitant when their children started joining the resistance movement, but later the parents themselves encouraged it, because they realised that it was the only way they could walk the streets with safety and dignity.

The archetype of the heroic mother who sends her children to fight has also been valorised as, for example, in the following protest song:

> We cannot survive without opening our mouths, how long are we to lock up our voices, the time has come to take to the streets. So Mother don't prevent us anymore.

> Mother, we have to go
> Join the demo in the street
> We have to face the bullets.
> Oh Mother don't forbid us
> Don't pull us from behind
> The streets quake
> With the slogans
> And the sound of protest.
> We all have to fight!
> Mother don't worry about us
> Stay calm and happy
> If we are killed
> Then think yourself to be the mother of a martyr.

The public sites of negotiating the conflict were therefore the streets, the market-place and the school. Hill people needed passes to go to the market. It was written on the pass—*Anumati deya holo, Bangladesh amar pran!* (Permission granted, Bangladesh is my life.) Women had to go to the market instead of men because men were more likely to be suspected and picked up than women. But women, too, were vulnerable and were open to harassment, sometimes physical but mostly verbal. Derogatory names like *chakku*, for Chakmas, *moghs* for Marmas, etc., were used as verbal abuse by security personnel on the streets. Security personnel searched buses coming in and going out of the hills. Bengalis and Paharis were separated and Paharis were searched. Bengali women recruited in the Village Defence Party were used to search the women and were particularly rude. This humiliated the Pahari women even more.

Inter-communal Relations: Paharis and Bengalis

As mentioned earlier, a distinction was made between old Bengali settlers with whom the Paharis had more congenial relations and those who were settled under the protection of the military. But during the late 1980s, when the more recently settled Bengali settlers were used by the military to work as their proxy in attacking Pahari villages, inter-communal relations grew tense and worsened. This led to a general deterioration in relations between all Bengalis and Paharis.

Schools were sites where Bengalis and hill people usually interacted with each other. Many respondents felt that normally, the relationship between them was smooth. But whenever tension rose due to some incidents, then the personal relationship between the two communities too would suffer. Even a small quarrel between class friends would be blown up out of proportion. Some however mentioned that if Bengali neighbours learnt of an imminent army raid, they would warn their Pahari friends.

Within the home and family, the crisis created difficulties and complications in personal relationships. It was particularly problematic in the case of inter-communal marriages. The hostility and rejection of mixed marriage needs to be understood in the context of the oppression of the hill people and especially the vulnerability of women in the face of the absolute power enjoyed by security personnel, as indicated in the stories of Kabita and Shikha, recounted earlier.

In these dire times, protecting young women in the family was a daunting task. Girls would go to school or out in the streets always in a group, seldom alone. Many stray incidents of rape or molestation have occurred when poor women have been caught working alone in the fields. As a consequence, for the hill people the concept of inter-communal marriages was anathema. In almost all the cases interviewed, it was stated that Chakma, Marma or Tripura men or women who married outside their community especially into the Bengali community, were not accepted by the *shomaj* (society). One person said that sometimes families would be bound by affection, to accept the marriage since it was their son or daughter, but not the *shomaj*. When asked why they would not accept such a marriage, the 50-year-old mother of a young activist said: 'We cannot accept the fact that our daughter [married to a Bengali] walks with her head held high, while our heads would be lowered in shame.' Marrying into the dominant society and one identified as the oppressor would shame the family.

Despite such feelings, intermarriages between hill people and Bengalis by choice are not few in number. When asked what the reasons could be for such marriages, many mentioned the insecurity of Pahari girls. Others said it was the parent's fault, they let their daughters grow up in luxury so that their lifestyle went beyond the average capacity of a Pahari family, thus making it difficult to find a suitable Pahari boy. My assistant (Shomari Chakma) told me of a family of 10, the father a government official and the mother a housewife who was so determined to give the best education to the children that she used to till the land herself to save extra. She was furious when one of her daughters who had a Master's degree from Dhaka University married a Bengali. The family has refused to see her even though she has been married two years and has a child. Women who marry outside are especially ostracised. Pahari men who marry outside are fewer in number but they do not face as much flak from society as women. Parents did not mind as much boys marrying Bengalis because the children stayed within the family.

Marriage was therefore an important marker not only of sexual and racial boundaries intertwining with each other but also of identity. Many activists believed it was necessary to marry within the community or else their very existence would be at stake. The woman's body therefore became a vehicle for reproducing racial, community and cultural identity. Moreover, many Bengalis, particularly those enjoying the power of 'ruling' the Hill Tracts, used inter-community marriages as symbols of assimilation as illustrated by the case of Shikha Chakma. Assimilative strategies were used as integrative mechanisms in which the nominal symbolic aspects of cultural difference, as for example, the difference of clothes and attire would be retained. This is amply illustrated in an advertisement of a detergent soap shown on Bangladesh television (BTV). Housewives from all the country's districts are portrayed, including a Chakma girl in her traditional attire and jewellery, called Tanya (a modern name) Chakma. The Chakmas, she indicates, are proud of their tradition, and they too find the product useful. In this way the Chakmas, as a distinct group, become integrated into the market economy of Bangladesh.

Women's Activism and Agency

Hill Women's Federation

The Hill Women's Federation emerged in the late 1980s to become the most organised form of women's resistance in the area. Earlier, women had been active in the students' front in schools and colleges. The struggle in the CHT did not register a large number of women combatants. Only two such combatants have been heard of. One of them, Madhabalita, is reported to be a member of the central executive committee of the PCJSS. However, a distinct characteristic of the CHT struggle was the very highly politicised and sensitised corps of women workers at the political and social level.

No doubt the issue of rape and harassment of women by security personnel was the single most important factor behind the formation and consolidation of the Hill Women's Federation from its precursor, Pahari Chattra Parishad, a student body. Army personnel allegedly raped Sujata Chakma of Guimara, Khagrachari. The Guimara HWF made its first protest to the District Commissioner in 1989–90. The rapist was caught red-handed by the Paharis in a public place and despite the threats witnesses came forward to testify. At a hearing chaired by the additional district magistrate, the victim, supported by the HWF came forward to identify the rapist. The chairperson of the HWF was made member of the enquiry committee but resigned when she saw that the information was being distorted. The HWF turned to street demonstrations. Three days of meetings were held with the authorities, but on the second day itself, nothing was established in the enquiry. A human rights team came from Dhaka to investigate, but that too did not bear fruit. The enquiry report was published. Failures like these strengthened the determination of women activists even more. They felt the need to build awareness both outside as well as inside their community. It was with this in mind that they set about recruiting women into their ranks.

When the HWF was formed, many activists from existing Nari Samitis or Pahari Chattra Parishads joined. For new recruits, they drew support from school and college going students, by engaging them in rallies, meetings and awareness raising gatherings as for example, Gonopicnics. Gonopicnics were mass picnics organised by people who were active in the movement but not necessarily by the office-bearers of the HWF and other civil society organisations. Sometimes whole villages participated in such picnics. They resembled any other picnic in the hills to the extent that people met, ate and drank together and basically had a good time. But the difference was that instead of playing games or gambling as was common in ordinary picnics, there would be quiz contests, to raise the awareness of the people regarding their community identity. For example, questions would be posed about the date of an important battle between Shanti Bahini and the military, or the birth and death anniversary of a leader of the movement. Gonopicnics therefore served as a mobilisation strategy.

Elder brothers and sisters inducted their siblings as activists. Many came of their own accord as a result of confrontation with the realities of oppression. Anuching Marma was in class III at school, when she witnessed the army raiding her house and ill-treating her mother. She was interrogated brutally on her possession of a syringe which she used for assuaging rheumatic pain. Anuching remembered the sheer insecurity of her daily life as she waited with two younger brothers for their mother to return from the market. By the time she reached class VIII at school, it was natural for her to join the demonstrations for autonomy.

The dangers of getting involved in the HWF and the PCP were obvious, but as the repression grew, even parents, at first, reluctantly, then gladly gave permission. They felt that it was the only way through which their children could walk down the street with dignity, the only way they could protect themselves from ruthless army operations.

The Hill Women's Federation has a structure very similar to the PCP. It has an Executive Committee led by a president, vice-president and a general secretary. Other posts in the central Executive Committee are that of the organising secretary and cultural secretary. These are all determined at their annual Council meeting. The strength of the HWF however lies in the effectiveness of its local committees. It has Branch Committees that are sometimes based on campuses, e.g., Dhaka University, University of Chittagong, Jahangirnagar University or Rangamati College; in short, wherever there is a large number of female students from the Hill Tracts. But in the Hill Tracts itself, the local committees are *thana* (police post) based.

Membership in HWF, PCP and the PGP is often overlapping. Depending on the situation, therefore, it is not surprising to find the decisions of one organisation influencing the other. In practice, it is useful to think of the three organisations as a loose coalition. After the peace accord, a split occurred in all three organisations between those who supported the treaty and those who did not. The supporters of the treaty back the leadership of Shantu Larma in the PCJSS. Their organisations function as front organisations to the PCJSS. The critics of the accord support the leadership of Proshit Khisa. The loose coalition of anti-accordists has acquired a formalised structure under the party banner of the United Peoples Democratic Front (UPDF). In both coalitions we see women's leadership being subsumed under a broader male-dominated mantle.

Despite this male dominance, the very nature of the struggle has brought forth the participation of women. Hence we see that in various periods of the struggle women members of the HWF were just as active and sometimes even more so than male colleagues. During the struggle the women of HWF have openly agitated against army rule and oppressive measures followed by the state. They have organised rallies and demonstrations against the genocide of the hill people propagating their message through posters, leaflets and other media such as art and songs. They have had an important role to play in bringing up the gender issue along with the rights of indigenous people. Several of the HWF members participated in international forums where they drew special attention to the problems faced by women of the Chittagong Hill Tracts. The militant role that women played on their home ground was perhaps best epitomised by the bravery displayed by the HWF organising secretary, Kalpana Chakma.

The Case of Kalpana Chakma

Army personnel abducted Kalpana Chakma, the organising secretary of HWF from her home in the New Laillighona village of Baghaichari *thana*, in June 1996. They also tried to pick up her brothers, but they escaped. Kalpana was a first year graduate student of Baghaichari College and a vocal and committed activist of HWF. Kalpana, an outspoken woman, had an altercation with a Lt. Ferdous regarding the burning of several houses in the village a couple of months before. Apparently, on 19 March Lt. Ferdous in an army operation had set fire to seven houses in the process of tracking down men belonging to the Shanti Bahini. Kalpana had protested and got into a heated argument with Lt. Ferdous. After that incident the Lieutenant had kept a watch on Kalpana's house. Many of Kalpana's friends and neighbours believe that her abduction was an act of revenge.

Kalpana's abduction spearheaded a nation-wide movement and national press coverage that was to bring the gender issue into the forefront of the struggle. A protest strike was staged by a joint front of PGP, PCP and HWF in the Hill Tracts. During the strike, clashes took place between the law enforcing agencies and protesters in which a school boy, Rupam Chakma, was shot dead and his body taken away. Three more persons were reported missing.

Kalpana's diary evocatively reveals the challenges she faced in the movement as well as the aspirations she cherished.[10] In depicting the life of a woman in the CHT she writes, 'On the one hand [the woman faces] the steam-roller of rape, torture, sexual harassment, humiliation and helplessness inflicted by the military and Bengalis, and on the other hand, she faces the curse of social and sexual discrimination'. Kalpana's understanding of oppression embraces all women of Bangladesh. 'I think that the women of my country are oppressed.' In expressing her yearnings for freedom from oppression, she uses a beautiful metaphor:

> When a caged bird wants to be free, does it mean that she wants freedom for herself alone? Does it also mean one must necessarily imprison those who are already free? I think it is natural to expect the caged bird to be angry with those who imprisoned her. But if she understands that she has been imprisoned in a cage and that cage is not her rightful place, then she has every right to claim the freedom of the skies!

For Kalpana Chakma, democracy did not mean merely free and fair elections. It meant participation in the political process and more specifically participation as a Chakma woman. She therefore stridently voices a critique of the student movement that remains male-dominated. She writes,

> Despite the fact that women constitute half the population, they are not taken seriously in any movement for social change. As an example one can point out that of the numerous demands voiced during the movement, even the 10 point demands of the Chattro Shongram Porishod [Students Revolutionary Council], do not specifically speak of problems faced by a woman. Many politically sensitive men seem to think that such problems are not important enough to be dealt with at this hour. Therefore the issue of women's emancipation has remained neglected in the agenda for class struggle and political change.

She also mentions in an article that a women's movement alone cannot solve the problems of Jumma women. The emancipation of Jumma women has to be constructed within the framework of the self-determination of the Jumma people. It is a struggle for emancipating both Jumma men and women. That is why both women and men must come forward. This she admits is a difficult task for Jumma women since they are discriminated socially, religiously, and politically. 'Our social structure is such that if women start to become aware, everyone feels threatened. The minute she tries to break her chains, people call her immodest. When she participates in the movement, people say she is without character.' But Kalpana eggs on her fellow comrades to disregard such comments and move forward. There are two bright role models to light their way— Rokeya Shakhawat Hossain and Pritilata Wadeddar. (Editor's note: Rokeya was a feminist writer and social reformer; Pritilata was a revolutionary activist involved in the Chittagong Armoury Raid in the 1920s.) Women's participation in the struggle for autonomy must be safeguarded.

It is an irony of fate that Kalpana Chakma, who became a victim of state violence should become the subject of a campaign which would help take the women's question onto another plane. This will be discussed in a following section which addresses the inter-locking and dynamic responses of the state, the Bengali community and civil society to the situation in the Chittagong Hill Tracts. Suffice it to say here that in the recent constitution of the United Peoples Democratic Front (the dissident front of the PGP, PCP and HWF), equality of women and men is one of the recognised objectives of the party. The PCJSS however continues to disregard the women's question as was evident during the peace negotiations with the government. I now deal with this question in detail from the perspective of some activists, both male and female.

The Woman Question in the CHT Struggle

The woman question in the CHT is still in its formative stage. The social implications of a changing gender role are still the subject of much heated conversation and lively debates. Both women and men activists acknowledge that the struggle has made them realise that women should have equality and be treated as human beings with rights. This is not something that is automatically enjoyed in traditional Chakma society, though Chakma women may enjoy more mobility than in Bengali culture. But when the problem is posed in more personal terms, as for example, how male political activists look upon or what they expect from their women comrades or even how women view themselves, then complexities arise.

Men asserted that they think that women activists have a strong voice in their organisations and that they have earned their respect. They also look upon them as companions in the social sphere. Women tended to differ. Some women indicated that though they were activists, they still looked towards settling down and having families while still performing their patriotic duties. However, a sizeable portion of women thought that this would not be easy due to the fact that Chakma men would not treat them equally. Even their own comrades were not free from male-oriented values. Many girls thought that most men still believed that their wives should be younger and less qualified or educated than they. But women activists were strong in their assertion that through the struggle they had at least earned the right to expect respectful treatment from their male colleagues and that they were comparatively better than men who were not politically active.

The fact that Pahari women have been highly politicised was evident in their answer to the question—what was their ideal of a Chakma/Marma/Tripura woman? Kabita says: 'Personal happiness is not an ideal which a Chakma girl should look for. She should contribute to her own society. I, myself, am committed to the *Dabeenama* [Charter of Demands] and will fight for women's rights, although it is secondary in our struggle for full autonomy.'

Mithila wants her daughter to be educated and at the same time contribute something to her own society. She cannot predict whether her daughter will marry outside her community or country, but she would not want her to. She thinks that even as a mother there are duties to perform, for example, bringing up her children in such a way that they learn to be proud of their Chakma identity. She then tells the story of her 2-year-old son, who while going to school in Dhaka, was greeted by a Bengali boy as 'Chakma! Chakma!' Obviously, the Bengali boy had intended it as an insult. But when her son came back home he told her with a sense of innocent pride, 'Ma, he called me Chakma! He must have recognised me!' Mithila was delighted that her son had learnt to be so proud of his identity that he refused to recognise it as an insult.

Moitri wants a future in which women can realise their full potential as human beings. Without full autonomy it was not possible to enjoy such rights. Their struggle was for realising ideals. The movement has to be led by conscious or educated people committed to building a nation where everyone will be seen equally, not as minorities or subjugated by patriarchy. An ideal woman for Anuching Marma is one who is dedicated to social work, educated and progressive.

Thus we see that while the gender question has been formally accepted as an area of struggle within the political agenda, it takes a back seat to the question of full autonomy. But interestingly it is not only men who feel that way. Some women too are of the opinion that autonomy should come first. This may be variously interpreted. It could be that these women are merely voicing the party agenda. But on the other hand looking at the depth of their experience and the nature and quality of agency which they have within their organisation, the issue may be looked at in a different light. Many of these women have been directly and indirectly subject to the hurt and humiliation of oppressive forces, and the humiliation which they faced as women was very much part and parcel of racial and communal domination and subjugation by the Bangladesh state.

Hence it is to be expected that their demands for gender rights would be incorporated within their demand for autonomy. However, how they prioritise them and who determines their prioritisation is a consideration which should be given serious consideration by feminist analysts and the women's movement in general. In the case of the CHT, men have largely dictated the prioritisation of the autonomy question over gender concerns. But since women's voices are not as weak as they used to be and since the women's movement in Bangladesh, in general, is gaining ground in certain spheres, they have been able to gain concessions as well. However, members of HWF who critique the peace accord agree that autonomy remains on top of their agenda.

Responses of the State, Class and Community

The Bangladesh government as well as the main opposition has remained more or less consistent in its attitude towards the CHT problem since the 1970s. It has been intransigent to the demands for autonomy and constitutional safeguards for the protection of national and cultural rights. People of ethnic backgrounds, different from that of a Bengali, have been persistently called *upajati* or tribes, something that the struggle has opposed from the beginning. It has also refused to recognise the Jumma people as indigenous people since that would mean conceding to them land rights in accordance with international laws and conventions. Instead, even after the peace accord has been signed, the government has tried to see the solution through the lens of a local governance framework. It has been emphasising the CHT as lucrative ground for foreign investments in oil and tourism.

The culture of the CHT has been projected in an orientalist fashion as a 'show case culture' where exotic 'tribal' men and women dance and sing without history or context, estranged from the forces of mainstream production. This is an easy way to marginalise and denigrate the rich potential for social change, which has been evident in the lives and livelihood of the people of the CHT as depicted here. Currently the Chakma elite also have taken to portraying Chakma culture. Unfortunately, the emphasis has been on individuality and not on the collective. This is evident in the focus on recording love songs around individual love stories, rather than traditional songs which talk of the people's love for their land. Protest songs, particularly, are not heard.

The following incident of a controversy over a TV drama brings into focus the interplay of gender, market and differing notions of 'tribal' culture. After the signing of the accord, Bangladesh Television started showing a drama serial based on the story of Chakma Rajbari. After the first episode, Chakma viewers vehemently objected. (Rangamati College had to be closed down due to violent student protests.) The main contention was that hill people in this serial were portrayed in an unrealistic and undignified manner. First, the Chakma prince not only wore the wrong clothes, but his household was portrayed in an undignified manner, e.g., the Chakma king kills his son's lover because he disapproved of her. Second, Chakma women were shown in clothes more suitable for Hindi cinema.[11]

For the Bengali middle-class which now constitutes a large part of the civil society, developments in the CHT have remained a delicate and sensitive issue, even after the signing of the accord. As a result, human rights violations there have remained the concern of a handful of lawyers, academics, human rights activists and left party workers and students. Many Pahari activists complain that national civil society organisations are reluctant to take up frontline activity.

The Hill Tracts issue did receive some attention in the national women's movement in the wake of the Kalpana Chakma's case. But women's organisations registered as NGOs are limited by their manifesto which prevents them from active involvement in political situations. However, the women's movement has been getting more 'political', i.e., taking up issues which have direct repercussions on the state. In protest against the murder and rape of a young girl in the northern district of Dinajpur, several women's organisations came together and formed a common platform, the Shommilita Nari Shomaj, which enabled them to bypass the limitations of their organisational agenda. The organisation has continued to protest state violence against women, including the Kalpana Chakma case.

Before Kalpana Chakma's abduction and murder, the Hill Women's Federation had managed to make its presence felt at the national and international level. They had participated in the 8 March 1994 women's movement rally on International Women's Day, with their slogan 'Autonomy for Peace'. They also went to the NGO Forum of the Women's Conference in Beijing in 1995 with the same slogan. However, although the National Preparatory Committee Towards Beijing, NGO Forum '95, constituted a separate task force on indigenous women, barely two lines were included on the topic in the summary of the official NGO report. This reflected the hesitation on the part of some Bangladesh NGOs to deal with an issue that had become a matter of political controversy. On the other hand, the movement, which rallied behind Kalpana Chakma, was exceptional to the extent that many human rights and women's organisations demonstrated on the streets and joined hands with the left and trade union activists to protest against the kidnapping in unambiguous terms.

This atmosphere has changed somewhat since the accord has been signed. As the ruling party has highlighted this as their achievement, and the opposition has opposed it, the media controversy over the accord has become highly politicised. A balanced critique seems not possible and the civil society (both Bengali and Pahari) too, has become divided over it. This has affected the women's movement as well. The same women's platform that had campaigned for Kalpana Chakma, has become divided. One faction supports the accord. The other faction raises issues of justice that remained unaddressed in the accord. But even this latter faction of the movement has failed to address the issue of the politics of nationality within the women's movement. As a result whenever the demand for autonomy is raised by the HWF (one section), it makes many women activists uncomfortable since in their minds they link it with challenges to state sovereignty. Therefore, the Bengali women's movement has been reluctant to address issues of militarisation and nationalism in a constructive and proactive manner. In this respect, there is no possibility of a dialogue between the HWF and the mainstream women's movement.

Post-accord: Women's Notion of Peace

Women in the Hill Tracts want peace and for most it means the freedom to be their own selves, to live without fear and insecurity. While there are claims and counter-claims of which faction—accordist or anti-accordist—constitutes the majority, there is growing disenchantment with the implementation of the accord reached between the JSS and the government of Bangladesh. The dissident factions of the PCP and the HWF, who oppose the accord, argue that the conditions of peace can be met only within the framework of full autonomy. Moreover, they maintain that the atrocities suffered by the hill people have been left unaddressed. Issues of justice and human rights have been swept under the carpet in the peace accord. It is well established that the process of reconciliation requires that there should be public cognisance of human rights violations—the massacres, abductions and rapes committed by the security forces in the name of counter-insurgency measures. It is necessary to publish all inquiry commission reports and to demand the trial of those responsible. Moreover, crucial questions of land and the Bengali settlers still need to be solved in a just manner. The peace envisaged, is a just peace.

Also, in the accord itself, little mention has been made about women's participation in peace-making or peace-building activities. The membership of the Regional Council does provide seats for women members. Among the 25 members, 12 are male ('tribal') and two female ('tribal') and six non-tribal male and one female. The participation of women is minimal, perhaps because the discussions preceding the accord negotiations were limited to a few leaders. Since the relationship between JSS and the civilian wings, the PGP, PCP, HWF was already strained both generally as well as over the accord, no formal discussion took place with the JSS leaders who were recognised as the sole legitimate spokespersons of the CHT struggle.

It is the demand for a just and democratic peace process which has made them dissidents in the eyes of the establishment, to which the JSS has recently acceded. The HWF along with those factions of the PGP and PCP which have critiqued the accord maintain that the JSS has compromised with the state politics of fomenting disunity among the hill people. The post-peace situation has been marked by inter-faction feuds and rivalry resulting in assault, abduction and murder. As a result, the democratic foundations upon which any peace process is built are on the verge of collapse.

Alongside, a promising development is taking place in the agendas of the HWF and the PCP factions which oppose the accord. It is taking place outside the mainstream women movement and has important consequences for the CHT activists and other indigenous peoples such as Garos. It is the emergence of a loose network of organisations and individuals under the banner of the Jouno Nipiron Protorodh Mancha (platform against sexual harassment). The initiative has come largely from women students in the country's university campus who are protesting against sexual harassment. Networks and alliances have been constructed in response to incidents of sexual violence which have rocked the country and could have the potential of being the basis of a sustained social movement. The Mancha includes both men and women and has on its agenda both the class and the nationality question, its constituency are left-oriented groups as well as indigenous peoples movements, like the PCP, HWF and the emergent Bangladesh Garo Chattro Shongothon. The PCP and HWF (dissident factions) are now reaching out to fledgling struggles of other indigenous people's organisations to build up networks among indigenous students groups such as the Garos.[12]

The Manch provides a platform to groups like the PCP and HWF (those still contesting state policies) to demonstrate solidarity with issues of concern beyond ethnic discrimination, thus building alliances and thereby strengthening their democratic foundations in the wider body politic. This opens up the possibility of linking up issues of gender and ethnicity from which the mainstream women's organisations have stayed clear.

Conclusion

It is clear from the above that women in the CHT have been especially affected by the armed struggle in the Hill Tracts. Not only were they victims of rape, torture, abductions and other forms of violence accompanying army operations, their daily lives too were transformed in ways which have had a long-term impact on their lives. For many women, normal activities like education or schooling were discontinued or suspended. When left to take charge of their families in the absence of male members, they had both to fend for their families as well as to protect them from army raids. Being the ones who were predominantly in charge of children, their task was doubly difficult during times of displacement or flight.

Amidst all this women had to prepare food for the family, negotiate with the army (often cooking food for them, or appeasing or negotiating with them for the release of their husbands), keep vigils and protect their families in every possible way. Survival strategies were often community based, mostly involving members of the same community, but sometimes with a helping hand or two from Bengali neighbours.

Oppressive strategies were aimed at the cultural identity of a Pahari, but in the case of women, their sexuality was under attack as well. For example, in the market-place and streets Bengalis and Paharis were openly discriminated against by the security personnel, but in the case of women, physical and sexist abuse was hurled at them. It was exacerbated by the different clothes Pahari women wore on the streets, i.e., the *pinon* instead of *sari* or *shalwar kameez*. It is for this reason that many Pahari women perceived gender oppression as part and parcel of ethnic discrimination. Consequently, hill women refused to acknowledge that there was any sexual abuse from their own community and maintained that it was a phenomenon associated with the dominant Bengali culture. Although many admitted that Pahari women were discriminated against by their own men, the level of sexual abuse against Pahari women was considered much higher within the context of the Bengali and Pahari conflict.

This affected the way in which the gender issue was constructed within the agenda for autonomy. It is clear from the excerpts from Kalpana Chakma's diary that women did argue the case for greater participation of women in the movement as well as the inclusion of the gender issue within the agenda of the party. But at the same time they recognised the need to be free of ethnic discrimination as well. Describing her vision of a peaceful world, Kalpana Chakma wrote, 'We want a society where men and women would enjoy equal rights. Also where one class of people would not exploit another class of people or where one community will not be able to dominate and abuse another community.'

In the struggle for autonomy in the Hill Tracts, women's activism had a practical importance and a symbolic significance. The immunity which women possessed as 'political innocents' enabled them freer movement in the market-place, access to officials and the opportunity to help the Shanti Bahini as undercover agents. But this immunity was intermittently threatened by strategies of counter-insurgency, when homes were raided, children tortured, women

raped with the purpose of destroying the last vestiges of civil society which the women were trying to uphold. Cumulative events
such as these often led women to transform their lifestyles quite
radically. From survivors they became militant activists.

Women were also used as powerful symbols of the struggle. The
participation of hill women was used to represent to the outside
world the all-out support for the struggle within the community.
The representation of women in the traditional roles of 'mourning
mothers' or 'bereaved widows' was used to mobilise support for
the cause. After the abduction of Kalpana Chakma, the national
press as well as posters of HWF carried photographs of Kalpana and
her lamenting mother. This helped to rally forth support for an
issue that the military establishment was keen on sweeping under
the carpet. However, such representations also have a dual effect of
making women susceptible to manipulation by their own comrades.
In the case of the Chittagong Hill Tracts there is still an ambiguity
as to what extent hill women have been able to represent themselves effectively in the recognised space of the struggle.

In the above discussion we have seen how women within the
struggle are still in the process of defining for themselves a space of
their own both within their organisation as well as in society. The
capacity for strong leadership is there, but it has yet to crystallise
itself in a more institutionalised form. As yet the Hill Women's
Federation of both factions is under the dominant influence of their
'master organisations', the PCJSS on the one hand and the UPDF
on the other. It is only in recent years that the gender dimension
has begun to emerge as a sub-text in what is predominantly an ethnic
struggle.

NOTES

1. Many of the interviews were done in Dhaka, since those actively involved
   in the movement were residing there for reasons of security. In Dhaka, I
   interviewed about 15 people, 10 of whom were women. The women belonged to different age groups ranging from housewives to young college
   going girls. The men were mostly students and members of Pahari Chattra
   Parishad. Some working men were interviewed together with their wives.

Most people with the exception of one or two originated from Khagrachari, and since my fieldwork was also conducted there this study will have a focus on a specific locality. In Khagrachari, about four women, two of them Bengali settlers, were interviewed. Tripura women were not available for interview. Apart from these in-depth interviews, detailed conversations with academic colleagues and lawyers helped me immensely.

2. The predicament of the Jumma people began with the building of a hydrodam in the early 1960s, which flooded 1,036 sq. km of land, submerged 40 per cent of their best agricultural lands and displaced about 100,000 Jummas from their ancestral domain. In 1964, about 40,000 displaced Chakmas and other indigenous people were forced to migrate into India and were settled in the state of Arunachal Pradesh. After Bangladesh became liberated, the founder of the Jana Samhati Samiti (JSS) Manabendra Narayan Larma was elected to the Bangladesh parliament from the CHT constituency in the first general election held in Bangladesh. As an elected member of the parliament he demanded constitutional safeguards and rights of the Jumma people in the Bangladesh parliament, but his demands were ignored. Following this effort, he led a Jumma delegation and submitted a written memorandum to Sheikh Mujibur Rahman, the then prime minister, with a four-point charter of demands for regional autonomy for the CHT. But not only was this proposal rejected outright, the Jumma leaders were charged with secession and for being anti-Bangladeshi.

3. Ameena Mohsin, 'Military Hegemony and the Chittagong Hill Tracts', in Subir Bhaumik, Meghna Guhathakurta and Sabyasachi Basu Ray Chaudhuri, eds, *Living on the Edge: Essays on the Chittagong Hill Tracts*, SAFHR, Kathmandu, 1997, p. 128.

4. Ameena Mohsin and Bhumitra Chakma, 'The Myth of Nation-Building and the Security of State', in Iftekharuzzaman and Imtiaz Ahmed, eds, *Bangladesh and SAARC: Issues, Perspectives and Outlooks*, UPL, Dhaka, 1992, pp. 294–95.

5. Father Timm, 'The Adivasis of Bangladesh', Minority Rights Group, London, International Report, Vol. 92/1, 1992.

6. Kalpana Chakma, 'Ronagoner Sharitey Amra Hobo Shoinik' (We Will Be Soldiers in the Frontline of Battlefield), in *Shongkriti*, Vol. 5, August 1999.

7. Meghna Guhathakurta, 'Overcoming Otherness and Building Trust: The Kalpana Chakma Case', and Ameena Mohsin, 'Military Hegemony and the Chittagong Hill Tracts', in Bhaumik et al., n. 3.

8. Hill Women's Federation, Leaflet distributed on the occasion of the NGO Forum on Women, 4th UN Conference on Women, Beijing, 30 August to 10 September 1995.

9. Gyanbikash Chakma and Farzana Nayeem, 'Pitritantric Shomajbaboshai Narir Obosthan' (Women's Position in Patriarchal Chakma Society), in Meghna Guhathakurta, Suraiya Begum and Hasina Ahmed, eds, *Nari: Protonidhitta O Rajniti*, Dhaka, Centre for Social Studies, 1997.

10. Chakma, 'Ronagoner Sharitey Amra Hobo Shoinik', n. 6. See also Meghna Guhathakurta, 'Overcoming Otherness and Building Trust: The Kalpana Chakma Case', in Bhaumik et al., n. 3.

11. Critiquing the serial, Lumbini Roy, a resident of Rajbari wrote in a daily: 'The Director in portraying hill women in indecent attire had humiliated them and given a wrong impression to others about their dress and character.' Lumbini Roy's protest itself took on the garb of male protectionism in his argument that no unmarried Marma or any other young women of the community in the hills wears only a blouse and lungi without a khadi, i.e., scarf to cover her breasts. Very obviously Ms Roy in critiquing the commoditisation of hill women by Bengali media has revealed her own class bias in her views regarding women's body and notions of decency or indecency, because what she says about the dress of hill women is only true of a particular class and age.

12. Bangladesh Garo Chattra Shongothon, Leaflet distributed on the occasion of demanding justice for the rape and murder of Garo domestic worker, Levina Howie, 25 August 1999, Dhaka.

Editor

Rita Manchanda is Programme Executive, South Asia Forum for Human Rights, Kathmandu, and coordinator of the women's studies and peace studies programmes. A journalist and a writer on South Asian security issues, she has contributed articles on gender and conflict to various edited volumes. Ms Manchanda is also a peace and human rights activist and a local partner of the Women Peace project of the Kennedy School of Government, Harvard University. She has earlier co-edited (with Tapan K. Bose) *States, Citizens and Outsiders: The Uprooted Peoples of South Asia*.

Contributors

Paula Banerjee teaches at the Department of South and Southeast Asian Studies in Calcutta University and in WISCOMP Fellow of Peace for 2000–2001. A Ph.D. in International Relations from the University of Cincinnati, USA, Dr Banerjee has published extensively on issues of international relations and gender studies in various reputed journals including the *Journal of Women's Studies* and *Canadian Women's Studies*. She is the co-author of *Women in Society and Politics of France*.

Amrita Banskota is an eminent freelance journalist and gender activist in Nepal. She is associated with a Nepali non-government organisation called the Institute of Human Rights Communication. As part of the Beijing plus five process, she was actively involved in preparing the Nepal country paper. A popular columnist in several Nepali publications and known for her writings on gender and health issues and human rights, she is also the co-author of *Situation of Women in Politics and the Media in Nepal.*

Shobha Gautam is a well known journalist and social activist in Nepal. She is currently associated with the Institute of Human Rights Communication and is an active member of the Progressive Writers Association, Nepal and the SAARC non-government organisation, Women for Peace. She has written actively in the Nepali press on issues of social and gender justice and has co-authored *Situation of Women in Politics and the Media in Nepal.*

Meghna Guhathakurta is Professor of International Relations at Dhaka University and Asia Fellow (University of Pennsylvania). A Ph.D. in Politics from the University of York (UK), she is also Research Associate in the Centre for Social Studies (CSS), Dhaka University and Associate Editor of the centre's *Journal of Social Studies.* Dr Guhathakurta is a well known human rights and gender activist in Bangladesh. Among her many publications are: *The Politics of British Aid Policy Formation: The Case of British Aid to Bangladesh, 1972–1986; Nari, Rastro, Motadorsho* (Women, State and Ideology) (co-edited); *Nari: Protonidhitto O Rajniti* (Women: Representation and Politics) (co-edited); and *Comparative Feminist Perspective* (edited).

Anis Haroon is one of Pakistan's leading women activists and founder member of the Women's Action Forum (WAF), Pakistan. She is also a well known Urdu poet and writer and has recently published a collection of short stories in Urdu called *Bada hai Dard ka Rishta* (A Painful Relationship) based on the narratives of the women in the Muttahida Quami Movement (MQM).

Darini Rajasingham-Senanayake is Senior Fellow at the International Centre for Ethnic Studies, Colombo. An anthropologist by training, she obtained her Ph.D. from Princeton University and is a Social Science Research Council, MacArthur Foundation Post Doctoral Fellow in Peace and Security Studies. She has written extensively on ethnic conflict and the problem of displacement in Sri Lanka. Among her many scholarly articles are: 'After Devolution: Protecting Local Minorities' and 'Democracy and the Problem of Representation: The Making of Bi-polar Ethnic Identity in Postcolonial Sri Lanka'.

Index

Shah, Nafisa, 202
Shah, Shahbir, 94
Shaiza, Rano, 169
Shalk, Pater, 113
Shangkham, Dr Gina, 162
Shanti Bahini, 257, 259, 263, 265, 266,
    267, 278, 280, 290
Sharif, Nawaz, 124, 181, 186, 200
Sheikh Hasina, 103, 261, 262
Shillong Accord, 137
Shining Path: Peru's, 215, 216, 219, 235,
    238, 243, 248n. 1, 250n. 31
Shommilita Nari Shomaj, 286
Shrestha, Nanda Kumar, 233
Shrestha, Sarla, 246
Shrestha, Shanti, 239, 244
Shrestha, Shyam Sunder, 231
Simla agreement, 48
Simon Commission, 134
Sindhiani Tehrik, 190
Sinhala Mothers Front, 21, 101n. 46
Smith, Dan, 12
Somalia conflict, 16
Sri Lanka Mothers Front, 25, 30, 96
state–community conflicts, 132, 143
Stri Shakti Jagaran Manch, 154
stridhan, 271
suicide bombing, 128
Suriya Women's Centre, 125
Swu, Isak, 137

Taliban, 127
Tamil Mothers Front, 21
Tamil Thesawalami, 119, 130n. 16
Tamil United Liberation Front (TULF),
    103
Tangkhul Shanao Long (TSL), 164
Tebhaga, revolutionary struggles in, 29
Tehriq-i Hurriyat, 60, 93
Telangana: revolutionary struggles in, 29
Terrorist and Disruptive Activities Act,
    78
Tezpur District Mahila Samiti, 144
Thiranagama: Rajini, 102, 125
total war, 14
tribal identity, 166, 173
Tripura Samiti, 270
two nation theory, 47, 179, 180

underdevelopment, 14
underemployment, 214
uniform civil code, 125
United Liberation front of Assam
    (ULFA), 22, 138, 146, 149
United Naga Women's Forum, 164
United Nations Commission for Refu-
    gees (UNHCR), 110, 117
United Peoples Democratic Front, 262,
    279, 282, 291
United Peoples Front, 217, 218, 219, 221,
    225, 236, 241, 242
University Teachers for Human Rights,
    Jaffna, 116
Unrepresented Nations and Peoples'
    Organisation, 137
upajati: identity of, 270, 285

Vajpayee, Atal Bihari, 11, 162
victimhood paradigm, 10, 15, 30, 32, 34,
    36, 43, 111, 120, 121, 123–24, 132,
    145–46, 174
violence: and dislocation in health serv-
    ices, 70

Wadeddar, Pritilata, 282
Wakhlu, Khemlata, 58, 59, 64
War against Rape, 191
Watsu Mongdung, 160, 163–66, 173
widowhood, 103, 122–24, 223, 230, 233
Williams, Betty, 156
women: as agricultural labourers, 141,
    214, 215, 222, 223; and autonomy, 13,
    19, 58, 120; as child rearers and
    nurturers, 16, 23, 24, 75, 95; and
    decision-making, 12, 17, 94, 109, 111,
    117, 154, 158, 183, 188, 189, 223, 226;
    income generating programmes for,
    32, 153, 209, 229; as informers, 81–
    82, 86, 87, 204; and inheritance of
    property, 37, 112, 118, 119, 157, 222,
    223, 227, 241, 271; mobility of, 106,
    109, 115, 117, 118, 120, 121, 124, 127,
    168, 183, 272, 282; and mortality rates,
    142; as negotiating conflict, 10, 27,
    28, 35, 44, 132, 144, 156, 165, 221, 246,
    273, 274; and politics, 10, 11, 12, 17,
    23, 24, 80, 92–94, 95, 96, 102–3, 144,